The Zodiac M

(Inspired by Christ)

A NEW REVELATION OF
OUR LORD AND SAVIOUR
JESUS CHRIST

VOLUME I

Printed and Published by
THE GREATER WORLD ASSOCIATION
3 LANSDOWNE ROAD, HOLLAND PARK
LONDON, W.11

> "*Glorious indeed is the world of God around us, but more glorious the world of God within us.*"
>
> These words epitomize the teachings given in this book.

CONTENTS

FOREWORD

In the former Revelation given to John he is shown the vision of the glories of the Heavenly Realms, and the " things which must surely come to pass ". In this new Dispensation the vision is widened, giving in greater detail the truths of the invisible kingdoms and their wonders. The Godhead is made plain to our understanding in the three aspects of Father, Son and Holy Spirit. The Divine Love is again manifested in the Person of our Lord Jesus Christ, who sends His messenger Zodiac to declare these things unto us.

It would be true to say that these Christ-inspired Messages—so vast in their portrayal of Divine Truth, so revealing in the loving Purposes of God for all His Creation, could, if their spiritual significance were fully grasped, transform the world! They are given in a surpassing beauty and simplicity of language which can be understood by the ordinary mind.

INTRODUCTION

In the year of 1921 there occurred an event of great spiritual importance to the world! A heavenly Messenger manifested to a small family group in the south of London, giving his name as " Zodiac ", and describing himself as a humble servant of the Master Christ. This was not his real name, but one chosen to lift up our thoughts from earth to heaven. His Mission was to bring to the world a new revelation of Truth inspired by Christ. His teachings, given first in the private Circle, and afterwards in public for more than twenty years, have been published regularly in " The Greater World ", and many have been inspired by their spiritual beauty and the deep love of the Messenger for all humanity.

The Messenger speaks " as one having authority ", the Voice is reminiscent of the Gospels; also the Messages bring to mind the words of Isaiah : " How beautiful upon the mountains are the feet of him that bringeth good tidings, that publisheth peace; that bringeth good tidings of good, that publisheth salvation; that saith unto Zion. Thy God reigneth !"

Instruction — Auras

M^Y children, tonight we have passed one more of those (to you) imperceptible stages and have started on a fresh portion of our work. I want you to throw out thoughts of sympathy, of love and of understanding, so that the good gifts of God, which are here in such generosity tonight, may contact with your own and yours, being gathered into that mighty Fount, can be used by God so that His will may be done . . .

My children, this is a very happy evening indeed ! I am speaking of the joy of the Spirit—of those things which lie far beyond the borders of the earth plane, which indeed are of the Bright Realms themselves . . . Therefore, in heart and mind rejoice, for I say unto you that in that inner self the Kingdom of God is at hand . . .

Yes, we go on ! gathering up sometimes, it seems to you, but little grist for our mill. But those in the Spirit have been adding and adding, and I tell you for your comfort that the resources are not only " enough " but are there in abundance. Out of the fragments of effort, out of the half-thoughts of holiness God has gathered the good grain and by the miracle of His Love has turned that which you value lightly into power that will be used again and again . . .

And now my children, as usual, we will talk over a few things, and tonight, in the beginning, I would speak to you of that which you describe by the word " aura ". There have been many upon earth, gifted with spiritual sight, who have been able to see in those around them some outward manifestation of the soul which is within . . . It is an interesting subject and much speculation has been forthcoming in regard to it; also much criticism too. And very often such descriptions have been dismissed as imagination—the distorted imagination of the person concerned.

Well, all those who have lived in the material world have found, over and over again, that that which is beyond the knowledge of certain persons is generally dismissed by them as non-existent—quite a common habit amongst the children of the earth throughout the ages. But you and I have learnt a little in regard to those spiritual laws which govern our life and being—I am speaking of the greater self within—we have learnt a little in regard to the wonderful Mind of God and His loving thoughts for the children He has created.

Well, in the first place, I will run over old ground in order to build up in your minds some faint conception (I can do no more) of what really is fact and truth . . .

To the majority of people the physical and the material exist only: in other words, the body and its clothing, and they form their judgments entirely on these outward indications of what lies within. And sometimes, dear children, they are an indication of the character of a person—I mean that you cannot think of God without, unconsciously, even to yourself, the physical body becoming spiritualised; you cannot wish to be pure and holy without that wish expressing itself both in your clothing and in the house in which you live . . . These things may be of a subtle nature but they exist in a definite form . . .

But tonight I want to take you much farther on than that. We will take for granted the physical body and the clothing in which it stands and get on to what is a little beyond the range of the ordinary physical eyes and physical mind—I speak of that in which you are enclosed.

My children, it has been discovered by certain students, on a purely scientific basis, that the human form has certain emanations—by which I mean that surrounding the body is that which can be seen and can be noted in detail—and yet those thinkers are, for the most part, quite unconscious of the significance of these " radiations " which are around you all.

In order to describe its shape and purpose (from a physical standpoint) I draw your attention to the parallel between it and the protective covering of an infant before birth, and I tell you that not only before physical birth, but right on through the many stages of spiritual evolution, there is that which is around you—protecting, guarding, warning and attracting.

Here I must draw your attention to the word " warning."

To most people attraction and detraction (or repulsion) is explained solely on physical grounds. In your daily life there are those for whom you are conscious of a feeling of sympathy, or of antagonism. Well, dear children, it is not necessary for me to tell you—you who have already learnt the rudiments of this subject—why this is so, but I would emphasise the fact that, as yet, you know only the outer covering of the great and important truth which lies buried underneath . . .

But let me get back to my description ! Picture to yourself this: that everyone with whom you come into contact, everyone in this great, vast world—as it appears to you—is enclosed in the vibrations which express their true personality. And those who have spiritual sight find it quite simple to see at a glance the stage of development which the soul has attained.

My children, there are some of you who have a very keen appreciation of the beautiful, and to you I would speak—I would tell you that could you once see the loveliness which surrounds a soaring soul, beauty of feature or of form would appear valueless in comparison. Those who wish to love God indeed are, as it were, swathed in a variety of exquisite colours, and, as they go on their way through life, that beauty is reflected on others, and so it is that some seem to gather unto themselves much, much love. I am speaking, dear children, of love and not of physical attraction—keep that point clear in your mind. Those who have taken the steep side of the hill are, as you can imagine, in a more favourable position in regard to displaying such beauty, and I want you to understand that as the soul gains its freedom—that is, as the soul gains domination over the physical mind—so it is able to expand those emanations with which it is gifted. The young soul—the soul who as yet is asleep, or only half awake —with these, dear children, you find that the light surrounding them is close on the physical body itself—it is an indication of that which is precious within but nothing more. Then, as the emancipation comes, so is it reflected in that beautiful encasement in which the children of earth live on the material plane. . .

My children, it is a little difficult to attempt to describe that which is of the Spirit in physical language, but I am trying

B

to build up in your minds some faint conception of the loveliness which surrounds the soul which knows God as its
Father . . .

And then we come to this: I said that this emanation
was a protection, and so it is. Remembering that others move
and have their being likewise surrounded, you can understand
that when a collision occurs between the vibrations of two
souls who are unequally developed a sense of shock is felt,
and that is what you call " physical " repulsion. It is not
physical at all, it is that which is of God guarding the sacred
self within. And when those who are attuned to evil rather
than to good come into your presence, contacting with your
emanations, so the warning is sent right through the physical
mind to the soul itself—a warning to take care, to be on your
guard because an enemy draweth nigh.

And so, dear children, it is not hard for you to understand
what a wonderful thing it is when two persons who both wish
to give out of their best come together in companionship of
any kind. Not only are the vibrations of each one in sympathy but, more than that, in coming together they recharge
each other, and that is how the joy comes. The power of each
one is doubled because the unity is complete.

You see, dear children, you have not to think very far
afield to realise what a wonderful privilege is offered you all,
and how sad it is that the children of the earth don't make
more of a struggle to gain and to hold that which has no
price. I tell you tonight that there are those upon earth who
are so spiritually awake that from two to three feet in breadth
all around them is the brightness—the reflection of the beauty
that is within. And these, dear children, quite apart from the
words they speak or the deeds they do (although these are
bound up in it) but quite apart from this, as they go through
life they are spreading holiness and truth.

When the body is laid aside and the children of the earth
come Home you can imagine their delight, their intense interest, to look at those who remain in the flesh and to see the
reflection of the real self within. Because—although it is in
a limited degree only—those vibrations which you contribute
to yourself are as near in appearance to the spiritual body as
possible while the physical remains.

My children, there is that word of warning to which I must revert . . . The vibrations which you call the " aura " are highly magnetic; for the want of a better word I will call them " electrical " vibrations, which possess a power which is not understood by anyone upon the physical plane. Yes, they have this power and it can be used or misused by the one concerned: and, in regard to others, can be used or abused as the mood takes them. You see, dear children, that we have to take into account that there are some men and women who, after reaching a certain stage of spiritual emancipation, fall from their heights to the ground beneath; and those who have never tried at all are the first to cast a sneer at their failure.

But I want you to understand this and to take to heart the responsibility which is attached to the vibrations which express your real self. I said, dear children, that those who have sought to scale the steeper side are very attractive to others; and I would add that those others need not necessarily have reached the same spiritual advancement to feel the attraction. In fact, in many instances you find a good man or a good woman rouses in one who is weaker or who is under the influence of an adverse force—rouses in these that tug of attraction to which they yield without any struggle at all.

Well, dear children, you know that the shadows are determined to block the progress of the more heroic ones and it happens sometimes that by the sheer power and beauty of their vibrations their downfall comes. Of course, they were off their guard at the time: it would have been impossible if close communion with Christ were there . . .

This is a difficult subject and I am hard put to make it clear. But I do want you to try and grasp that good men and good women—those who have struggled to free themselves from that which would hold them down—that these are not to be condemned if such a failure should come. Compassion of an unutterable kind is their right and what was not made good on the material plane shall be readjusted and strengthened when the body is laid aside.

My children, it is not a contradiction to say that those who are the most highly evolved spiritually are very often beset by the greatest temptations there are. This is only according to fact as illustrated in the life of Our Lord—for on those with a lofty purpose the evil concentrates its energies in order to pull down that which has been built up with so much strain and effort—but, as you know, Christ knew no weakness at all, yet He knew fierce temptation—temptation unparalleled by any other soul that has ever been created.

And then I pass on to this: The mere fact, dear children, that these vibrations are so interwoven around you carries also with it what would appear to you a disadvantage in regard to sensitiveness—and that sensitiveness gives some slight indication of the sensitiveness which is experienced by all when the physical body is laid aside. You have heard that when the tabernacle of the flesh is discarded nerves, as nerves, exist no more—but you must differentiate between nerves and sensitiveness. One is of the physical and the other is entirely of that spiritual nature which expresses your real selves.

My children, in regard to this subject I want to draw your attention to a little point, and that is in regard to this same sensitiveness—which you will find will increase as the days go on. I want you to realise that it is as well to protect it as much as possible—to look ahead, as it were, and to be on your guard against that which would cause it damage. It seems strange to you to speak of sensitiveness in this way, but it is really that outer expression of the soul-body which is within and it is not wise in such cases to do certain things . . . For instance, one should not be wakened unexpectedly from sleep: it is dangerous from a physical standpoint because during the sleep state still more so is that emanation apparent. If you could see with the eyes of the Spirit it would look like this: The physical body seems strangely shrunken; in fact it is more an indication than anything else, and around the sleeper are waves upon waves of light. The body is, as it were, enclosed in a cone of the finest woven strands of silk (I must use these material illustrations) but each thread is so definite, so perfectly formed that though they appear as of gossamer quality yet they are strong and vibrant with feeling . . .

Well, dear children, it is not difficult for you to understand that it is like plunging your hand through that which is not of the earth at all and touching a tiny bud inside. It is not only touching in act but when you call unexpectedly that is the effect it has upon the person concerned and that is how it looks to us. The very voice, the calling back, breaks a million, million of those most wonderful lines of light in which the sleeper is enclosed . . .

My children, you see how difficult it is for me to portray spiritual facts in physical language ! I must ask your great indulgence tonight but I have done my best with the tools at my disposal . . .

In a lesser degree, as you had demonstrated just now, it is not wise to touch suddenly any highly sensitive person, more especially those who are dedicated to this work. There, in quite a definite way, you get the same thing demonstrated, but in a slightly lesser degree—unless the one concerned is what you call actually " under control " when, as you know, they must not be touched at all . . . In regard to these " sensitives " special treatment should be meted out to them and they should be doubly on their guard against any concussion between their vibrations and those of others in an unexpected way. I refer to the so-called " chance " collisions which occur so often in daily life. My children, those who are out to destroy are vigilant indeed and when it is in their power they seek to injure, and in every case much work has to be done by us in order to protect and to make good afterwards . . .

You see, dear children, you get the two sides and you cannot have the one without the other. When those who are attuned to God come into contact with others like-minded, all the joy and the gladness is there; in fact, it expresses the highest form of happiness which the earth can know. On the other hand, you have the element of danger and certainty of discomfort when you are brought into contact with those who are keyed to lower vibrations than yourself. But God protects ever and ever again, as you were told by one who has seen God's Love and who has dedicated himself to the demonstration of that Love unto others . . . (Dr. Bottentuit).

My children, as you go on—as you evolve spiritually— you will find that this sensitiveness will increase. And I want you to take it, not as an added burden, but rather as an outward and visible sign that you are shedding the material and that the spiritual is claiming you more and more . . . This will comfort my little secretary (Dorrie) I hope ! It is necessary, my child, that you should know the why and the wherefore of these experiences as you undertake them. There is not one which will not be justified in the days to come, and only by experiencing these different phases can you help or guard others on their upward way . . .

My children, I find on going back on my words that I have left several loose threads and that is against my custom. But with a subject of this kind—with which you are only barely acquainted—it is difficult to proceed without taking you out of your depth. Yet believe me that as the time goes on I shall come back to that which still remains hazy and make all clear; and in the making clear you will see something of the marvels of God's protecting care, and how each one, from the weakest to the strongest, is held—" involved "—in that which is of God. And that all that is left to them to accomplish is, by their thoughts, their efforts and their endeavours to increase the beauty—to enlarge that which expresses Spirit. And in so doing not only to add joy and peace to the soul within but to shed on all beauty and grace as well . . .

And now I leave you ! There are messages tonight which have their work to do, and this being so I ask for your complete and undivided attention and help . . .

Taking Control

GOOD evening, my children ! and in the very beginning I am going to say that the darkness and the density of conditions outside is not apparent in this room tonight. Here, could you but see things with the eyes of the Spirit, you would find beauty and brightness and holiness past all belief. I say " past all belief " because with the finite mind of the body it is impossible to grasp that which is of God. So, dear children, banishing for this short time when we meet together the remembrance of the physical world and its many discomforts, we enter into the brightness which is of the Spirit, and those good gifts of the Spirit are being poured down in an unlimited measure upon you this evening—as they will be for ever more —although sometimes you forget it.

Tonight, dear children, we have several little things to talk over and I want you to give me your complete attention: but first of all I must rid myself of the covering my child has put on upon herself. You see, dear children, that when those come into the physical body of another, under any conditions there is a sense of restriction, of being compressed into a space which is not adequate; in fact, as some of your friends have expressed it, side by side with the joy of coming is the sense of being suffocated, from a physical point of view.

Now this is rather an interesting subject, for many there are who are puzzled—looking at things from purely practical point of view they are puzzled as to how it is possible for those who obviously are taller and broader in proportion to occupy the physical body of another built on a much smaller plan. You have to remember that the body is material—it is not only physical but it is related and keyed and built for use in a material world—while those who are free from the flesh are, on their side, adapted solely to spiritual or immaterial conditions. They have a body, it is true, but although it is solid from one point of view in no sense does it represent flesh and bone and muscle. Yet I have said that in coming into the body of another a sense of restriction—sometimes of suffocation—is experienced.

Now we have got to harmonise these two points and to bring them to a logical conclusion. I send your minds back on my remarks in regard to the " aura " and the breadth of the emanations which are possessed by those still in a physical body. You can understand, dear children, that that reflection of the spirituality within, of necessity, gives an impression of size which is not borne out by the form of the owner; but I told you that those emanations were an expression of the soul-body which, during its earthly experience, is cabined within the tabernacle of the flesh. Well, those who have passed out of physical existence have it in their power to do this: In order to enter into—and I use this term in its literal sense—in order to enter into the physical body of another built on a much smaller plan it is necessary to, as it were, draw in that which represents themselves until the body is actually occupied.

My children, I want to make this quite clear. This process (which is at will) the process of repressing themselves is necessary only in order to get a lodgment in the body they wish to speak through. When that is accomplished—in the same way as I described to you the emanations surrounding the physical body of those who love God—just in the same way those emanations which reflect the personality are able to come through that which is physical and expand themselves round the body so occupied.

Now, dear children, you can understand from this that the difficulty, the test of endurance—and it is considerable— is confined to the act of what you call " taking control ". It explains also how it is that even the inexperienced, after they have once, as it were, got their bearings, are able to speak through and use the body of another with freedom. The body being occupied by that which is of the Spirit (in the sense that it is not physical) is able to spread itself beyond the body and gain ease in that way.

You will ask me then why was it necessary to discard the little covering that my child had put on to protect her from the cold. Well that covering would accentuate the sense of repression and lack of space, and I was thinking of those who have to follow. It would have been impossible for one who was inexperienced to have overcome that added handicap.

And then I pass on to this: I want you always to take a perfectly commonsense view of the process whereby those who have vacated their own physical bodies are able to come back and speak to you in person. In your world " communication " of this kind is graded under many headings, most of them entirely misleading. For instance there is that word which has almost lost its original meaning which is used as a matter of course—I refer to " mysticism ", which in the mind of man today does not express close communion with God, but rather dabbling with that which is a danger to himself and the community at large.

You see, dear children, that simple truths, as time goes on, can be lost in a conglomeration of thoughts entirely unconnected with the spiritual world. In the days of old a " mystic " was one who was trying to get into direct touch with his Maker; today it is a term used mostly in contempt to describe those who are unpractical, who are dreamers merely and who involve themselves in a mass of theories or intellectual entanglements. I am not denying that the word holds good and will for ever, but you and I have to take things as they are and you would not dream of describing an earnest, diligent follower of Christ by the term of " mystic ".

Therefore, dear children, tonight we will make things clear as to what we are and what this sacred communion represents. We are the children of the Master, following as closely as possible the teaching of Our Lord Himself, given through the physical body which He took on to demonstrate that God could control that which was of the earth. Our precepts are His precepts; our very actions in seeking to break down the barriers between the two worlds is but following in His steps and endeavouring to obey His will. And I say to all—all who read these records—that they have only to turn to what is called " The New Testament " to find illustration and example of what we are trying to do, in Christ's Name.

" Mysticism ", as the word is interpreted nowadays, has no part in the work on which we are engaged. As in the days of old, Christ our Lord directed His disciples to seek God and to find Him, to allow themselves to be guided solely by Him, through direct contact with the Holy Spirit, so you and I, in our humble way, are trying to do likewise, and, thank God ! are succeeding far beyond the comprehension of the minds of the children of the earth.

I think I have made our position clear, and I want you next time you hear anyone refer to such " communication " as coming under the heading of mysticism—I want you to say: No ! but as followers of Christ, trying to do His will—as laid down by Him during His earthly experience—seeking to obey, wishful to be used, we offer our hearts and minds to the One who is Love Itself.

And then, dear children, there is another point which I wish to talk over and that is in regard to the " sensitiveness " to which I referred the last time we met together. Children, that same sensitiveness is given to you for a great and glorious purpose. Not only is it an accompanying gift with the shedding of the material but far more so it is the gateway into spiritual consciousness—by which I mean, the understanding of those things which are connected with the Bright Realms and with many spiritual laws which are in operation both in your world as well as in our own.

Now you know it is impossible to plunge into anything suddenly without due preparation. From the beginning I have tried to show you that not only must we build brick by brick but, first of all, must the grains of the bricks be brought together and made into a firm whole in order that they may be used. It is no use, with the things of God, to build hurriedly; we build with care, with great painstaking and, sometimes, we build and rebuild again. So, dear children, in regard to the uncovering of your spiritual consciousness: of necessity it must be a slow process. The means by which it can be done have to be gathered together in minute portions—in that steady building up of character and of self-control and, what is more, by the even balance of the physical mind.

It does not need me to tell you that self-control is perhaps of all things the least practised by the children of the earth in their general every-day life. I am not referring to those big and, sometimes, devastating impulses which occur very often when least expected—I am referring to self-control in daily life. Now, dear children—it will make you smile per-

haps—but do you know that you have been building up something which is going to mean a lot in the days to come by
the mere fact of your concentration and the control of your
physical mind during the hours when we meet together. Look
around !—few there are who have sufficient control over their
nerves and physical minds to sit still for ten minutes together.
It is a little point but it is a most important one. Gradually
I have trained you so that now for two or three hours my
children can forget themselves in listening to the things which
are of God. You have been told—and I emphasise it more
and more as we go on—that repose of mind, the quietening
down of physical thoughts and the controlling of that network
of nerves connected with the body—that this self-discipline is
not only going to bring you much in the days to come, but
is essential for the carrying on and the expansion of this work.

You see, dear children, this is another point which you
have not taken into account. In the beginning, out of ignorance of spiritual laws, you did not realise that quietness, that
stillness, that the control of that most natural desire to "fidget"
was essential in order that we might build up the conditions
required. The moment the understanding came you started
immediately to train yourselves and to obey my injunctions to
the best of your ability. Soon the sense of effort passed away,
and now I can say that my children are able to do that which
the vast majority in the physical body find it quite impossible
to accomplish: my children can be still, my children can control those nerves which, from long habit, it would be thought
had the upper hand.

You see, dear children, what can be done when the will
is there ! Only in the silence, only in the quietness, in the
quiescence of that which is of the earth can the Spirit be
released. So long as the tug of this and of that is hearkened
to, so the door between you and the Greater Wisdom can be
no more than just opened. It is essential as we go on that
you should cultivate—not only during the time we meet together but during your daily tasks—that you should cultivate
the habit of mental repose and of keeping the physical mind
as much as possible under control—under the control of the
Spirit. And the moment you can do this that sense of worry,
the fret, the ever-repeated desire to anticipate the future in an
adverse sense—all these things will gradually but definitely

fall from you and you will be untrammelled by the physical in its most hampering form . . .

You see, dear children, that I am obliged to urge you on. It is not for me to say that you have got so far and you have done well and now you can rest and enjoy ! Indeed I should be your worst enemy; and tonight I speak to Margaret particularly, in this sense: I ask her a simple question—has she not, during these months of preparation, asked to get on, to get nearer to those things of God which now hold her heart and mind ? She will answer " Yes !" and so, without beating about the bush, I tell her—as I tell you all—that for the children of the Light there is no lingering at this spot or that— it is upward and onward ever and ever again. And if at times the weariness grows great, yet I would remind you that God provides, when the need arises, those resting places into which you can retreat, getting recharged with courage, with strength and with determination to continue the journey whatever may lie in front. Yes ! I repeat—whatever may lie in front ! And tonight, dear children, it is my great pleasure to tell you that what lies in front is brightness surpassing anything your minds could conjure up—brightness and that ineffable joy which is of God alone . . .

That is the future, and the past—with its entangling sorrows, with its haunting sadness, with its questionings as to why this should be so and why that should be so—these things shall be left behind; they belong to you no more, they are of the valley beneath. And strengthened with the strength of the Spirit we go on, fired with the inspiration which comes to all once they have seen and felt the Love of God. Weariness is unknown because on either side there are those Messengers of Christ who are there to warn, to guide, to protect, and all you are asked to do (although even this may sound hard to you) is to listen to the Voice of the Spirit . . .

And that brings me back to that same " sensitiveness " to which I referred just now. Only by and through that sensitiveness can you hear the Voice direct; and to those who hear not the Voice of the Spirit as a Voice, I say: Be of good cheer, for there is that within you which listens and understands, and if the Voice fails to penetrate the mind of the body yet in your heart there is the wish to do as God would have you do, you cannot go astray. Unconsciously to you, you are hearing, with nothing in between, the Voice of God: nothing in between, for when the greater you is attuned to the Divine the physical mind ceases to exist in any sense there could be, as intervening between you and what is your own.

So, dear children, I leave it here tonight. On another occasion I have much to say about the unfoldment of spiritual consciousness, but, first of all, you must enter in through the door of that sensitiveness of perception before you are in a sufficiently responsive condition to take on the next step . . . Therefore you see, dear children, that the experiences you have been through and are going through are not that which has gone wrong, not something which you had overlooked or that which you had stepped into unaware. They are part of the training, part of the preparation, and not one incident in your life at this stage is not there for a purpose—a Divine purpose: the attuning, the refining, the harmonising, so that when the time comes (only waiting, dear children, for you to be ready) you may take the next step in confidence and there may be no retracing at all . . .

On, on we go—slowly, it is true, but surely—which is best; and that is my last word tonight before I leave you to enable others to come. Slow and sure, and that which is best in every sense there could be; to look around on your conditions, on the routine of the day and to say: In this and in that I see God's Hand and all, all is wonderfully well ! . . . Faith shall be justified, hope shall be turned into fulfilment, blindness into sight, misunderstanding into comprehension— that spiritual comprehension when you shall find that all doors shall be opened to you and welcome, sweet welcome on either side . . .

Father, we thank Thee for all Thy many good gifts and protection. Father, we thank Thee again and again . . .

Mans
Treatment of Animals

MY children, tonight, perhaps, is one of those evenings when, from an outside point of view, it would seem that conditions were adverse because of undue strain upon my child. But, as you know, God is so good, and when any one of His children have suffered—because they have suffered so He sends down power and grace in order that it may never even be thought that the Father is not mindful of both the small and the great things which concern His little ones. So, dear children, starting perhaps a little slowly, we shall work through that which is not up to standard and the evening shall show God's blessing all round.

Tonight, dear children, there are very many things which I should like to discuss but, as usual, we are limited for time; and so in order to distract your thoughts a little I think I will speak to you in regard to man's treatment of animals.

Now, all of you, and the vast majority, are singularly compassionate towards the dumb creatures created by God. Some there are who lavish much love upon their pets; and, if not robbing another, then I say this is good in the sight of the Father. But, as you know, it could not be pleasing to that which is Love Itself to overlook human creation in favour of any other . . . I do not say a " lower " creation, dear children, because in God's sight these grades do not exist. Humanity and the animal, vegetable and mineral kingdoms are separate states, each demanding and receiving the necessary care of which they stand in need . . . And in regard to plants, later on in our studies I will try and show you how the Love of God is shown in them and how they, in turn, reflect the love of the Creator.

Tonight, however, we are considering animals and their

part in the scheme of things; and I say at once that it is not pleasing to God when excessive love is bestowed upon these and hardness and coldness of heart is shown towards the little children who stand so sorely in need of another's care.

My children, some there are who say they find it far easier to love a dog or a horse than one of these little ones, whom Jesus blessed (for in blessing one child He blessed children as a whole) and you do not need me to put it into words in order to grasp it—in an unlimited sense.

Then, dear children, we will turn to the other aspect, which is terrible to some to contemplate. I mean that, now and again, you hear of cases of intense cruelty to one of God's dumb and helpless creatures; and I want to give a word of warning on this subject.

But, first of all, you must remember that death, as death— by which I mean the taking of the life of any animal—is, in reality, bestowing upon it a gift of price. Now keep this point clear in your minds: I say that the surrendering of " life " and the suffering entailed by the brutality of another is, by reason of what it cost, turned into unparalleled gain to the one concerned. On the other hand, I tell you—and I emphasise it with all the power at my disposal—that those who, out of carelessness or cruelty, inflict one pang of pain on another who is unable to defend itself is piling up that which can only be worked out by much, much effort and suffering.

And then, dear children, I pass on to another point, which naturally, comes into the consideration of this subject—I speak of the slaying of animals for food. Well, dear children, some have debated this as it concerns the law of creation; and I want you to do your best to follow me in what I am going to say:

These animals used for food are a provision of the Almighty for the needs of the physical body, and there is not the slightest responsibility placed upon anyone who kills an animal in as humane a manner as lies at his disposal. But mark you, that which does not come under the heading of " humane " is a tremendous mistake, viewed from the physical aspect and the evolutionary processes of the soul . . .

But I want you, dear children, to hark back to the remark I made—that the taking of the " life " by another does not do

anything but render a service to the creature concerned—
because according to the proportion of suffering, and by the
very fact that the carcass is of service to others, so that greater
life which was within is helped and is added to in a way you
cannot yet understand.

Is it not feasible that God, Who is mindful of every
sparrow that falls, should be concerned with the suffering, the
persecution and the brutalities inflicted on those entrusted to
man's care ? It is a tremendous responsibilty and many there
are who on laying the physical body aside are appalled by
the spectacle which meets their gaze—that massing together
of the small brutalities which, e'er they can continue the upward path, have to be made as non-existent.

And this applies, dear children, without reserve, to those
who, under the name of " sport " torture that which God has
created. Yes ! I know it will be said that it has been done
throughout the ages, that it is a healthy exercise, that it is the
custom of the world ! But the day will come when those who
took their amusements in this unspiritual way—when these
with sorrow, will have to go back on their tracks and make
good that which was so sadly missing.

Selfishness or, rather, love of self, sometimes can do as
much harm as deliberate, preconceived evil thinking. God is
not unmindful of the hare or of the fox: each pang suffered by
them is reflected in the Heart of Love; and because they are
His creation never would He separate Himself from that which
is His own . . .

The world has to change its attitude of mind over many
of the so-called customary things of every-day life. And I
entreat you, dear children, when the opportunity arises to put
in a word for Christ on this tremendous subject which is so
misunderstood.

And then I must refer to another point which in the minds
of my children has caused serious misgiving—I refer to the ex-
termination of so-called " pests " which, if allowed to increase
unchecked, would soon make life quite unbearable from a
physical point of view.

My children, a little incident in connection with this has
almost passed out of your minds; but we do not forget. I
speak of the little mouse and its distressing end, which caused

tears from at least one of my children and prayers from others. Well, dear children, I want you to know this for your comfort: that you are well within your rights—indeed you are called upon to so regulate your household that only that which promotes health is allowed to obtain a footing. Yet I would add just this: that your tenderness over the sufferings of the helpless can be, and has been, used by the Mind of Love to mitigate that pain which follows as a natural course.

You see, dear children, how wonderful are the spiritual laws that govern your life and mine; nature in all its forms and every living creature. No thought of compassion, no shrinking of the heart from the pain of another ever falls to the ground unused by the Father. So you see, dear children, that even in this way you can soften the suffering of others. There is not one of you who has not again and again thrown over some dumb creature, as it were, an anodyne which mitigated its suffering. I tell you for your great comfort that God is happy in His children when they send thoughts of healing —which compassion means—in the direction of that which is helpless to defend itself.

I think I have made the matter clear, and I cannot tonight go into the part which animals have in the scheme of things. But you have been told that certain animals have been seen on this side and, therefore, know that they have their place amongst those who are free from the body.

Everything has its place ! That's what I want to leave on your minds tonight. To you very often nature appears as a cruel and pitiless monster, and the suffering that goes on, on either side, to you, is appalling in its many ramifications. But I beg you next time when such a thought arises to remember the words which appear in your own precious Record—that the Father is mindful of every sparrow that falls. You cannot grasp this and neither can I, but I see and I know that in each living thing is God (in the sense that it was created by Him) and He acknowledges His responsibility towards it.

You have much to be thankful for, my children, and one of the things which should call forth your greatest gratitude is that sensitiveness over the pangs of others, which are so often overlooked by the many who are immersed in themselves. It is a privilege to feel for others, and even—or rather because—

C

you suffer in so doing, so it is adding power and enlightenment to yourself, because sympathy is an attribute of God and each one of us who can gather it unto ourselves shortens the length of the bridge between us and that which we want to be and that which God intends us to rise to !

Well, my children, I must not stay any longer tonight because last week, as you know, the personal messages had to be severely curtailed and I do not like this to occur because your dear ones so look for the opportunity to speak direct. You cannot understand, my little ones, what it is to us to come in this way and to express in words the love and the understanding that we have for you all and for humanity at large. And in connection with this there is one to whom I would direct your attention. Those who are bound to you by ties of love, of relationship and by those strong cords of friendship—these pass through your minds with regularity and they are able to take advantage of their turn when it arrives, without undue struggle to overcome the opposing forces. But there are others who, from your point of view, are strangers both from a physical standpoint and also so far as their characteristics are concerned, for as yet they have had little opportunity to demonstrate these in person.

There is one tonight to whom I refer directly—one who by long years of service, of watchfulness, of unceasing prayer and unbroken patience has linked himself to your lives and to the work for ever more. When you come here, dear children, you will be amazed to see the close and loving friendship which exists in the Spirit between you and what you would call " total strangers." It will be a wonderful revelation; and if a pang of compunction is felt as well, then love will soon cover that over and all will be as God intended.

The one to whom I would direct your attention has appeared in these records under the name of " Mr. Taylor ", and by God's direction I bring in his loving personality tonight. He will come when an opportunity offers—not necessarily this evening—but send him thoughts of friendship, of gratitude and of sympathetic understanding, for he has done much, has suffered much, has overcome much in order to make his presence known among you. And there I leave it.

False Pictures

GOOD evening, my children, and once again we meet together in great peace. Sometimes, my little ones, it seems to you that peace has slipped a little over the border, but if you could see things as they are you would know that this was but a misrepresentation on the part of the shadows who, as I have told you before, spend much time and effort on building up false pictures: and the children of earth, in ignorance, think that these travesties of the real represents life as ordained by the Father. When, however, the children get a little older they are not so easily deceived, and when such mental pictures are presented before them they say: " No ! before I accept this I am going to get down to facts !" So with a will, point by point, they compare the features of the counterfeit picture with the details of their life at the time; and if this is carried through faithfully, before long they discover they have very nearly been tricked again . . .

My children, in this there is a warning for you all—for all those who are going through their earthly experiences. In regard to my own children, I am, as it were, the guardian of their happiness—for this glorious quest on which we have embarked is the only true happiness there is—and I, as guardian of their happiness, bid them take care: It is only just, when two points of view are brought before your attention, to analyse them both with equal patience and thoroughness. It is no use taking the one and agreeing that it is accurate and refusing to examine the other side of the shield . . .

My children, sunless days upon earth have a way of lowering the vitality of the body, as you know; it is a disadvantage which has to be fought against. But I say this tonight: Is it wise to shut out the sunshine of the Vision Splendid, and so add to the darkness of the physical world the twilight of the Spirit ?

You see, dear children, I have a great responsibility in

regard to you all. I have called you out of the beaten track;
I have urged you to try the sharp, steep road which leads into
the understanding of the Greater Wisdom; I have bidden you
forsake much which the majority rightly consider an integral
part of daily life—all these things I have done, and more. I
did them deliberately—I did them by instruction of my Master,
Christ. But in no sense does that lift the responsibility from
me, and I say tonight that I am conscious of this—I accept it
down to the tiniest detail or portion.

On the other hand, dear children, you must remember
this: that in calling you out of the busy, careless crowd I did
not do so without good reason. In the first place, I saw that
you would listen to my voice, that you would heed my guiding
care. Then I saw the next stage and the next—the strain, the
weariness and the struggle; and what was more I saw (and I
told you at the time) I saw the fierce battles which must come
as an inevitable part of the journey—the battles with the evil
forces, which have shaken older and stronger pilgrims than
my little children here tonight.

You see I am keeping back nothing—I kept back nothing
from the beginning, if you will consider my words—but God's
gracious goodness threw a veil over their meaning, in the sense
that He would not allow you to live through those troublous
times in anticipation. The Father knew that when the test
came you would want all your courage and endurance—that
you would also have to fall back on those resources which had
been gathered together by the many years of preparation . . .

Well, dear children, from an outside point of view, it
would seem that I have played rather a cruel part. I led my
children away from their kind; I induced them to give up
the few toys which remained in their possession, and I started
them on a very hard and difficult road which I knew held
determined enemies—I will not say " dangerous " because I
have told you from the beginning that the protection is complete . . .

Ah ! my children, it sounds rather a sorry story; and yet
it is the brightest and the best and the most beautiful that
could be imagined. For, remember, I saw too the enemies
overthrown, the sadness despatched for ever, and joy and gladness and unity on every side; my little charges no longer bent

beneath their burdens but rejoicing in the brightness and the sweetness that is all around.

My children, it was necessary to speak on this point to-night, because we have reached a stage in our journey when it seems to those gifted only with half-sight as if darkness lies before even as it lies behind.

So you see, dear children, that I, as your loving companion, as your guide, as the one who in Christ's Name calls you on—I am sensible of my responsibility; and I want you, as much as possible, to forbid the dark days in your world to cast a shade over that part of your mind which, of necessity, is in an extremely sensitive condition just now. These encounters, dear children, leave their mark for the time being; and there are those among you who are only conscious of the wounds, and the sense of victory has been obliterated by the weariness of the contest . . .

I speak to all, for each, in a different way, according to the point they have reached, have had these struggles and, in proportion, they are suffering from a sense of shock. But oh ! dear children, isn't it wonderful to think that in comparatively so short a time we have got so far ? Isn't it glorious to think that we can mark off so many of these encounters as that which has taken place and not that which lies before us ? Yes ! I think, viewing things in the broad way—in the way of the Spirit—it must impress you that you have every reason to rejoice and that really at this stage mourning is a little out of place.

I want you to consider, dear children, one thing more, and that is the generosity of our Father, God.

Put it to yourselves: Just suppose that there were friends who loved you well enough to undertake a long and dangerous journey (dangerous so far as physical well-being was concerned) that you heard that these dear ones had started. And you were in the position of witnessing, although, apparently, afar off, their many trials and vexations; then, as they proceeded, the real suffering which came as an inevitable result; and, again, those treacherous passes, those sharp rocks on either side—that from your point of vantage you were able to witness their sense of dismay, their wondering how it would be possible to proceed. And then you noted with pleasure that after a little consideration, and perhaps delay, they go

forward braving the anticipated dangers and certainly enduring both weariness of mind and body . . . Well, I think as you
watched your friends advancing and as you saw how strong
was the love within their hearts; how anxious they were to
see you—well, dear children, wouldn't it be only natural that
you would look round and see how you could welcome them
in a way that expressed something of what you felt . . .

It is a crude illustration but it must serve. Of course the
great difference between you and Christ lies in this way: that
the Saviour never watches merely, but shares; that the Saviour
is never afar off but at your side, and that the Saviour does
not wait until the journey's end to show His love in an outward and visible way, but, step by step, as the pilgrim progresses, so are the gifts of the Spirit found on either side . . .

You see, dear children, that when I talk to you everything
is so beautifully simple, so straight forward, so exactly like
Love Itself. And so I would remind you of the picture, the
false picture which evil builds up so eagerly, hoping that it
may catch your eye. Tonight I am presenting the truth as it
stands; and I think you will allow that it is only fair to view
both the real and the unreal and to see to which your heart
responds the most.

Once you can get firmly fixed in your physical mind the
companionship of Christ—that intimate, personal companionship which is never absent from you for one second—if once
you could get a grip on that then I should not have to point
out the glories and the beauties of the quest on which you are
engaged: and it is that great comfort which the shadows are
so determined to prevent. But, children, as you have been
told before, in everything there are two voices—one the Voice
of God and the other the voice of the world. If you listen to
the second you cannot hear the first: and, again, if you listen
to the Voice of the Spirit its sweetness blots out any other
voice there could be.

Oh ! it is not so hard; it is far easier than man understands: but the first stages are difficult, I own. Once the tests
have been put and accepted; once evil has been faced as evil
and overcome, then, dear children, comes the dawning of that
harmony of the Spirit, and its influence is so great, so attractive, both to the mind and heart, as well as to the soul, that the
struggle is o'er. The real self within yields itself up to the

Divine counterpart. It is, as it were, as though for a time something had come in between two great forces—the force within and that all-enveloping force which you call " the Spirit". But I tell you—and this applies to all, although with some the breach indeed seems great—I tell you the force of the Spirit is of so dominant a character that that which is within—its counterpart in miniature—must be reunited, must go back to its Source. And though all the powers of evil may concentrate on preventing this, yet because that which is within belongs to God nothing can prevent the unity in the end. The Father stretches out His Hand and the soul, waking from its sleep, gets one glimpse of Beauty—nothing more at that stage. But that revelation of Beauty—which can be made its own—so rouses within the desire for the highest and the best that it is only a question of time . . .

And here, my little ones, once more I bring in the exquisite patience of our Father, God. It seems to you sometimes that you make so little progress; that, in going through your own heart and mind, you see so many weeds and the flowers are delicate indeed. But, children, have I not told you that the first thing a gardener has to learn is patience ? And so it should not be difficult for you to grasp how your Father feels—He who is patience itself; patience in a way that can think of eons and eons of time and build for the future, knowing that although man may stray far from His loving guidance, yet His care can reach to the furthest point. And though the guidance has been rejected, yet His Love, at last, shall turn the steps of the wanderer home . . .

Oh ! my little ones, do not lose heart. I am in rather a difficult position: If I tell you not to grieve over your limited spiritual resources then I am blocking your progress; yet, dear ones, if I say to you that you should have done better, then I am not representing the Father's attitude towards you at all. Keep these two points clear: The Father calls you on and on because He knows that safety and happiness lie in front; because He knows that once passed this difficult stage you are protected from sorrow, as you regard sorrow, for evermore. But, at the same time, the Father understands that to children the road is heavy indeed, and though the call rings out again and again " Come up higher and I will show you the things I have prepared for you ", yet even as the words go forth, the

Father understands that it is difficult to hasten the pace; and His love and protection and companionship are with you every step of the way.   There is no blame in the Mind of Love because the steepness of the road brings forth your sadness; nothing but perfect understanding of the child's view towards the unknown . . .

My children, tonight I am most anxious to comfort you in every way I can: I am so anxious to bring into your midst —nay ! into your hearts and minds—some realisation of God and His unlimited Love.   It is terrible to us—we who have seen and who know that Love (so far as we are able to take it in)—it is terrible to us that the little children of the earth find it so hard to get the " personal " aspect of the Love of Christ.   " God so loved the world !" . . . Yes, but even that statement does not convey the personal side, which the Father has tried, is trying, and will never cease to try to force upon the physical minds of His little ones on earth. The "universal " Love of the Father presents one element of danger, from our point of view: In saying that " God so loved the world " it conveys to the mind of many, unconsciously, a generalisation rather than the personal aspect, which is literal fact.   Say then to yourselves, dear children: God loves me; Christ is my Saviour; the Father has me under His direct care !   This is not selfishness—I put that in because to some minds it may read thus.   But what humanity is crying out for today is a personal Christ, a personal God, an individual Father, and until we can force this on the physical minds of men and women so will the mourning and the grieving and the misunderstanding go on.

Because God is the Father of the world, of the Realms of the Spirit and of all those states and conditions which are far beyond your range, it does not alter this Divine truth: that from the highest to the lowest and from the lowest to the highest, so far as spiritual attainment is concerned, God is the personal, individual Father of each one; that He is the Christ, the Saviour, the Redeemer of each one, and you are bound to Him by that strongest tie of all—you are of Him. Because within there is that emblem of God, that aspect of the Godhead, that priceless part of the Creator—within you is the Holy Spirit, which is God—and in recognising your kinship, your sonship and your daughtership you are only acknowledging that which is your own . . .

My children, it has been difficult to convey my meaning—difficult because your language is so limited, your conception of Love so limited, your understanding of the Father so terribly limited as well. But just try and take from my words something of what it means to be a child who wants to love God; something of the happiness, the harmony and the infinite joy of—when you are free from the body—meeting your Father face to face and receiving from Him the kiss which a Father bestows upon one whom He has cherished and guarded and watched right back through those long periods of time which entirely escape your imagination . . .

There I must leave it. I pray God that greater understanding may come, that the joy (which you have worked for) can be taken—taken as your right, taken as an inseparable part of your physical daily life—and in so making it your own you may get some reflection of the illimitable Love behind it . . .

Finding Christ

WELL, dear children, we meet in the Silence of the Spirit!
And I want you to so attune your hearts and minds
that your undivided attention may be given to God—to banish thoughts that are not entirely of Him—for if you will endeavour to do this, to the best of your ability, then I can
promise, with so much happiness, that indeed you shall contact with Holiness itself. Offer then your hearts and minds to
the One to whom they belong.

Tonight, dear children, the opportunity has been provided to discuss with you one or two of those points which
cause difficulties in the physical mind—points, moreover,
which are used directly by the shadows to, as it were, cast a
slight shade between the Spirit within and the Great Spirit to
whom we owe our being . . .

(Subject: The Divinity of Jesus).

Children, there are many ways of finding God, as you
have been told. There are many ways also of following His
teaching; and it is not necessary for me to emphasise the fact
that he who wishes to do or to think aright shall find, when
the physical body is laid aside, that indeed he worshipped God
with a clean heart.

Yet, dear children, it has saddened you—as those countless millions in the spirit—to find, sometimes, that the full light
of revelation, as it were, shines not directly on the person concerned, but at a slight angle.

It is difficult for me to express in words my meaning, but
think you of what you call " astigmatism ", as it relates to
physical sight. You know that in the eye so built that the
light without fails to shine on a given point within: and, therefore, while the owner is able to see much—the beauties of
nature, the glories of the sun, the moon and the stars—yet he

knows, and you know, that although " sight " is there, as sight it is imperfect.

Children, there are some still cabined in the physical body who are in a similar position in regard to spiritual sight and understanding. The revelation—that magnetic beauty which shines upon all without distinction—that light from the All-Light is hampered by the fact that the physical minds of some are not quite in focus with it; and although many powers are theirs, yet the full splendour of illumination just misses them by that tiny fraction which differentiates between true vision —perfect vision and that which is one stage less.

Children, tonight I am going to give you a plain statement in regard to the " Immaculate Conception ", as some name it, and the birth of He whom you call Christ.

In the first place I send your minds back to a very early evening when we talked over together the character of Mary, the Mother of Our Lord. I told you then that she had been prepared for this sacred use, that much experience, in a spiritual sense, was her own before she entered on her earthly journey.

Now, dear children, I am not here tonight to argue or to try and tear down any theories or doctrines or beliefs held by others; I am here to make a clear and definite statement of facts as they were and are and will be for evermore.

Mary was not protected from evil except by her own purity of heart, gained and fought for through those long periods of time which are beyond your imagination. It was because of that preparation that she was chosen. And, as I have told you before, the whole reason and purpose of that earthly experience undertaken by our Father God, was that man should never be in a position to say: " God cannot understand !"

In regard to the conception, the purity of the girl and the part she played throughout: I state definitely that she was of God in the sense that she had tried to follow the teaching laid down by Him—to get nearer in spirit to the Great Spirit. And although I allow that her physical mind may have appeared limited indeed, you and I, dear children, know that independently of the physical mind and its powers the soul within, unrestricted, can soar and can contact with God.

It seems curious to us why the " miracle " of the conception should provide such a stumbling-block in the mind of
man.   That the Creator of all—of those marvellous details of
nature, of the heavenly worlds and constellations, of the secrets
of so-called science: it seems curiously strange to us that the
One who brought into being not only your little world but
those vaster, greater worlds and spheres and states beyond:
that He who thought out the construction of that physical body
in which Our Lord was carried—that this simple miracle, if
you like to call it thus, should be considered beyond His power
or imagination . . .

My children, this is a very serious subject.   It is as a
jewel which has been given to mankind: that priceless gift of
God, as man, going through the same experiences as you and
I, knowing and feeling just as the least of His little ones;
Divinity taking on so simply, so wonderfully simply those experiences with us on earth—that this should be discredited,
that this should be ruled out of court as something which
strains the powers of reasoning to breaking point . . .

My children, it is not easy to find suitable words with
which to treat this subject.   It is difficult for me to adequately
express even a tithe of what this gift means—I mean the
coming of Our Lord as an infant, in a home which was not
congenial from many points of view, in an environment which
meant a stern hold on the physical mind and physical will—
not favoured by circumstances in any sense: that Child bearing
all, overcoming everything; always with one thought in view
—the revelation to man of Love Divine.   Not of power, not
of greatness, not of Godhead (in the sense that the physical
mind accepts it), but to reveal Love Divine, unlimited in
understanding, in compassion and in hope.

And then there is another point which I would bring in
here: Some of you think, or have thought, that humanity as
a whole is not ready yet for the further gift of Truth which
is even now being unfolded to you; but, dear children, I ask
you to go back on the life of Our Lord.   In looking at things
dispassionately, comparing the times then with the time now,
you would be forced to say that the coming of The Messiah
was even less opportune than the presenting of this further
explanation of Truth today.   I remind you that when Christ
said " I and the Father are one " they stoned Him.   Yet, dear

children, you have only to look round and you will see that
although those of His own generation and kind stoned Him
for expressing Truth, little by little, slowly—yes, slowly indeed that statement became an accepted fact by countless
thousands and it stands today. Today, my little ones, there
may be some who, as it were, find their minds fixed not on the
Light itself but on the reflection of the Light; yet for your
comfort I tell you all that in the years to come these same
earnest seekers shall come back to the children of the earth
and announce with joy that they have found the Truth indeed
—the Truth as expressed in Christ our Saviour, God: Father,
Son and Holy Spirit; One yet Three; Three but One ! . . .

Children, there are those who cannot wait for the full
revelation to come; I mean in this sense: I have told you before that the unfoldment of spiritual consciousness, of necessity, must be a slow process; I have told you that, in God's
good time, the petals of the flower will be unravelled and the
beauty will be complete. But the conditions of the physical
world do not tend to promote swift growth in this direction;
and some there are who cannot wait for the consciousness
within to come—the mind is so active, so full of vitality that it
has got to answer every question now—and that's where the
mistake comes in.

My children, there are many experienced ones on this
side who never attempt to express a final opinion on any
subject which has come under their attention, even though
they may be gifted with spiritual sight. They speak with due
reserve, as you have noticed again and again with your loved
ones. Within them is the warning that finality can never be
reached, and the only One who understands the beginning
and the end is God, the Creator of us all.

You see my point: that when it concerns great truths,
or what you sometimes name as " great mysteries " it is wiser
to be silent—wiser in this sense: Not because the God of Love
is injured or damaged by an open expression of these half
denials, but because when fuller understanding comes, the
one concerned, who was so anxious to get to the heart of
things, will suffer in proportion . . .

My children, when you hear the God in Christ denied do
not feel indignant for His sake but send out your compassion
to those who are held back—held back, remember, only by

the construction of the physical mind, only by that tiny lack of focus—send out your prayers to them because, loving God so much, they will suffer when they come here and it will take all our love, and more, to heal the wound . . .

You see, dear children, that we punish ourselves. There is not one thought which fails to come up to the highest which does not, even in your daily life, bound back and strike you e'er it passes beyond your memory. This is a spiritual law— Love Itself—when you understand the principle underlying it. Only by the working out of that which is " error " against the Divinity within; only by that process which you call " cause and effect " can the soaring soul step into radiance when it is free from its physical bondage.

Let that thought sink in and know, dear children: that because compunction comes for this or for that, when you realise you have failed your better self—that this is God's most loving way, so that the multitude of definite formations which, unconsciously, you have built by thought, that these may not have to be grappled with when your earthly sojourn is ended.

Then I want you, dear children, in your daily lives to bear this in mind—and it follows on quite naturally on my remarks last week in regard to a personal, individual Christ and Father—I want you to remember that as you are able to bring Light to others (or in failing to do this pray that the fuller Light may be born within)—as you are able to reflect the Love of Christ to others so, unconsciously, both to them and to you, you are demonstrating the Divinity, the Godhead of the Man of Sorrows, who was acquainted with the griefs of physical existence. That, dear children, brings me down to the whole meaning and purpose of our Father God dwelling amongst us: that purpose of demonstrating to those on earth that Love stopped at nothing in order to express Itself and to bring reassurance to the little children that wandered hither and thither in ignorance, or in spiritual loneliness.

There is one other point, dear children, which I cannot leave untouched, and that is in regard to the great and holy men who, by many, have been looked upon as God, or an expression of God upon earth.

Children, there is not one, from the strongest to the weakest, who has ever helped another to live more spiritually who has not gained the direct blessing of God. And these great teachers who, to an enormous extent, influenced the minds and lives of their fellows—these great and holy sons of God have entered into unspeakable conditions, have gathered unto themselves those rarest gifts of the Spirit and are centred in Love Divine for ever more.

As you know, theories and dogma and doctrines are swept over the borders by the strong wind of purity and holiness of thought, and in your minds you are perfectly right to give honour where honour is due. But there is one thing which I must emphasise tonight: Following on my statement that it is the " life " that counts, then I ask you to take the life of Our Lord from childhood until the physical end and to compare it point by point with those others—and you will find that Christ stands alone. I am not speaking of His miracles, of the power He had over the elements or over the wayward hearts of the children of the earth—I am speaking of that simple, patient life of service, that great Heart, that perfect charity and forgiveness, that perfection of Love—and I say to you all, dear children, that you have your answer there. Yet, in so saying, I belittle not the great and holy lives of others—the sacrifices, the stern self-discipline—they are, as I said, centred in Love Divine for ever and for ever. But there was One who was greater than these, greater and simpler too. Keep that simplicity definitely in your minds because it so expresses Love in its highest form—the Love which could strip itself of everything, everything that makes physical life bearable to a sensitive soul—and in poverty, in loneliness of mind He trod His earthly way, shedding those imperishable flowers of holiness and of tenderness. And when every prophet shall be forgotten, as such, He who was stoned for expressing Truth, He shall remain enshrined—I do not say " enthroned "— but " enshrined " in the hearts of His children because He expresses Love—unlimited Love—and Love has to be answered by us all . . . yea, even by those who as yet know nothing of the meaning of Love. But so great is that Love that it shall draw them in and raise them up, for the patience of Our Father, God has no beginning and no end . . .

My little ones, you will have seen once more that I am

trying to express the inexpressible, that I am trying to describe that which baffles all description. But yet I pray God that He will, through that inner consciousness within, allow you to fasten on to something of the great and glorious Truth I am seeking to unfold . . .

My children, I am loth to leave you, but there are others who are equally anxious to make their presence felt in this way, so with deep, deep love and perfect understanding we part for a little while—part ! yes, it seems thus to you, but where my children are there gathers Zodiac, for you are my own—in Christ's Name I say you are my own. My little flock is precious indeed to me. I not only know you all by name —those names which belong to the Spirit—but your hearts and minds are as open books and there is not one tiny item which you could ever say has eluded my tender and loving attention. Yes, dear children, the cords between us grow tighter and tighter, as was promised to me by my Father, away back in the dim and distant past. Yet in so promising I too had to wait for the fuller revelation of what this implied, because the Mind of Love not only gives but gives so lavishly that we cannot take it in. And so we leave it—leave it until we have grown a little more: but when we've grown a little more, why then we find that the generosity of God has grown greater still—and again we leave it. And this goes on for ever . . .

Suffering

MY little children, we start rather late tonight (8 p.m.), and it seems to you a curious thing why so much on the physical plane is allowed, apparently, to interfere with our plans when those plans are formed solely with the idea of following obediently the direction given.

Well, my children, looking at things from the earth point of view I allow that there are many things in your daily life which seem to run diametrically opposed to all-pervading Love, a sense of which I am determined to instil into your physical minds. Yet, dear children, viewed in the big way, in the way that you will regard it when you are free, you will see that nothing has gone amiss—there has been no miscarriage of justice—but all is as it must be in order to produce the beauty and the power which will be required later on. Because some suffer under the process would you that the plan should be thrown aside ? For, my little ones, how often must I tell you that it is suffering which produces the highest and the best; it is suffering which provides the necessary working power; it is suffering which brings you closer to the Spirit than anything else.

Yet again I say I can understand the earth point of view. Human nature has its limits, and the thought that only by so much discipline can the real self emerge causes a chill to the heart and mind of each one who listens to me and to those who read my words. So tonight I am going to make things clear: I am going to tell you that suffering was never meant to last throughout the physical journey. It is, as I have said, required to provide the strong staff, the experience and the guiding instinct to lead you unto God, and when once these have been obtained then the necessity for suffering is at an end.

You are concerned, very often, about the sorrows of others; the almost devastating experiences, so you think, which

D

they have to face: you are troubled, both in heart and mind, that there should be so much poverty and hardship in the world at large. The recital of another's earthly experience causes deep dismay. And yet, my little ones, while it is necessary that you should listen and enter into the sorrows of others I bid you also try and take a wider view of that which, of necessity, must pass away in time to come. I am not underestimating the grief in the world today. It is caused partly by the hardness of heart of those who are better placed; it is caused also by that lack of self-restraint in the centuries long past, which has allowed the evil forces to gain a much stronger hold than ever was intended. Yet, dear children, as you realise, freewill cannot be interfered with. And so our Heavenly Father has taken that which has been done to wreck and wound, and, by the miracle of His Love, has turned loss into gain, suffering into happiness beyond all expression.

You see it very often happens thus, because the freewill of the individual is a gift from God, never to be thwarted— never to be influenced except by love. And because of this, God has chosen another means of working out His wonderful purpose. And though the evil may strike you and others again and again, the Father takes the very blow itself to bring you gain, to give you your heart's desire in that day when the vision comes and you see the splendour of the Life which has no end.

My children, I am very near you in thought tonight. Nothing makes a barrier between me and those I love, although, dear ones, you find it so hard to take this in. Nothing in the world or in those conditions where darkness reigns— nothing, nothing can separate me from my children, to whom I am bound by every tie and link there could be: and those links are sealed by God, to remain unbreakable for ever and for ever.

And now that I have got you all safely under my wing once more we will talk of other things: and first of all I have just a few words to say about one who has called forth your love and admiration—admiration because the Spirit within is strong and courageous indeed. (Mr. Ernest Meads.)

Tell him from me, my children, that the work goes on apace; that the love of God which is in his heart has brought him into conditions which shall defy trouble and sorrow and

suffering. That one, dear children, has suffered much, he
has been through deep waters. And yet, keeping his eyes on
the Light above, safely he has swum from shore to shore and
ever the land grows firmer under his feet and he is blessed
of the Father indeed. Shut not your love off from such a
one; cast aside those crippling thoughts of the earth which
forbid this and forbid that. Love was given to each one to
give again: and he will understand. Ah ! yes, he will understand that Spirit calls to Spirit and that the tie is one of God
alone.

I give these few words, dear children, because I want you
to know that, more and more, I am leading you hither and
thither where help and strength may be found: and yet you
cannot imagine that after directing you to take I should tell
you not to give in return. The power of love is greater than
anyone on this plane has ever grasped; its healing, its sustain-
ing power is unlimited when the love is pure. And so I say to
you and to all who read: Give out of your love and restrain
it not, because God said " Little children, love one another "
. . . love one another !

And now, my little ones, speaking of love I will pass on
to a subject which, in the physical minds of many through the
ages, has caused perplexity and sometimes that which is far
less pleasant—a certain lack of delicacy, which is hurtful to
them and to those who hear . . .

I refer, dear children, to Our Lord's statement that there
was no marriage or giving in marriage once physical life was
ended.

Now here, dear children, we are brought up against two
attitudes of mind, because, as you know, that which you call
" marriage " has not been carried out as Our Father intended.
To those whose experience has been bitter or disillusioning
the thought that once physical life is over marriage, as marriage, exists no more is greeted with a sense of thankfulness
which goes too deep for words . . .

Then, dear children, there are others—many others, thank
God !—who have got fairly near to the ideal; and when death
steps in the one who is left behind is conscious of a sense of
loss which even the knowledge of reunion later on cannot wipe
out. Children, they view it somewhat like this: they say

" Oh, I know we shall be together again, but it will not be the same !" And by this they mean to imply that that which awaits them will be far less complete than the union during their physical lives.

Well, dear children, with a subject like this, on which so many queries arise, it is well, I think, to give a plain and straight forward statement, so that you, and others, may readjust your minds to the truth as it is and has been from the beginning.

True it is that there is no " marriage " in the bright spheres, but, my little ones, there is a unity between soul and soul which far transcends anything that has ever been experienced, even under the most ideal conditions, upon earth. Because humanity, as a whole, has been unable to get the true vision of unity of Spirit it goes to the other extreme and rules out that "wedlock" between individual souls, as non-existent.

It is strange to us, dear children, that the word " wedded " should represent to you only a state which is possible while the physical body remains: it is strange to us that man should be so blind and that love should have been allowed to fall so far from its high estate !

Little children, do not misunderstand. Those laws of nature are necessary for the working out of God's plan, necessary because there are countless thousands wanting always to undergo their experience on earth. But, dear children, love is a far more subtle thing than that. The attraction between individuals on the earth plane is simply and solely the bare outline, the merest indication of the unity of Spirit in the Realms where Spirit has full scope.

I want you to get your view point right; I want you to be able to say to those who have suffered under the conditions of marriage—I want you to tell them that there is in store for them a unity, a wedlock, in its spiritual sense, which will reveal to them God's mighty Love. And I want you to reassure those who feel that something has been taken from them which will never come back in the old sweet way again —I want you to say, with faith and with certainty, that beautiful as that love may have been; complete, in the earth sense, the sympathy of mind established, those things were but a reflection of the real. And when they come Home they will find their loved ones waiting for them, and in that reunion—which means a unity which it is impossible to explain in words, because it is of the Spirit and not of the body—joy and perfect happiness becomes their own . . .

My children, here I interpose one remark, for fear I may be misunderstood: There are many marriages on earth in which the Spirit takes by far the largest part—these unions are the only ones which are of God. But within your own knowledge there are countless numbers who have entered into this holy state with minds which are unholy indeed, with motives which are of the lowest, with that base misrepresentation of love which, in itself, is a desecration to them both. You can understand, dear children, that it is indeed a farce to say to such as these " Those whom God hath joined together let no man put asunder ". God was not asked, God had no place in their thoughts. But the evil, seizing the opportunity of their " unawareness ", brought into being a state of things which wounds the Tender Heart indeed.

Children, there is not one who has suffered under these conditions—suffered through no fault of their own—who will not reap the blessing of the Father, and joy and power in the days to come. They have not failed their vows. And because another forgot, even as the words were spoken; God holds the injured pure and free. And in place of hurt and that deep anguish of the mind, gives healing, gives grace, gives that understanding which will not only help them on in their own spiritual progress but will enable them to help others—for only those who " understand " can heal like wounds or can restore that which has been broken . . .

Oh ! my children, there is so much more in this statement than you can grasp just now ! But I say to you that the linking up of two lives in this way should be regarded indeed as a sacrament, not in name but in essence and in the very spirit of the word. Names count for nothing: but the sacredness of these unions should never be forgotten. Children, I have told you before that those who provide the opportunity of allowing others to take on their earthly experience—that these if they are in touch with God, are indeed not only following His Will but are lending themselves to the working out of His unlimited purpose for the raising up of mankind . . .

There is one other aspect which, perhaps, it is wise to underline tonight, and that is in regard to the unity between Spirit and Spirit once the body is laid aside.

Children, when you come here you will find that there are many others who are linked to you and to whom you are linked by the closest ties of love imaginable. And so it is that very often, during the early stages of spiritual emancipation, there are those who work together, who are linked in this way, because at that particular stage they provide for each other the necessary help, or the one has certain qualities which the other is trying to develop. I don't want you to get confused. You must remember that love, as love, represents a very high state of spiritual progress. And once the body is discarded those who wish to climb are the first to realise that, as yet, they are not ready for that perfect union—that complete unity of Spirit and Spirit to which I have referred—so voluntarily, looking into the eyes of Christ, they start their preparation, and this goes on, sometimes, through many stages and, to you, it would seem that much time elapses before the final linking up is there. But, as you have been taught, where love is there are no barriers. Spirit can commune with Spirit whether in the body or whether free from its restrictions, and this is worked out throughout the spheres. Yet I would have you consider that love is so of God that much preparation is necessary before you can make that most precious gift your own, in the sense that God intended.

You see, my little ones, how perfect is the Mind of God. Nothing is withheld, but once the sight is there you see for yourself that it is better to wait awhile so that when that which is your own is made your own you can hold it fast and may fail it not.

Now, my little ones, I leave you. Yes ! I know you want me to stay, but there are duties on every side and these duties cannot be ignored. We are one in love, one in sympathy, in aim and in purpose, and meeting thus nothing which is not of God and Light can enter in.

Reincarnation

GOOD evening, my children! First of all I will ask my little secretary to turn the light round a little more . . . Well, my children, tonight, as you will have noticed, I said that it was a " good " evening—good not only because we are together but, still more so, because the goodness of God shall be seen on every side . . . Yes! though the enemy may be strong the goodness of our Father God is far, far stronger still and thus the work goes on.

Tonight, my little ones, as usual, there are many subjects which I should like to discuss with you, but it is not wise, on any occasion, to crowd too much in. I mean that in order to assimiliate things in a right manner the physical mind must have time to, as it were, turn over each fresh point before it passes on to the next stage and the next.

So, my little ones—and I speak to all my children, whether they call themselves by that dear name or not—I speak to them all and I say that, as opportunity offers, we shall touch on all the many subjects which arise in the mind and which, as yet, have not been satisfactorily dealt with by those who are cabined within the physical body . . .

My children, this sounds rather a proud statement to make—but you know me better than that! I would just remind you that why these so-called difficult points remain unexplained in a way which appeals to both heart and mind is that man so often seeks in the material world for his answer, forgetting that the Great Spirit, the Creator of all waits—ah, yes! ever waits to listen to His little ones and to give them the key to this problem and to that, if they will but show a little of that patience which He expresses in an unlimited way.

And while I am speaking of my " greater family " I want to make it quite clear that in choosing to discuss any certain subject with you here I am mindful ever of the needs of the whole—and that is why, dear children, so often another, far away, tells you that Zodiac has answered just the very question they longed for most . . .

I speak with great, great love and understanding in regard to my children who, for obvious reasons, are unable to be present with us, (at the circle). I tell them all that no thought passes through their mind which is not noted by me, no hint of sadness approaches these, my dear ones, without my instant aid to drive the enemy back . . .

I want you all to get a wider and more comprehensive realisation of the love which surrounds your lives—the love of many who are outside your physical thoughts. And I want my children far away (or so it seems to them) to remember that by the miraculous power of love, distance and time cease to exist. Zodiac is never too occupied to attend to the half-expressed wishes of his children upon earth. And so I would remind you all that if there seems a little delay sometimes in giving the spiritual aspect of a statement in your own precious Record (Bible), or of one of those many queries which arise so fast in conversation—I want you to remember that each one has been noted by us and will be dealt with in God's good time—dealt with in as adequate a way as you can take in; and then, later on, a fuller explanation will be forthcoming, and so the unfoldment will go on, and all will be as God intends.

My children, this evening I am going to touch upon that very interesting subject which you call " Reincarnation "— but, as I explained, it is only possible to give just an outline of the vast scope and possibilities which are contained in that state of change or transition which all must go through.

Now, dear children, there are many in the world who are convinced that as the generations go on the greater self within comes back to this earth in varied forms. You see, my children, there has been much said which gives rise to this very natural explanation of the progress or the evolution of the soul. It appeals to commonsense ! Man looks at himself and at his fellow beings, and his practical side acknowledges that neither he nor they are ready for the powers of the Spirit or for the joys of the Realms of Light . . .

I want you always to take a very broad view in regard to such theories. As you know, dear children, our understanding Father does not say to His little ones: You must not think of this; or you must not try and explore that channel of thought, which is long indeed. No ! our Father God wishes His children to use their mental powers to their fullest extent; but you can appreciate this without much explanation from me: That the Father does not like to see His children worrying over, apparently, insoluble conundrums when the solution lies so near at hand. I have emphasised this point before, but I do so again, deliberately, tonight—I say that the secrets of physical life and its many phases, together with the unravelling of those glorious truths of the Spirit, can be attained by retreating into the Silence of the Spirit and communing with God in that intimate, closer sense, when, in one way or another, an explanation will come . . .

Children, I make this statement with a perfect appreciation of the responsibility of so doing; and I tell you that there have been those who, loving God, have laid aside self in that entire sense, who have put this into practice and have not been disappointed.

But let me get back to the first point in regard to the passage of the Spirit through its many stages of experience.

Now, dear children, I have taught you from the beginning that you and I and all the countless millions who have lived and are living on any plane—that these are of God, that they are part of God, that they emanated from Him, that, in the first instance, they were as a spark from that which is Unlimited and Divine—God giving out of Himself so that others should share in the joys and the powers which are His own.

Having reminded you of this, then it is not difficult for you to imagine that starting from that which is All-Holy, these " expressions " of God had to go through many processes of " involution " before the stage of " evolution " was reached.

This, dear children, takes you back so far that the mind is quite incapable of taking it in; but, never mind ! all you are asked to do is to reconstruct in your mind your ideas of the time of creation. You must remember that this little earth of yours is but one stage—a most important one, as I have said—but one short stage only in the process of spiritualisation which all have to go through.

You see, dear children, that in using the word " spiritualisation " at once I get the thought from you: " But if we started off from God, Holy as He is Holy, spiritualisation seems the last word to use !" Yet, have I not said that the journey of the Spirit was one of experience ! The Divinity which is within us all is a gift from God; but only by the process of overcoming and of rising above that which is evil, can the gift of Divinity be made our own.

You are asked to believe, then, that starting from the point of Perfect Purity you went through stage after stage of experience before the point of " evolution " was reached; and, as a result of experience, you are making that gift of God your own . . .

There is one point here which I want to bring in and emphasise—and that is this: When God gave out of Himself, with the gift was that of " free will "; and that gift has never been interfered with, and never will. You see, dear children, that if man—if we had all been stronger, more watchful than we were, we could have gone through our experiences without losing so much of he holiness and the purity with which we started . . .

I want to make it quite clear: As you have it stated in your Bible, man was made in God's own image; and that image, it was His intention, should remain for ever more. Yet there have been many who, as you know, have not only fallen to the level of the animals created for their use, but indeed have shown signs of far less advancement, in a spiritual sense, than the animals possess.

This is your explanation, and I give it tonight as plainly as I am able: Because there have been those who have found traces of man on a level with the animal creation—because these types have been found, it only means that during certain stages humanity, as a whole, forgot its sonship and its daughtership with the Most High. The power of evil had far too great a scope, and thinking and living as the beasts they drove, so they degenerated into that which, as I have said, in many cases was far worse than the lowest in the animal kingdom. Now, dear children, I want you to remember that you can think only of finite things, and then to recollect that this little world but represents one short stage. Those processes of experience have gone on in states and conditions which are entirely beyond your imagination; and during certain phases of the world in which you now live the conditions there were only suitable for those sons and daughters who had forgotten the link between them and their Maker.

Get things in their right perspective. You cannot expect to understand just yet the gigantic nature of the subject on which I speak; but, as time goes on, the dawning will come, and later, when the physical mind is laid aside, so the revelation and the understanding shall be your own.

The " missing link " will never be found, because man— so characteristically—carries on his researches on the material plane alone, searching in nature for the solution of these difficult problems; ignoring the fact that the great Mind of Love, which created nature, reserves certain parts of knowledge as His own; and only Spirit can contact with Spirit, and Love provides the key.

You will see, dear children, that the physical mind has very good grounds for the assumption that " Reincarnation " only provides a workable explanation of man's being; yet, as I have told you before, into a physical body you will not enter again; but the next body, in many cases, is not so dissimilar as you might think. Those who have neglected the opportunities provided on earth find their powers are very little greater; and those who have wilfully shut themselves off from the Light (which is all around) these are severely handicapped, and the physical body, when looked back upon, represents power and freedom indeed.

Once more I say—" get things in their right perspective ", keeping always in mind the order, the magnificent order, of God's plans, the unparelleled justice of His laws and the infinite patience of the Father Himself, who waits and waits and waits !

What I have said tonight, dear children, answers also the very natural query which arises as to the spirituality shown by some even in those times which you call the " dark ages."

It was possible, as I have indicated, that the experiences taken on by the individual soul could be worked out, could be made their own without alienation from the Father. These so-called " saints " just illustrate this.   Yes ! they have passed through many fierce battles, many temptations, which to the minds of the children of the earth would be inconceivable because they are not subject to them themselves.   That is another point which I want you to remember—that there are states and conditions where those who are out to find God have been tried even as by fire and have come forth suitable vessels for His use.   It sounds, as I speak, rather awe-inspiring; but, dear children, before you entered into this world, of necessity, you must have gone through that, otherwise, I could not teach you or speak to you of the things which are of God.

It was the same with those who loved our Saviour during His brief sojourn among them. These, in spite of weakness shown, perhaps, in the physical mind—these had tested themselves, had voluntarily taken on those deeper experiences which you cannot understand now, so that when God was manifested among the children of the earth He might find a few to whom He could impart the Truth and to whom He could entrust the gifts of the Spirit . . .

Children, I am having a little difficulty in making this subject clear, but I think, on reading it over, you will perceive that which I am anxious to convey.   It is impossible to do more than outline something of the gigantic pattern which the Creator set into action in those distant periods of time which are beyond us all.   Yet it should do this: it should give you a sense of responsibility and also a feeling of great comfort as well.   Thinking of the past, of the many stages, of the experiences lived through and overcome, surely then you should rejoice that so much lies behind.   And if, at the same time, so much lies in front, yet each stage—indeed each year —brings you nearer to that which is Love Itself; each minute of your life contributes something which is going to provide just the necessary power which, later on, will enable you to step into the illumination of the Spirit, when misunderstandings pass away never to return again . . . Then onward into the   Unlimited,   into   Eternity,   into   Completeness—which means joy upon joy.   But I cannot take you more than a step on this road because the mind is bound by the definition of joy upon earth, and that, as you know, is just as the reflection of a tiny beam of light in comparison with the power of the sun itself.

My children, I will leave you now for a little while, but I shall want all your help tonight because my child is tired and cold, and these conditions make it a little difficult for the inexperienced to work against. It creates a sense of dimness or of elusiveness which is hampering to those who, being free from a physical body, have somewhat forgotten the restrictions and limitations it imposes. Yet I know I can count on you all and the evening will be shown to be God-given indeed.

Plant Life

MY children, tonight we are drawn together for God's purpose, remember that—remember that the desire within you, even if it but half expresses God's purpose, yet, in time to come, must be brought up to that high standard. Remember, my little children, that Christ has called you, that the Lord of Hosts is in your midst tonight, that the Sacred Presence always is there when those who wish to serve meet together in this way. Give out, then, of your love to the Great Lover of all, give out your adoration and your most tender thoughts to the Father Who waits upon His little children, seeking ever to acquiesce to their wishes, seeking every means to bind each one more closely to Himself.

Children, when we meet together in this way it takes a few seconds, as you know, to break the thoughts which are fastened too securely on physical things . . . Now, my little ones, I have told you before that the things of the world have their place; but, now and again, comes that most blessed privilege of all—the power to disentangle yourselves from the body and bodily things and, free in spirit, to penetrate into that inner sanctum of the Spirit. Just a step—it may not be more, as yet—but even this one step is a gift beyond all price. Into holiness we pass, and God shall use these precious hours to sow many seeds which shall bloom in the years to come . . .

Children, I told you once before that I had much to tell you in regard to Plant Life and its place in God's purpose. But, of necessity, I cannot take you far on such a wide and extensive field; yet, as you know, the first few points must be explained in the beginning in order to prepare your minds for that which lies ahead.

Many in the physical world, by studying nature—in particular the details of nature, under what you call the microscope—have discovered that the Mind of God is a wonderous thing indeed. In the tiny leaf, in the delicate petal lies re-

48

vealed beyond physical sight, beyond the physical mind in very truth. For, dear children, even the finest instrument cannot tell you how this marvel and that came into being. It can show you the exquisite tracery, the marvellous constructive thought in the flowers—in those tiny particles of flower and stem—but the door to the wider knowledge is shut, closed fast, and will remain so until man learns the great lesson which I am trying to impress upon you now : . . Until man lays aside his intellectual pride, and with humility approaches the Great Creator, the Great Constructor, the Great Architect of nature and the realms beyond and above, so the door remains un-opened.

Children, I want you to regard the flowers, simple as some of them may be—I want you to regard them as sacred in this sense: that because they express a thought of the Most High therefore they must be tended gently and with care. I want you to realise that in the lavishness of the gift of nature, there you have one of the most beautiful symbols of the Mind of God. I want you to try and understand the inner life of the flowers and the trees; I want you to listen for the voice of nature as it runs through the long fresh grass; I want you to hear in the very leaves which sway in the wind the voice of wisdom, the voice of the Spirit, trying to teach those who will pause and listen.

Yes ! my children, I can quite understand that, for many, the study of what you call botany is impossible. Neither the time nor the necessary instruments are there, nor are there such patient teachers as God would have who, gifted with physical knowledge, could pass on from that—out of the physical and the material—into the spiritual and the Divine.

I know that to few the opportunity comes to delve into the secrets of nature in the way I have explained; yet to all there is the open road to knowledge, there is the unfettered path to wisdom—that which can rise above physical conditions or the training of the physical mind.

Children, from our point of view it does not avail very much to be able to enumerate the number of veins there may be in a certain leaf, the signs of age in a tree, or any of those many facts—tabulated facts—which man has prepared throughout the ages. These things have their place, as I said just now, along with the physical; but the hour approaches when that physical side will be lost—will be allowed to slip away into the past—for those who love God shall cross the threshold of things material, of things " known ", and shall enter into that vast sphere of the spiritual—the so-called " unknown "—yea, even while the physical body remains !

You have heard me say before that the only barrier between mankind and the higher knowledge is lack of dedication, lack of simplicity and purity of heart. By laying aside self, by preparing the physical mind, by the discipline of the physical will, man—no longer bound to that which has been " proved ", to that fickle mistress called " science "—freed from shackles, born into a new freedom, the valiant soul goes forward to see for himself, not only how God has made this or that, but something of the stupendous purpose underlying everything which has been created . . .

Children, I ask you to listen to the voice of nature. Some of you already have heard these faint voices; some of you, when alone in a forest or out on the wide hillside, have felt and heard that which lies within . . . These things, as yet, are misunderstood or, perhaps I had better say, not understood: misunderstood in the sense that man, in sensing these finer vibrations, takes all the credit to himself; not understood by the majority who, having never listened themselves, rule out this spiritual law as non-existent.

Those who have trained themselves for pursuing the path to the higher wisdom would tell you, dear children, that from certain trees they are able to get certain emanations which express that particular tree. And it would be possible to take these so trained, so " sensitive "—to take these blindfolded into a forest and, standing in front of that which has known centuries of time, they would be able to say: " This is an oak, because I can hear its voice !" and so on and so on . . .

That, dear children, is the first stage but the first stage only. To you it sounds difficult even thus far; but I say to the earnest, to the strong, to the pure, that the gift shall not only come but shall develop in a manner absolutely beyond your imagination now.

When the spring comes tripping in, when nature takes on new beauty, new expression, get out by yourselves and listen to the many voices of nature—nature trying to teach you, trying to train you, trying to show you how beautiful is the Mind of God: how exquisitely merciful and loving as well !

The trees will answer to the faithful; the flowers know those who love them best. And if, perchance, you understand but little at the first attempt, then go back to the flowers, go back to the example of the trees: wait, and try again. That perpetuity of effort which is expressed in nature is a lesson for us all ! Because a tree fails to come up to standard one year, yet e'er the spring comes round again new strength has been gathered to its roots, and the second year atones for that which was lacking in the first.

Nature is so restorative !—and this is another little thought to make your own: that if you fail in the first or the second or the third experiment, remember that the God-nature in you has powers of restoring, of rebuilding, of re-charging, and what you cannot do to-day is but held in store to be granted in the happy days to come . . .

Children, I want you to regard the gifts of nature in a very wide way indeed. I want you to realise that in regard to those gifts under your care you are, as it were, a custodian —a custodian of the thoughts of God. And if a garden be denied you, then with the flowers which others supply you can show your appreciation, your gratitude for these little messengers of Love, which are sent indeed to lighten and to gladden your lives; to express a beauty which, perhaps, is absent from your own, to demonstrate a hope which perhaps has not occurred to you before—that hope which always tells you and explains to you that the beauty or the happiness or the brightness which passes away only passes to return again in a new form—and, if you have acted worthily, in a sweeter and lovelier form as well.

There is nothing in physical life which has not its spiritual counterpart in the Realms of Light. Those things which surround your lives—they were given to you in order to try and prepare your minds for something of the gigantic, the magnificent manifestations of the Mind of God which are everywhere in the Spirit. Even the houses you build, the furniture you make—these but tell you that harmony and good work, stability and firm foundations create something which will stand and serve; something which, even though it concerns the most mundane things of material life, by its harmony, by its orderliness, by its good workmanship expresses God—the God within . . .

Children, I have not been able to take you very far; but on another occasion we will go a step further. I have asked you tonight to set about the preparation, the listening; the sending out from yourself of those sympathetic vibrations which can, and will, contact with the vibrations of that which you wish to understand—the " sensing", the " hearing ", as well as the " seeing ". That is the next stage towards understanding the place which nature has in God's great scheme for the raising up of mankind . . .

Children, there is one other point—quite on practical lines—and that is to remember, in regard to flowers and plants, that even as a surgeon treats his patient so should these be served. When a limb fails to do the duty which has been laid upon it, then, with a sure stroke, the surgeon removes that which offends. It is done in the quickest and the most skilful way, according to the knowledge available. It is but a little thing, but I want to teach you that flowers and plants have their capacity for feeling which, though not in the sense of physical " pain ", yet is definite; and rough handling causes a wrench, a jar, a " sensation " to that which is delicately poised.

The flowers shed many tears in secret; and this, dear children, is not pure fancy only. They long to be loved, they long to be regarded in the way that God meant them to be regarded—they long to have their place in your lives and in the lives of the children of the earth—and so you can understand that, in the matter of care, of consideration, the flowers have their rights as well as the rest of God's creation.

It is true that the little ones err in this respect. They pick the pretty blooms and soon, withered and broken, they lie on the ground to perish: their effort to express beauty has aroused neither the desire of the heart or mind, but of that lesser self which seeks but possession . . .

Teach the children then to be merciful; and still more so warn the older ones who so recklessly and heedlessly destroy loveliness without a pang. Tell them that these things must not be. That the flowers which are given to them are trusts which will have to be made good some time, in other conditions; when they will see and know that, in God's sight, the tiny daisy has its place—and that place is for the raising up, for the expansion, for the releasing of the closed-in spiritual mind which is struggling to get free from its physical toils.

Yes ! in the daisy as well as in the rose God's love is shown: in the beauty of the sky is reflected the beauty of the trees; in the beauty of the trees you get the contrast of the sky. Each has its place; each draws its strength, its vitality, its being, its life from God the Creator; and to God these things belong. Gifted to the children of the earth by a generous Father—ah ! yes, my children, gifts bestowed with so much love. But it grieves the Giver of All when those who take seek but to destroy instead to preserve; seek but to make void the beauty He has created, instead—by their thoughts, by their gratitude, by their acknowledgment of God in the flowers—to send those flowers onward with new strength, with greater possibilities of beauty and a higher expression of the Mind of the Divine.

Children, now I leave you. Keep your thoughts well under control. Who ever comes, be they for you or not, send them your love and sympathy, because each and all belong to the one Great Family—the family which is joined together for ever and for ever . . .

Influences

MY children, we must go a little slowly in the beginning, because the enemies of the physical have been rather troublesome today; and, as you know, the effect of these struggles is a weariness of heart and mind, which hampers the Spirit a little—in the measure that the physical and spiritual minds are not in harmony. You have been told that physical weakness and the vicissitudes of daily life are a source of gain to the Spirit; and I would not have you overlook that point. But it is quite consistent to say that, at the time, there is an adverse effect which such encounters leave behind; and it is with " the present " I am engaged now . . .

Children, there are so many subjects to discuss that, although these evenings were arranged for in that far yesterday, as you have been told before, yet the events and the thoughts and the conditions in which my fast-growing family is placed make me hesitate a little in regard to the presentation of those grains of knowledge which I have been instructed to impart.

You see, dear children, that when we are free from the body and its many restrictions; when we have seen and have heard a few of the many wonders which are everywhere in the Realms of Light, then it is a little difficult to choose just that aspect of the grain of Truth we wish to teach—just the aspect which, at the time, will be most acceptable to the physical mind.

You see, I am treating the physical mind as a thing of some importance; and so it is. It is the weapon, the tool, the vehicle of self-expression which is tangible to you during the earth stages. Comparatively few people ever stop to consider or to analyse themselves—I mean they are quite content with the physical aspect of their lives; indeed, the body and its needs, its desires, its many requirements provide such an interesting topic for conversation and for private thought that they do not wish to be bothered with anything further.

Look around you ! How few there are who are conscious

that, primarily, they are Spirit; how few who realise that the physical body is but a garment to be worn for a little while, until that which is within, having out-grown its use, lays it aside; when, so far as the actual " body " is concerned, it will be forgotten and unregretted.

You see, human nature is still in a very elementary state in regard to those higher things of the Spirit; which, however, one day will have to engage the attention of all whether they will or not.

I want you to think very seriously about those two instruments of use with which you are provided—I mean the physical and the spiritual minds: and although I refer to them under separate headings, this is entirely and only because man, as a whole, makes the division himself.

The physical mind is even as a sensitive plate, as you have been told before. It receives countless impressions; and, in its turn, through the vehicle of speech and of action, is able to pass on those impressions to others. You call it " influence " and it can well come under that designation: but, after all, what is influence ? Influence is the domination of a stronger thought, a stronger feeling, or a stronger vision over that which is weaker; and, as you know only too well, " influence " can be detrimental in the extreme.

Now, in regard to the physical mind: that mind, to a certain extent, is at the mercy of its environment. The people you mix with, the books you read—these and a multitude of other emanations from things as well as from people—these being focussed on that which is intensely impressionable builds up the thought and the attitude of mind which you carry on from day to day.

It is an interesting subject; but when you come here, dear children, you will see that indeed it has its sad aspect as well. There are so many " influences " at work of which the children undergoing their physical experience are entirely unaware. But Our Lord and all who followed in His steps have ever exhorted mankind to keep close to God—close to the protection which He provides in so lavish a way.

Can you not understand that it was not possible to tell the people of that generation how the position really was: to tell them that not only those in the body, in their daily life, were influencing and swaying that physical mind—(not yet closely fettered to the Divine) but there were countless thousands, free from the body, it is true, but, alas! not free from the memory of physical thoughts; and these, dear children, do destructive work indeed.

I speak most seriously tonight, because, unfortunately, those who are in a sensitive condition of mind are influenced to an enormous extent by those others, who never cease to force their evil and harmful thoughts upon those who are out to climb.

Cannot you grasp what I would warn you against? Yes, there are those among my children who have suffered grievously from these attacks; and sorrow and heart-break and something akin to despair has been their portion as a result.

Children, if once you could see these enemies of Our Lord and Master you would spurn them for ever more. It is because you cannot see them, and because you are scarcely on your guard sufficiently to " feel " the nature of these destroying forces, that you allow them to approach.

There is so much underlying my warning; and I speak in most compassionate, most understanding tones, especially to the younger ones among you. I entreat you, for the sake of your Spirit, for the sake of that God-given happiness which awaits you—I entreat you to meet these enemies as you would meet an enemy in physical life: Not to quail, not to cringe, not to ask for mercy; but in confidence, with perfect self-control to say: " I am linked to One who is stronger than you all !"

Oh! my children, how I long to help you more; yet if you refuse that unlimited help which is offered to you what can we do but to pray and pray again! The Spirit is held free and untouched by those attacks, but (as I explained in regard to the weakness of the physical body) at the time, there is damage done which we find it very hard to work against.

But let me go back! We were thinking of the physical mind; and while I am on this subject I want to take you a little further in regard to that much-discussed gift which you call " imagination."

Now, dear children, as you know, it is against my practice to attempt to destroy any of the many theories, so care-

fully thought out, concerning these different questions; and
when you get on a little farther you will find that the position
is this: That I have destroyed very little that man has attemp-
ed to explain. I have merely taken you on from the physical
aspect into the spiritual; and, it all fits in quite harmoniously
and no blanks or awkward corners are left behind.

My children, imagination is a gift from God; but, as you
are well aware, it can be used by those who are evil indeed.
That "image-making", which those who have studied the
question find it quite easy to explain, on physical grounds—
to their satisfaction and to the satisfaction of the majority—
that word is, purely, a misnomer. Image-making, or imagination is something which is built up by other "suggestions",
influences and scenes; yet tonight I tell you quite simply that
imagination—true imagination—has its roots in the Spirit and
is of the Spirit alone.

Children, not only when you are asleep but for a large
portion of your waking hours, the real you is not fettered to
the physical world at all; it is wandering in the Realms of the
Spirit. And when you say, or you see, that a person is "lost
in thought" it means that the real self is functioning in one
of the countless spiritual realms; while the body remains on
earth, doing its duty, following out its mundane tasks, may be;
but only that which is akin to the world remains behind.

Children, in regard to the physical and the spiritual
minds: when you get on a little you will find that they can be
so intermingled that it would be difficult to draw the dividing
line. And yet I must explain this, otherwise you will get a
false impression:

Now, the physical mind is the tool, the vehicle, which
even the youngest souls bring with them for use during their
earthly experience. As the soul evolves it disentangles itself
from that same physical mind, in one sense. Or let me put
it another way round: that physical mind is slowly but surely
becoming spiritualised. And if you could draw a map representing the two gifts you would find that, as you grow spiritually, as experience is made your own and overcome, so that
which represents the physical mind is slowly but surely submerged by the spiritual. And it is possible. It was worked
out by those servants of Christ who carried on His ministry,
and it has been illustrated, again and again, by the so-called

saints and holy teachers of all time: it is possible that e'er the body is laid aside that that which represents the physical mind exists no longer, because the Spirit, rising and dominating that which is of the earth, is able to bring about this transition; which appears even as the " destruction " of that which is associated with the body.

My children, I want you to get this clear. I want you to realise, more and more, that the physical and the spiritual interpenetrate again and again. It is purely a matter of personal effort: there is no division, so far as the Father is concerned, between that which is of Him and that which is of the world. Your part, during your earthly sojourn, is to take that which is not of Him and, by prayer and effort and understanding, to change it from greyness into brightness— change it from that drabness which represents the thought of the world into the Light and the Joy and the Beauty which is of God . . .

Never despair, little ones, if, on going through your physical minds, you feel that your task is only just begun— never despair. Because all have been through that stage—all those whom now you long to be like, all those dear ones; the bright ones, the visitors who come to you in this way—they have been through the hard stages too: and many—yes, many are going through desperately hard stages now. The only difference being that they know, they are certain that that which is not allied to the Spirit can be and will be made one with the Divine within . . .

Children, talking thus intimately with you, I take little points, here and there, which I think will help you on your upward way; but again I come back to the chief subject, as it would appear to you:

What is that illusive thing called " Imagination ?"

My children, it is at once a complex and a perfectly simple thing. It is memory, pure and simple—memory which brings its responsibility as well as its privileges. During those periods when the mind of the Spirit escapes from its imprisonment it receives impressions of a varied kind; not only conceptions of things scarce understood by the physical organ— revelations of the wonders and the beauties which lie everywhere in the higher realms—but also impressions from those darker planes of thought, which are gathered close round each one in the world to-day.

Children, it is very much the same as listening to a complicated and intricate explanation in the form of a lecture: only those highly trained can bring away with them an accurate and comprehensive impression of what has been said. The majority, for the most part, are glad to fix upon given points; and, holding these " points " firmly in the mind, at leisure, to go back over them and, by that same " memory ", fill in as many blanks as possible.

There, in illustration, you get a simple explanation of " imagination." The mind of the Spirit soars out and away. During the sleep state it is taken on many journeys far, far from the earth plane indeed. So much is acquired, so many sights and sounds and wonders and marvels are thrown upon that exquisitely delicate mechanism of the mind of the Spirit which, by their very spirituality, cannot be transferred to the mind of the body. Yet, what happens is this: A thought, an " inspiration " is able to penetrate, but nothing more; yet from that thought, that inspiration the busy physical mind starts to build, and (as with the lecture) the individual, remembering a point here and there (by the aid of the Spirit power which is all around them) is able to conceive something which is harmony of sound, of beauty or of structure.

And there you have the explanation of " genius ", whether it relates to the fine arts or whether to that greatest gift of all—the gift of understanding a little more of the things which are of God . . .

Children, this is a vast subject; and I want you to give me your full attention tonight. I am seeking to make the tangle straight, to give you a clear and lucid idea of the processes of the physical mind and its relation to the mind of the Spirit.

In regard to " imagination "—and, of course, all the great " masters " of art, in every form, have this gift in great proportion—in regard to imagination it can be a gift of God, or it can be turned into a wicked gift—as one of those so " inspired " has put it. (Tennyson ?)

Here you get your warning; here you see the sign-post ! Those who are sensitive in the degree that they retain the

" memory " of what they have seen, what they have experienced through the mind of the Spirit—those so sensitive have
their choice. They have their choice as to whether they will
walk in the Fields of Holiness, or on those lower planes of
thought and feeling which have been built up by the thoughts
and feelings of men and women during their physical lives . . .

Now think you of this as it stands: It is possible for you,
or for anyone, even during your waking hours, to send that
mind of the Spirit—which is free to wander where it will—to
send it into conditions which are intensely harmful.

Children, free-will is never interfered with. And although
" imagination ", so-called, is a gift of God, yet, because of
that freedom of will, it is quite possible—indeed it happens
more often than not—that that which is so free wanders in
planes of thought which are destructive to the work which
the Spirit has set itself to accomplish. And here you get the
desecration of art, here you get " genius " used by the evil
indeed.

Children, there are many in the material world who,
under the name of " art ", do much destructive work. They
concentrate on the things which are of the earth, on that
physical body which, as I have said, is but a garment to be
laid aside and forgotten. Under the name of " art " thought
influences which are dangerous to others go forth; and I would
warn all those who read my words against this great mistake.
Because that which is impure comes under the heading of
" art " it does not make it pure; and, in God's sight, that
which is built, that which is created, that which is portrayed
which appeals only to the lower emotions—in God's sight that
is enemy work indeed.

Children, never allow yourselves to be persuaded that
because thoughts which are impure, thoughts which are destructive to the Spirit within—that because these are presented
to you as " art ", never allow yourselves to be persuaded that
this is excuse enough.

So characteristically—so terribly characteristically—man
concentrates on the body, on that which is physical—on that
which never becomes anything more than physical—ignoring
the quest of the soul within, ignoring the fact that although
the body in which it is encased may be beautiful, according
to physical standards, the Spirit, which is of God, is lovelier,

far lovelier in every sense there could be. The time will come when that which they regarded as beauty—that grace of form or of feature—when they will turn from the remembrance of that with loathing, because it signifies the state of bondage they were in, and how that "imagination", how that "memory" illustrated the journeys the mind of the Spirit undertook. (Using that term "Spirit" purely in the sense that it signifies that within which is free, free to wander where it will outside your limited earth plane).

My children, the responsibility towards the real Spirit, in regard to these journeys, is terrific. Cannot you see that your-self! The Father gives you unlimited freedom—except so far as that little which is "physical" is concerned—the Father gives the real you that wonderful freedom to roam where it will; and, more than that: helpers and guides, trained servants of our God, wait to take you into those higher realms where holiness abounds on every side. Yet the freedom of the will cannot be interfered with; and so it is that during the hours of sleep many wander, not in planes of evil, it is true, but in those destructive planes of sadness, where "the past" and all the "questionings" are held . . .

Children, cannot you understand! Think of the count-less thousands who have lived and had their day: their regrets, their repinings, their backward thoughts, their prayers against the Spirit. These "influences" stand, remaining until the soul within humanity has grown sufficiently strong to destroy them: and in these planes of twilight many wander during their daily life, as well as during the hours when sleep claims them.

I want you to look at things in a practical way. Life, physical life, may not be easy for many; it is difficult, indeed. Yet, in addition to grappling with the inevitable strain—un-consciously though it may be—the lesser self sends the greater self through those planes where misunderstanding has built up an atmosphere of sorrow and depression.

Oh! my children, let it be your part not only to control your own thoughts, but also to warn others of the danger which lies so close at hand! At will—mark you, at will—that which is free within can soar into the spheres where dark-ness is unknown; but you must send it thence deliberately and with intent. And then, dear children, I can promise you, and I can promise them, that the "imagination"—that all those thoughts which float through the mind, coming from you know not where—all these shall bring a reflection of the brightness which the real you has left behind—left behind because you could not grapple with or bear the Joy which is the keynote of those conditions which are of God. Yes ! as I said, enough brightness to gladden your lives and to change the whole aspect of your point of view. This you shall bring back to the mind of the body: and then no more will the days seem long, no more will time pass on leaden feet; because, though imprisoned in the flesh, you will be living and acting and functioning, and even seeing, in the Spirit—the Spirit which is all around, ever more pressing, ever more persistent, and, by its magnetic force, pushing further and further away—or, if you will—covering more closely, more effectively that which still remains " physical " in the minds you use.

Children, after all I have been able to say very little. There is, as you can understand, a variety of aspects in regard to the physical and spiritual mind, which must be understood either in your world or in those conditions hereafter. But I want you to think over what I have said: I want you to give that gift of " imagination " its rightful place, and also to control its going out and its coming in—to allow yourselves no latitude in that direction . . .

The fields of Light, those realms of holiness, of beauty and of power are open to you in a way you little dream. Then send the mind of the Spirit upward and ever upward, and close the door for ever on that which is destructive indeed.

My children, I will leave you now but I must return to this subject again in the days to come. Prepare your minds so far as you are able, and remember what I have said: that if you could once see, with the eyes of the body, those " influences " who masquerade as " holy sorrow " and " rightful grief "—if only you could see them you would shrink from them in very truth, shrink because you would know they are allied to that which is of darkness, using their powers solely to strike the Tender Heart of God. Because, remember, when you suffer He suffers too, and when you grieve and when you feel the journey is over-long, then, because you are His own, so that which is Love Divine is hurt and hurt again . . . And now I leave you.

Christic, the Judged

GOOD evening! my children, and I am going to say at
once that I am very glad to see that others have listened
to the Voice of the Spirit and have come, instinctively, to
that which teaches them a little more of the Mind of God,
of God's wonderful thoughts towards His little ones cabined
within the physical body.

Oh! never think that because you wander here awhile—
outside, it seems to you, the range of things celestial—never
think that more than that infinitesimal part of you remains
outside! You cannot think one thought of unselfishness, one
thought of self-discipline, one thought of God without immediately entering into that which is of the Spirit. Never think
that the Father waits for the physical experience to lapse before giving you of His gifts. Remember that He has said:
" Come unto me ": and in coming the gifts are vouchsafed . . .

Oh! my little children, if I could portray but once something of the Tender Heart of God you would indeed feel that
the material things of the life which you now live are as
naught: you would feel that being in touch with Him you
could let all else go by. Some of you have thought a little on
my words. I told you that when Christ came into my physical
life what the world had to give or what it had to take away
was as nothing—nothing to me. And why was this? Simply
dear children, that (as I tried to explain to you before) my
real self—all that felt and thought—was free, free from the
tempestuous conditions in which I was placed, free to commune direct (the Spirit within with the Parent Spirit)—not
above, not beyond my physical reach—but companioning me,
by my side, accessible at any moment—mine, mine to call
upon for strength, for endurance, for all that sweet peace in
which my soul was bathed.

And that is the position of man today, but he heeds it
not. Again and again you have it laid down in your Scrip-

tures—plainly and with no reason for twisting its meaning—
you have it laid down that God is amongst you, with you
all, in you, and you of Him . . . Oh ! my children, tonight I
ask you once more to stand free—free from those entangling
thoughts, free to grow, free to be and free to act !

This is the future, this is what lies before you in a way
impossible for you to grasp now: The life of service—which
is of joy, which is of peace—that life which knows no ending,
which can defy physical death—for it shall come to you and
you shall know it not. This is the future, and it goes on for
all Eternity, because you are linked to Christ—Christ, who
never rests, who never grows weary of helping, strengthening,
calling His children on and on . . .

On earth valuable time is wasted; on all sides you see
your fellow-beings pursuing that which is but an echo of the
real. But when this brief experience is over then they will
have to go back on their tracks and, with sorrow and with
suffering, rebuild, re-create, remould as the Spirit within
directs.

Yes ! there is much that lies in front, but tonight, for a
few minutes, I want you to think of Christ . . . On other evenings we have taken various subjects which have raised queries
in the physical minds of one or the other; and, as time goes
on, I intend to deal with all those questions, with all those
debatable points, in order to clear a space—to clear the
vibrations so that the mind of the Spirit can be free. It is
impossible for you to understand the things which are of God
while these teasing queries remain unanswered; but, mark you,
I do this for one purpose only—to prepare, to attune your
minds so that the Greater Wisdom may find a lodgment within . . .

Tonight, then, we will take the highest and the best and
the sweetest—we will think of Christ: Christ—not only in
those days of old, living amongst men, teaching, helping, healing—but Christ, the same Christ who was from the beginning
and will be unto the end. For, as I have told you before, the
Lord God Jehovah was and is the same gentle Shepherd who
was slain by man.

But think you, my children, of this: Christ said: " For
judgment I am come . . . that they which see not might see "
and I want you to consider this statement in its true aspect.

You have it on record that the Saviour also said that He came not to judge the world but to save it, and that stands for all time.

Christ, God, the King of kings came into our midst with a simplicity, with a Love past all understanding—came not to judge others but to be judged by us. And those who had eyes to see, those who had tried to cleanse their sin-stained hearts—they saw the Divine, they saw that which was Tenderness personified, tenderness demonstrated as never had it been before . . . God came into the midst of mankind for judgment —judgment by the children which He created—saying to them—saying to you, to the world at large: " Look at me, examine me, judge me; because you belong to me and I belong to you."

Children, the physical mind finds it impossible to grasp such exquisite humility; the physical mind, so glorying in its own petty powers, cannot understand that the One with all power, the One who created everything, who thought out the marvels of this and of that—those marvels which, dear children, you know little about and of which man, as a whole, is entirely ignorant—the glories and the wonders which are of the Spirit: the God who made us all, the God who gave us life, who has endowed us with His Spirit—part of Himself— that He came down to earth, and before His children submitted Himself for judgment, so that they who were blind might see, that the Voice of the Spirit should be heard, should answer and break free . . .

Children, as you know, Love, Divine, past all understanding was, by the few, deemed deserving of death . . . Listen and take it in; visualise that scene yourself—not the agony of the Cross, not the torture of the body—but the anguish of the Spirit within, the anguish of Love refused, the anguish of seeing His little ones bind themselves to the forces which are of darkness. Here you get the true representation of the Crucifixion, before which the physical suffering seems as nothing: God crucified by those He came to help, to heal and to save from their lesser selves; Love—understanding Love—spurned and despised. This is the real lesson of Lent, this is what I would have you ponder over; for then you will see that it is in the power of humanity to crucify God again and again. True, the physical body is no more, but, as you know full well,

Christ is bound to you, walks with you through your physical experiences, suffers with you—indeed is anguished when you turn from Him, not understanding the gift which is held out . . .

That is the lesson of this season of sacred memories. Christ came for judgment; and Christ is judged by you all during your daily life. Is He worth following ? is He worth fighting for ? is His Love worth having ? These are the questions put to each one again and again. The Lord of all waits —waits with that exquisite patience—waits for man to judge Him and to say: " This is my God whom I adore !"

Yes, dear children, the days go on; time is flying fast; thousands pass over spiritually unawakened, totally ignorant of the duty they owe to the Divine within. And then, when they have laid the body aside, they see and they understand. Not at first, it is true: you cannot turn your eyes from Love during the physical journey and then, when that is o'er, look at the Divine. No ! the eyes are chained to the earth, the evil which they have sought, deliberately, has closed them in; and because they preferred darkness, when the Light was all around, so they must wait—wait until the stifled desire of the Spirit within gains strength to assert itself once more.

Children, you know that I have told you often that Christ's Love is around the lowest, the weakest, those who have betrayed the Spirit most. The Father and His children are never separated, but the child turns from the Father and heeds Him not. Yet you must know that time so wasted takes much effort to make up, that death, the death of the body, changes you not at all—in this sense: That where your desires are, there do you go; each goes into " his own place ", and that place is being built up, point by point, as the thoughts, as the actions, as those worst emotions surge through the mind. They are there to be faced, to be conquered and to be overcome, and that which was not done when the opportunity was offered, during the earthly experience, then, when that time is over, he who was blind has to learn to see . . . Changed, and yet not changed when the physical body is no more . . .

Yet I have a word of infinite comfort for those who have tried and have failed again and again. To those I say: As you have striven, as that greater " you " within longs to soar, to be free of the cloying thoughts that seek to hold you back; as the desires, as the aspirations, so you shall find, when this garment is laid aside, that you step free into that which you longed to be . . .

That is the pilgrim's progress, and so, dear children, I want you tonight, as always, to get back, back to the Christ way of thinking.

First of all, in your mind, to build up a portrait of The Beloved—yes, of the One who understands you best, the One who loves you whatever you are, whatever you fail to be. Get before you that Image of Love, and then call out the Spirit of God which is within—and you can do it, by thought. You can do it in your daily work, in the most mundane tasks which make up your lives. All that is necessary to contact with the Divine is just the wish—just the thought: " God hold me, God keep me."

Prayer is thought, remember that. You were told to pray—to withdraw from others and to kneel in prayer. This, as the Father knew so well, was of aid to you in raising the mind from those multitude of physical distractions; but with the soul who knows and who recognises his Saviour, he can contact with the Divine on a second's thought . . .

Remember that whatever you do Christ is by your side, Christ is there to help you, to guide you and to restore; and if this one thought is stored in the mind—GOD, or CHRIST, or MASTER—just the one thought—then the communion between you is complete . . . That is prayer, prayer penetrating into those Realms of Holiness which represent God—my Father, my Saviour, my Beloved !

Children, there is one other point which I should like to speak about tonight. It is in regard to the quest which is in front of you all. I am not speaking of physical conditions just now; I am speaking of those journeys which the greater mind takes when sleep claims you, or even during the busy day when your thoughts travel off on their own.

I want you to know whither your steps are trending; what is the task which lies before you in regard to the spiritualisation of that which must be allied to the Spirit within . . .

Children, it is a little difficult to put it into words, but I have to tell you that a " trinity " lies before each one in regard

F

to the expansion and the development of your own individuality.

In order to be used by God after the physical body has been relinquished—in order to do that pioneer work, that work which allies you to the peace and the joy which is of Him, in each man and in each woman there has to be a " trinity " of development.

It is as this: In the days to come, when you will see with the eyes of the Spirit, there—contained in you—must be the perfect man, the perfect woman and the perfect child . . .

Now this statement may seem a little confusing; but wait and I will explain:

You see, dear children, in the God-Mind there is completion; and yet, endowed with a physical body, of necessity your characteristics are those associated with the masculine or with the feminine, as the case may be. At once you see that, to a certain extent, during the physical experience you can only develop along the line of the characteristics which you possess; but—and this must strike home to all—there are certain characteristics which, more or less, are reserved for the man or for the woman; and of course with the child, there are those gifts of the Spirit which are lost or submerged as the years go on.

Some there are who have noticed with disgust that woman is inclined to show tendencies which are rather masculine than feminine; and, again, the accusation is brought against man that he, in some respects, is losing that manliness which marked him off from the woman . . .

Let not these things distress you. True it is that human nature mistakes the guiding path and takes the wrong road which brings pain in the end; yet I would tell you this: that if man would choose to emulate those higher qualities of tenderness, of sacrifice and of devotional love which the woman possesses, he would find that he was growing nearer to the God ideal. And if woman, instead of aping those characteristics which so often indicate the lesser side of man— if woman would focus her attention on his strength and stability, his courage and the executive power to act in times of need, so she too would grow nearer to the Divine within.

You see, my children, where I am leading you. This is

the meaning—the purpose of God's plan in linking men and women together, but how humanity as a whole has marred that plan !

Yes ! each should draw strength from the other—that is the ideal; and although certain qualities may be associated with a feminine or a masculine body, yet, through companionship, each may catch the reflected light from the other, when seeing its beauty, they long to make it their own . . .

And then we come to the child. My little ones, after you have traversed far, after you have experienced much, then it will dawn upon you that there is only one thing which can give the finishing touch to that which has been brought together by much labour, by much discipline of self—the purity, the faith and the trust of a little child ! That lies before each one. Though their minds may be saturated with the material things of the physical world, that is their quest, and what has to be, and will be accomplished, although aeons and aeons of time may elapse before it is done.

Think you of this ! . . . There are some things which go too deep to be put into words. As you know, I saw Christ— I was with Him, I listened to Him, and I loved Him as I never knew it was possible to love before. And then, when my body was laid aside, I entered into those sweetnesses, those inexpressible joys which are part of the vibrations which He pours out upon us all. The power and the glories and the wonders—I mention them not, because once you have seen something of the Love of God, then you have got the highest and the best !

Think over my words and let the Spirit within guide you and teach you and lead you on. God will help you—He will never cease in His efforts to break down those last defences of the physical mind; and once these are laid low, so you too, little children of my heart, will enter into that peace which passeth all bounds . . . And so I leave you.

Children

GOOD evening, my children! You will have noticed that tonight, for the first time, I dispensed with the few words of prayer which you say together. I did this for one reason only: I found it advisable to release my child from the physical body at the earliest possible moment. You know, dear children, that at times the prison-house of the flesh seems almost more than you can bear; but I have told you that God never allows the breaking-point to be reached. In some way or other the tide of adverse conditions is turned, and, in the pause, the mind is able to gather together its resources—to meet the enemy not only with courage but with the ammunition necessary to drive it back.

Well, dear children, when anyone has given themselves up to this sacred work for God it is the easiest thing to release them from the physical world; and by allowing the Spirit to rest in this manner it quickly regains its poise and continues its way re-charged direct from God.

I give this little explanation because, otherwise, you might think that the words of dedication—with which you start our little conversation—lest you might think that these words were not acceptable to the Father.

Well, dear children, the time has been rather taken away from us tonight, as it would seem to you (9 p.m.) so I will not dwell unduly on these opening remarks, but would assure you—for I know how much compassion, real compassion there was in your minds—I would assure you that my child is now quite happy and content; and—I am bound to confess it—the chief reason of her happiness and contentment is that she has got rid of that " incubus " of the body, as some of you regard the temple of the soul. Ah! my little ones, you will never know until you stand with us and look earthwards—you will never know what the same troublesome physical body, what those irksome conditions in the physical world, the irritations, the strain, the selfishness of others—or what appears as lack of consideration of some towards their fellow-beings—not until you stand with us and look over that plane which you call "the earth" will you understand and appreciate all that the physical experience has done for you . . .

Well, dear children, never think because I point out these things to you that I do not understand, that I cannot enter fully into all your lives—what they hold and what has been cast away. Never forget that we are as one; yet only can that at-one-ment be possible because Christ has given you into my care, and Christ's Love has made the link between us. His strength, His power holds them intact, and His mighty understanding foresees everything that might seek to break them in twain.

Christ, the Gentle Saviour is in your lives, in your hearts in a way you little understand. Yet, as time goes on, those grosser layers of physical and material thought shall be cast aside, shall be removed one by one and, as the refining process takes place, so the realisation shall come that the love within for the Tender Shepherd is stronger, greater, more lasting than anything else, and has been from the beginning.

And now, my little ones, there are several things which we will think about together; and tonight I am going to lessen the personal messages in rather a drastic manner, because I am anxious and ever more anxious to teach you and to expand the borders of the spiritual mind, so that indeed the physical shall be ousted out never to return again.

There has been a little said already in regard to the work which the children undertake for the Father, and this evening I rather want to underline the children's side: I mean those who have been with you just a little while and then, e'er the bud had opened, the flower was gathered into the Gardens of the Spirit, there to bloom under the Sun of Holiness, there to bring sweetness and renewal of faith to those who have lived the allotted span . . .

Children, you will recall my remarks in regard to those who have cultivated their physical minds to the fullest extent. These have contributed more or less valuable and useful information to the world of their day, and also to the generations which are coming along. Yet, dear children, I told you also

that physical thinking and spiritual thinking were not connected, in the majority of cases. I put it that way because I
want you to understand clearly that the man who trains and
schools and feeds the physical mind to the best of his ability
and opportunity, that if he were so minded he could carry
the mind of the Spirit along with him, point by point. But
it occurs very often that the physical mind and its powers—
its vitality—is sufficient; indeed it is all-satisfying to the possessor and he is quite content to, as he might put it, " let Heaven
look after itself."

Well, dear children, when such as these pass out of the
physical body they have to leave that same physical mind behind, in the sense that memory only is taken with them. Mark
this clearly: I have told you that during the sleep state and
times of meditation you pass out of the physical plane into
one or other of the spiritual realms, and I said it was " memory " which allowed you, sometimes, to bring back a faint impression of what you had been witnessing. Now dear children,
when you are in the spiritual body you are again dependent
upon memory in precisely the same way in regard to events
on earth—for physical facts, for those things which are not
connected with the mind of the Spirit. But affection, compassion and tender recollection of the kindnesses of others—
all those gifts which have been acquired and used while undergoing the physical experience, these are carried over with
you . . .

But let me go back. It was necessary to give that little
explanation, otherwise you might become confused.

When these highly trained mental characters leave their
bodies and the physical side of their minds behind they feel
strangely lost—lost and bewildered—just the same as if you
awoke without preparation and found yourselves in a Chinese
village. I use that illustration because there are no words
which can express the sense of bewilderment and, in some
cases, childish apprehension with which the highly trained
mentally, but not spiritually, meet their new conditions.

Well, dear children, such as these—unless they have kept
a definite place in their heart and mind for those attributes
associated with God—these are very difficult to help. You
cannot spend the greater portion of your physical life teaching others, laying down the law, producing facts and state-

ments which you affirm cannot be denied—you cannot suddenly throw over this attitude of mind; and so it is that although they are confused by their new conditions, yet they resent any little explanation which others would make in order to help them . . .

But after a little while, after the bruised feeling, resulting from the dim consciousness of being betrayed—or, as some would say " let down " by the physical mind—after that bruised, sore feeling has passed then they are more approachable; but still great tact is required, and here it is that the children are invaluable. The little ones just dance into their lives. Their youth, their innocence, their purity catches the attention of these world-worn, somewhat hardened travellers, and it would delight you to see how, from the most trivial little thing, a friendship springs up. First of all it is an attraction by the eye: the children are very sweet to look upon, and the colours which are the emanations of purity and simplicity are exquisite indeed . . . Later on, when the trust between them has been cemented, then it is that the children commence to teach them something about the wonders of the Love of God.

I want you to try and visualise this: A child when she has found a treasure is always anxious to show it to others— to disclose the little secret spot which she thinks she has chanced upon in her play. Now I want you to understand that the children over here are children; they are not precocious, not the " old heads on young shoulders " which perhaps are rather in evidence in the world today. That is entirely " physical " and, for the most part, on the destructive side. No ! the little ones here are children, children in every sense that you could think of, with this exception: Very soon after they are gathered into the Realms of Light the harmony and the love and the beauty—well, that overrides any little naughtiness or wilfulness that may remain; also the force of example has its influence in a way which those on earth cannot understand . . .

So, dear children, I want you to realise that when the little ones take under their care those who have excluded the things of God from their physical lives, they teach them as a child would—by showing them their little treasures, by a simple description of something they have seen, which, because of their childish frankness, convinces the older one that it must be true.

And so it is that the children work for God, work in their own way, I mean; and love, of course, plays an enormous part, for when the older ones begin to see and begin to try and understand something of the gigantic plan in the Father's Mind, then they are overwhelmed with humiliation and self-reproach. At these times no one could help them except a little child. They, as children would, see that something is wrong, so their little arms go round the sufferer's neck, and in that sweetest of all links the real man is able to emerge and to grow stronger.

Children, there are many, many aspects of this particular work, yet I am bound to stop at this stage because tonight I want to emphasise particularly that what was said in prophecy regarding Our Lord—" A little child shall lead them ", applies to the Spirit of every child who has taken on physical existence. Yes, a little child shall lead them out of the winding paths of physical thought, out of all those thickets of deduction, out of the twilight into the Light, when those so bound by the capabilities of the mind of the body will realise that those capabilities, which they prized so much, were gifts direct from God, only they had put them to a use which was never in the Father's Mind . . .

" A little child shall lead them !" There are countless thousands in the Realms of the Spirit who never would have reached the Light of Holiness had it not been for the children, had it not been for the little thoughts, the tender fancies and the exquisite simplicity of the infant mind which was under the direct influence of He who blessed the little ones . . .

Yes, dear children, there is a lot which arises out of this subject, and tonight I will just touch upon the little ones who are everywhere in your midst today . . .

You see, dear children, that it was the Father's intention that not only should the children in the Spirit impart to the older ones something of the things of God, but that those same older ones on earth should learn from the examples in their midst a little of the beauty of purity and simple faith.

A child's life is a great responsibility. Some of you, I know, have exaggerated that responsibility until it has grown into an apprehension of ever taking on the responsibility your-selves, but that is not right. Yet, dear children, I admit that it is true that many parents regard their little ones as requiring from them far less thought than a business transaction; indeed, in the planning and construction of a house in which to live, a hundred-fold more thought and care is bestowed than in contemplating that little house of flesh in which something of God is stored . . .

We will try and get this matter a little clearer. So many theories there have been, and are, in regard to the upbringing of children, and as the centuries go on you see the swing of the pendulum. One generation, perhaps, shows signs of harshness to those so entrusted to their care; then the next generation goes to the other extreme, and the result is rather damaging to God's plans for lifting the children of the earth above their environment.

Now, dear children, the reason why these mistakes are made—and you see them constantly on either side in rather a bewildering way—the reason is that comparatively few parents regard their little ones in the way God intends.

First of all get back to the purpose of physical life. You know the Spirit within each one is of God—a part of Him—which has started off on its long journey in order to make purity and holiness its own. You know that the Spirit chooses certain conditions in order to bring out those higher qualities, or to eradicate those characteristics which hold them back; and the homes in which the little ones arrive are chosen entirely as a background for the working in, and the working out of the experiences which that which is Divine within the body intends to undergo.

So you see, dear children, that after all when a mother or a father is particularly proud of the appearance, or the cleverness of the little one they have brought into the world, it is taking upon themselves rather a lot. They are, as it were, appropriating that which belongs to another. It also shows you the fallacy of comparing one child adversely, or favourably, with another.

You have been taught by me that many of those who come into the physical world ill-equipped bodily—yes, and sometimes mentally as well—that these are the strong souls, these are the ones who were inspired to do as much as they could in the shortest time possible . . .

You see where I am trying to lead you. Real parents, intelligent parents, in looking at the beauty, or the health, or the ability of their little ones, first tender thanks to God, and from that point realise their responsibility begins . . .

The gifts are there: will they be detrimental to the progress of the Spirit within, or will they add a little to its store? And this explains why it is that some mothers—especially mothers—have such a wonderful love for the child who is deformed, for the little one who comes into a rather sorrowful world even more restricted by the physical than the majority. The mother's heart, her spiritual instinct—although she may not know it—but that spiritual instinct within tells her that the little maimed form in her arms represents a strong Spirit indeed, one who is allied to God, one who, out of love for Him, throws aside all those attractive possessions of the body and intends to fight through without them . . .

Again I say, you see where I am leading you. Get these things into their proper place in your mind and think them out for yourself.

The gift of a child is a responsibility indeed, but not in the way in which men and women on earth regard it.

The child mind—the tiny physical mind which is so gradually unfolded—to what does it unfold itself? Is it to holiness and truth, or is it to the soiled aspects of a material world?

Don't you see that during those early stages much can be done. The undeveloped physical mind, gathering in in the vaguest way impressions—mostly through the eye or through the touch—that tiny mind is like a clear garden, and what are the seeds that you are to sow therein !

Yes ! I know all about those discussions which come under the heading of " Heredity ", and I intend to deal with that subject as opportunity occurs; but I say that the influences, that the vibrations of thought focussed around the unfolding baby-mind are of such transcending importance that no words can be found to express it.

And remember this: That when both stand free in the Spirit—the father and the daughter, the mother and the son; not in those terms of relationship, but as Spirit and Spirit— then those who had the training of the younger physical life will, in many cases, recoil with horror to find how they were used by the evil to harass and hinder and retard those in their care . . .

You see again, dear children, where I am leading your thoughts. No one in your world, nor in those many planes beyond are free from this responsibility. Whether a child was committed to their charge during the physical stages, it matters not. Here or in the Beyond each Spirit has to go through the same experience, the same training in regard to helping the younger ones to grow into maturity . . . And I say there is no anguish compared to this: when a mother or a father sees the effect of their thoughts, their interests, their lives upon the tiny mind opening to the world in which it has chosen to learn its lessons.

When you look at it in this way harshness towards a child, or that deceptive " spoiling "—each falls into its place; or, rather, both are submerged by the truth, the truth as to the real position between parent and child.

I want you, as much as you can, to put others on their guard; to try and induce them to regard their little ones in this way: as souls which, unconsciously to their physical minds, are struggling and striving to make the Divine within their own possession. To point out to the older ones that this earth's experience is even as a training school. You know how it is in school life: that if you do your best to learn your lessons quickly—why, not only is life easier and you escape many punishments for evasion, but also, by application, you pass on from stage to stage, eventually emerging into that freedom when school days are no more, and, perhaps, you begin to teach others in your turn.

That is how physical life should be regarded by the parents, by those who have been entrusted with the privilege of helping another soul on its upward climb. Therefore, my dear children, you will see at once that by influencing the little one towards the gifts of the Spirit—and it can be done from the earliest stages, by ever and again showing to the little flower-mind how much beauty there is in the Father-Mind, and by instilling in it a love for growing things, using nature as an illustration—imperceptible though it may be to you, yet you are providing for the opening out of that physical mind the environment which is the highest and the best.

Yes ! when you come here you will see how malleable is the mind of a little child. I do not say its " will " because— well, the majority have come up rather abruptly against the baby-will, and they consider it a question that has yet to be solved. But don't you see that in influencing the thoughts, unconsciously to the little one, you are bending the will God-wards, drawing it from the attraction of the earth side and physical things; and, later on, that will, strong as it may be— well, then it is strong for good, and that is what it was given for.

In regard to the subject of the children's part in the Great Plan of Creation you will find, all of you, that the importance given to the young is, on the one hand, exaggerated, and in an unwise way as well; yet, on the other hand, God's side is, for the most part, overlooked. It hasn't been sought for, it hasn't even been thought about amongst the many other things of daily life.

To the mothers and the fathers who so love their little ones I give a special word: I say that when they see things in God's way they will find it hard to forgive themselves if, on looking back, they see they delighted only in the love and companionship of their children and did not give to God in return: and you know that the only way we can give to God is by helping others to get a little nearer to Him. It is the only thing that we can do for the Father; and if you would remind me of " love ", then I answer at once that, over here, love is translated into " service ", and so you have the thing complete.

Then, dear children, there is another subject which I should like to refer to tonight, and that is in regard to daring much for Christ.

I have in my mind at this moment the little story of Peter—Peter who left the safety of the boat and tried to reach his Master.

Well, dear children, the mind of man, to a certain extent, has misinterpreted that little incident. So often it is told as a warning against lack of faith, and you are reminded that Christ Himself said to Peter: "O thou of little faith, wherefore didst thou doubt ?"

Now I have been commissioned to unveil, in the little time

at my disposal—to unveil to you something of the love of God, something in regard to His attitude towards the children that He has created; therefore, my little ones, when this passage comes up I want you to interpret it thus:

As you know, there were others in the boat with Peter; but when Peter saw Our Lord walking on the waters, within his heart and mind (unconsciously to the lesser self) there arose that great spiritual ambition to go to Him, and, disregarding the physical conditions and the obvious danger which lay between him and his heart's desire, he threw himself out of the boat . . .

Now, dear children, think with me awhile. From the world's point of view, from the so-called practical point of view, Peter's act would have been considered not only foolhardy, but lacking in even the elementary principles of commonsense.

Between the boat and The Master there were the waves and the dangers they represented; and yet Christ, standing there, seemed, by His love, to urge Peter to try . . . And so it is that, now and again, there are men and women in the world who rise above physical thinking, above all those thoughts of caution—those destructive thoughts of caution—and they defy that which is of the earth and, from the strength which is within, gain, anyhow, sufficient courage to attempt the seemingly impossible.

Children, from an outside point of view this is a fairly adequate illustration of the position in regard to this Truth. You have the arguments of the logical mind: " If you attempt to cross the waters of the river of death, then you are asking for trouble, and, probably, will meet with utter destruction " . . . Yet Christ, the Light of the World, stands on those " dangerous " waters and, by His love, beckons you to His side . . .

And then, dear children, I come to this: I ask all those who read these records to try and interpret The Master's reply to Peter's effort in the way in which it was said and meant.

I take you back to the little child—the little child which the mother is trying to induce to walk alone. The little one, urged by the love and the desire in the mother's heart and voice, attempts what is soon proved to be impossible. And what does the mother do ! After the first faltering steps, e'er the child falls, the mother has clasped it in her arms, and she says, as a mother should: " Oh ! why were you afraid ? Mother is here and she would not let you fall !" . . .

You see, dear children, what I am trying to impress upon your minds: That those words of Our Lord were never intended to imply reproach—they represented Love, exquisite, tender, understanding Love . . .

Think then of it in this way: Peter, with a courage greater than the others could find, Peter throws himself into the water; and then, being in a physical body, bound by the restrictions of physical thinking, he feels that he is on the point of sinking. But Christ catches him e'er he goes down, and with an out-pouring of love for the one who tried to show his love for Him, He says: " O thou of little faith, wherefore didst thou doubt ?" . . .

It is the Mother-heart of God stretching out and gathering in the child who is not yet strong enough or experienced enough to walk alone . . .

Yes, dear children, these thoughts of ours go very deep, not only in a physical way but in that far better way which belongs only and solely to the mind of the Spirit. Think you of these things, and when there are those who would say to you, in regard to this work: " Isn't it a dangerous undertaking ?" then answer them with faith: " Christ is there to hold me lest I fall; and because He has passed through physical death and proclaimed that life is everlasting, so I too will do my best to meet Him where He bids me come."

Never go back on the thought that Peter failed. Peter's " failure " was a success that the others could not rise to. You see my point: Here and there there are those who will attempt; and these, called by that which is Love itself, shall, in God's good time, see for themselves that even though they seemed to sink, yet e'er the waters closed over them the Master had them fast, and with gentle—yes, and playful tenderness He says to them, to you and to Peter: " O thou of little faith, wherefore didst thou doubt ?" . . .

You see that you have got to look at things in God's way if you are to make any progress towards the Higher Life. You have got to readjust these statements in your Sacred Records, and to regard them by the Light which shines from

His Love. Over and over again, what man has interpreted as censure was but as the loving assurance which a mother—a devoted mother—would give to her little child whom she is watching, guarding, tending and trying to teach the rudiments of physical life, so that the limbs, the mind and the Spirit may grow as God intends . . .

The true Mother reflects more nearly the Mind of God than anything else in the physical or spiritual worlds—the true, unselfish, far-seeing, spiritualised Mother, spiritualised by her love, is very close to the ideal—that ideal which interprets to us something of the heart and mind of God . . .

And now, my children, I will leave you. There is one who would speak to you tonight; and then, as the evening is slipping by, I think we must draw this time of sweet communion to a close—but that is as the Father wills . . .

Work

GOOD evening! my children. First of all, I want to say a word to my little secretary, who rather anticipates that tonight is going to present obstructions which will not be easy to overcome. I want to reassure her that she is companioned on either side; and the Father does not ask from any child—whether they be old or young, in a physical sense—the Father does not ask from any child more than they can accomplish. Let her then give up thoughts of strain and rest her Spirit in all the power which is around.

My children, tonight it seems to me that there is a promise of spring in the air. Yes! I know it happens very often that these " promises " are only half worked out, yet, even so, that sense of new life, of brighter, warmer days to come—with their accompanying flowers and sunshine—does hearten all of you, who, more or less, are very much affected by conditions. And I want you to realise, if you can, that as with the promise of spring—of new life, new hope, wider joys in every sense—so the promises made in regard to your physical lives not only stand firm but ever are nearing that time when you will see that the fulfilment is being worked out . . .

My little ones, I find this evening that in your minds there is an element of peace. The peace to which I refer is that restfulness when the physical mind can say to the Spirit: " I hand over the future to you !" Of course, dear children, the physical mind, being very much like a little boy, does not give up the reins of government for long. Yet, as all Mothers know, even that brief space of time when their little son can say to them " You do it !" is a relief, and the remembrance brings a sense of comfort when the position is reversed . . .

I just give these few opening remarks so that you may know how we watch for any little signs of acquiescence to those marvellous spiritual laws which are operating—if the world could but grasp it—operating entirely in favour of the children of the earth.

Some of you have noticed that there are times when it is possible to get into vibrations which are as harmonious as the earth can offer. And then it seems that everything goes so wonderfully well; and those who wish to love God—well, they feel they are at last in harmony with Him and His purpose, and they rejoice to think that the shadows have been so far overcome.

My children, I can understand so well how it pains you when, all unconsciously, you step a little to the left or to the right and find yourselves outside the direct rays of the sunshine of God's Love; and tonight I want you to try and make a big effort to keep this promise to yourselves: that when you feel those sympathetic vibrations are getting a little knotted up, to pray—yes! to pray earnestly, even though the physical mind may be unwilling to do its part. These times are tests, and they are severe ones when the pilgrim is strong enough to stand them. Yet, dear children, the enemy could be despatched in the easiest, simplest way imaginable if only you would remember that Christ is waiting—waiting for you to appeal to Him direct.

You see, dear children, it is not that the Tender Saviour waits in the sense that no help is forthcoming until you ask. The help is there in an unlimited way, but free-will cannot be gainsayed. It is just as though you were offered that best gift of all—best from a physical standpoint—the gift of water, precious indeed to the parched or to the one who is stricken by disease; yet, dear children, as you know, it is most difficult to force that liquid through the lips when those same lips are closed, and the teeth behind.

It is exactly the same with the gift of God's unlimited peace—you must do your part as well. And I entreat you, with all the force of my love for you—I entreat you to appeal to Christ more and more in your daily life, during the trying moments, during those periods of " tests "—tests to see whether you are ready for use, whether the Father can count upon you what'er betide . . .

You see, dear children, privileges bring always their responsibilities. They bring their joys and powers as well, but it is impossible for anyone to have great possessions without at once incurring deep responsibilities, not only in regard to others but also in regard to themselves.

G

Yet tonight I would not have you think that I am scolding anyone. My children make mistakes it is true, but never willingly, never without regret; and so these few words are rather in the nature of an assurance that those times of strain and chill—spiritual chill—can be lessened until they disappear never to return again. God wishes the children of the Light not only to demonstrate a little of that Light to others, but also to be centred in that perfect joy, that exquisite harmony which is their right by service. Yes ! their own in every sense there could be, and soon, thank God !—soon they will have learned enough to be able to grasp and hold that which the Father has given . . .

Now, my children, I want to talk to you a little about Work—or, perhaps I should say, about the Toilers—those who, whether they will or not, have to work the long day through, and sometimes give even of the hours of sleep as well . . .

As you know, conditions are very much better today than they were a generation ago in regard to the rank and file, and I am quite prepared to admit that very large sections work only as much, or hardly as much as their physical strength allows. Yet, dear children, we—looking at things with the eyes of the Spirit, going through not only the details of many lives but also the hearts and minds of countless numbers—we see that there are many, yes ! far too many from Love's point of view, who are working (as I said) throughout the long day, with very little rest at night.

In the first place, dear children, I want you to try and realise that in regard to such as these—who are hard-pressed by physical conditions—that those in the Spirit never cease in their efforts to help; indeed were it not for the tremendous power built up around such toilers it would be a physical impossibility for them to get through the tasks they have in hand; moveover, the body itself would refuse to act under the command of the will . . .

Some of you have experienced the kind of help to which I refer. You know quite well that in physical tasks—by which I mean those which make a demand upon the muscles and the strength of the body—that in regard to these tasks our power is enormous; and if you, and others, could remember to call upon that power more consistently than you do you would have a revelation of its unlimited strength and durability.

You see, my children, it is not selfishness to ask the aid of those in the Spirit when you are hard-pressed by conditions which are beyond your control; it is not selfishness in any sense of the word; in fact, it is conferring upon us a privilege —a privilege which, in a way, impossible to explain to you at this stage, has a far-reaching effect, not only on the ones concerned but on many others.

Tonight I want to speak to you a little about those same toilers—unnoticed, for the most part—who indeed are working into the pattern of their lives something which will stand for all time. And, children, there are many such as these in the world today; many in your own city, in your own country, and many more in those countries which you regard as separated from you by customs and conditions.

My children, the Father never expects His children to undertake these great tasks—in the sense of using that word " expects " as an injunction. No ! you will find as you go on and expand the borders of your thoughts that, so far as God is concerned, it is He who gives and gives and gives, expecting nothing in return except that His children might love Him, and seek to get free from that which comes in between them and their love for Him. Yet, as you know, there are certain strong souls who, in taking on the physical experience, were rather drastic over the programme they laid down for themselves; and so, dear children, I would ask you more and more to try and look at the hardships in the lives of others solely as a mark of spiritual progress—of the ambition and the determination of that which is Divine within.

You will find in the world today that there are large sections who do not wear out their bodies with work which has any relation either to service to their fellow-beings or to the Creator of mankind. It is more common, my children, for a man to over-work in order to gather something unto himself which he prizes, and that " something " is generally of the earth. The body is a tool, the mind a weapon, and with these two confederates he sets out to conquer and obtain.

Then, of course, there are many who over-strain that same physical body in their pursuit of pleasure—of those transitory joys which seem so attractive until they have been tried; then once again on these restless ones go, seeking to obtain something a little more satisfying and lasting.

These, dear children, work hard—both the ambitious and the pleasure-loving—and very often the body suffers considerably in the process; and, sad to relate, so much effort, so much planning and contriving and looking ahead leaves no mark on the side of the Spirit at all.

I want you to get this clear. Those who work for others, those who strain their mental powers and physical capacities in order to provide the necessaries of life for their dependents, these—unconsciously though it may be to themselves—are dominated by the Divine which is within. But, as you know, with so many, ambition, power, self-advancement—these are the glittering baubles which they pursue ever more feverishly as the years go on.

And then, dear children, I turn to a brighter aspect of this subject—to those who are anxious to do, as they would say, their " little bit " before they pass Yonder. There are countless thousands who, in their free time, throw themselves into social work, trying in one way or another to serve; and these, whether they blunder in that service, whether they fail to do what the Voice directs, whether they leave but little mark behind—these indeed are the servants of God—useful servants, just in the same way as you regard your limbs as servants to your self.

I should like this to be known by those who have given up so much time and thought to these tributaries of service— I use that word because they work out of the great, broad river of service. They are just pulling their little boat up some side-stream, out of sight, forgotten, unmarked by the great majority who are doing the big things which will stand for all time.

Those who are working on a big scale have their reward both now and hereafter, and I am not belittling their magnificent results by drawing your attention to the efforts of those who are limited by reason of time and opportunity. But there are many who get rather tired of giving in this way; they feel they are working on a pattern which never grows. Yet I would remind you that the seeds strewn on the mind of the body shall make a showing in the mind of the Spirit, hereafter

—if the soil of that physical mind was not quite suitable for production.

Well, dear children, I have gone rather a long way round, perhaps, but I wanted to show you the broad aspect of work, and then to bring you back to those who have not even the satisfaction of feeling that they are contributing something toward that " service " which God has entreated for His little ones on earth . . .

Yes ! I have come back to the plain toilers in the home and in those many cul-de-sacs of employment that exist in bulk and which the world, as a whole, so often forgets.

You have one in your mind (Mrs. Beams). She is often in your minds as typical of those who toil and yet finds at the end of the day that there seems nothing on the gain side, certainly not in a material sense; those who work not only in their own homes but in other people's homes as well—work as you would say, to keep body and soul together—and it seems hard, strangely hard that more help is not forthcoming to lighten the burden.

Well, dear children, I brought in this sturdy soul in order to point a moral. You will remember that she has said— and she meant it: " I'll never give in !" In those few words you have the quest which is ever before her Spirit, and that will carry her through not only the physical stages but through many of those stages which lead ever from brightness into greater brightness, from peace into the peace which is of God.

I want you, in thinking of the one I have used as an illustration, to make it applicable to countless numbers whom you know not with your physical minds. There are multitudes of such toilers—patient, unknown and, for the most part, unthought about by their fellow-beings.

Let your prayers go out to those—not that their burden should be taken from them, but that the power of the Holy Spirit may be so built up around them that, even though the body faints, that which is Divine within shall rise triumphant again and again.

You see, dear children, there are many in the world who are working—unconsciously, may be—on a very big pattern. They work with the eyes bound, yet the instinct of the Spirit guides them and leads them along the narrow, up-hill path.

And when the body has finished its part, so will the bandage be removed, and then with joy they will see that not only was it well worth while but that all along God's Love, the power of the Spirit and His messengers not only helped them but literally supported them as they climbed. Yet because they knew it not but went on in faith—or, sometimes, with determination only—but because they knew it not they reap alone what they and others have together sown.

I want you to take a very wide view in regard to Work. You have been told by me, many times, that the physical body should have its share of attention, that it should be treated as something of great importance because of the Holiness stored therein. Yet, dear children, I should be misleading you if I did not say at the same time that those who work so hard, straining the resources of mind and body almost to the breaking-point, that such as these if they work for God directly— or indirectly, in the sense that their labours are for others— these, dear children, are building up strength and power and wonderful opportunities in the life which has no end.

There is another point. You have been told before that those in the Spirit have very active lives; indeed you have suspected that this activity is on so large a plan that it escapes your comprehension altogether; and this is true.

When you come here, free from the restrictions of thought, of effort and of action, you will find that within you you have a capacity for work enhanced beyond anything your imagination could conjure up. Yet, dear children, you can understand when I say that those who on earth had never trained themselves for service for God cannot step into that knowledge; moreover, in regard to the physically indolent—well, that habit, being cemented by years of practise—that habit is brought over with them when the work-reluctant mind has been left behind. You cannot alter yourselves by stepping out of the physical tabernacle. If a man or a woman preferred ease to work while upon earth, that will be their attitude of mind when they come here, and it will take many, many experiences to eradicate it.

You see what I am trying to bring out: That the capacity for work while on earth is building up for you something which will give you a joy and a power when you are in the

Spirit, something which will represent to you then your heart's desire. The hard workers—those who toiled, ignoring the calls of the physical—these indeed shall work for God, and the pains and the weaknesses they endured in the flesh shall be as weapons before which evil will give again and again. That concentration, that spirit of never giving in is wanted in a way you cannot understand until you come here. There is so much to do, there is such an enormous work before each one; and those who, as I said, have steadied their will for work while on earth, they indeed shall reap a glorious harvest when they work in the Gardens of the Lord.

Keep the point clear in your mind. God does not lay upon anyone those heavy burdens, but the Spirit within, determined and valiant, says " I will !" and because of that the power of the Holy Spirit works with them and for them, from the beginning until the end . . . that " end ", dear children, which, as you know, is the beginning again of work so akin to joy, so expressive of the Love which is everywhere in the Realms of Light, that you cannot think of one without the other. You cannot think of God without thinking of work in an unlimited sense, for while our little efforts go on the Father works on the big plan—works and works and works . . .

Well, dear children, I think I will leave you now, although there is so much more to be said regarding the inner aspects of Work, regarding the special gifts it develops, regarding also the power that it circulates both on the earth plane and in the Realms of the Spirit. It is as though the one concerned were pouring out power—power which, when it contacts with the power of the Spirit (which is everywhere—in all the vibrations) is, as it were, transformed into part of the Great Power which dominates all the worlds—all that is and has been.

Remember this: That, unconsciously to yourselves, you are circulating power—power which is wanted urgently by those in the Spirit—to be used and re-used again and again . . .

On another occasion I will try and tell you a little more about the motive power of work . . . And now I will go . . .

Spiritual Laws

WELL, my children, tonight we have much to do together, and I want you all to give out as much strength and power as you can. You will see in the days to come that this evening typifies constructive work, and, therefore, in the measure that we can use it for God's most holy purpose so the blessing will rest on you, the little children who contributed to that which the Father had already provided.

This evening we are in tune in many ways. I would like some of you to go back on the events of this little day, and you will see that harmony and peace held and maintained their place. This was the preparation—the necessary preparation—so that your minds might be in suitable condition to listen to the Voice of the Spirit, to take in, in some measure, what God has directed me, and others, to impart.

Well, dear children, in the first place, I have a little to say in regard to those spiritual laws to which I and your loved ones have referred in a general sense. I cannot tell you much tonight because you are scarcely experienced enough, but unless I put in the first few bricks then you will have nothing on which to support the bigger and more beautiful construction, which is only waiting your readiness to be your own.

In the first place, dear children, as you have suspected, these laws—which are intangible and indescribable, for the most part—these spiritual laws have an importance which cannot be over-estimated.

As a crude illustration of their working I would refer you to what is called the " wireless." Yes, to the physical mind the wireless is inexplicable, except by results. You see my point ? Certain rules are followed, certain equipment is used and " result " is obtained; but no one can tell you why, or how such simple mechanism can produce such gigantic results. The thing itself eludes entirely the physical mind of the most highly-trained.

This is indicative, to a degree, of those same spiritual laws which govern your life and mine, your world and all the bright and glorious Realms in which holiness and happiness reigns.

My children, I want you to consider this: That if you send a thought to another—whether they be on the earth, or whether they have laid the physical covering aside—that thought, unimpeded, reaches their Spirit with a rapidity impossible to put into words.

Again: you have been told that in regard to prayer, the Listening-God hears not only as the words arise, but even as the thought is being gathered together in the mind . . .

There are many such illustrations of spiritual laws—of those multitude of spiritual laws, which are worked out in rather a beautiful way in the flowers, in the growing things, in the power which nature shows on every side.

You must remember that when God created—and I am speaking of creation long before this little world of yours was concerned—that when God's thoughts were manifested in form—even before that time these marvellous, detailed spiritual laws had been set into being. They were the first thoughts, they were the preparation for the Life—life unlimited and unending—the Life which was to follow . . .

It is a little difficult to make this clear. You are bound by finite thinking; you are bound by that indication of time which is connected with the inhabitation of your little earth, and it is difficult to take you outside its borders in imagination.

Yet, dear children, I want you to do your best and I want you to consider, among other things, the body with which you have equipped yourself. The power of the limbs, the wonderful mechanism, in a physical sense, of the blood and nerves, bone and muscle; and the harmony—yes, in spite of conditions of civilisation—the extraordinary harmony between all the organs, and how they, sometimes against enormous odds, work out on to the side of health and strength and beauty.

You see, dear children, I have always given the body its rightful place; yet I have never allowed it to over-step that position and to approach upon the domain of the Spirit within.

In illustration of this I want you to consider the relative

importance of the strength of the body and the power of the
Spirit, which it seems to guard even as a prisoner whose freedom has been forfeited.

In the hands there is much power, much that causes
amazement when looked at from the physical point of view.
You had it described that the most marvellous piece of machinery, the greatest invention of man is as nothing compared
to the perfect mechanism of the hand and what it can do. Yet,
dear children, I should be misleading you if I did not take
you on from the thought of the powers of the body to those
greater, stronger, far more wonderful powers of the Spirit. In
comparison again (only enlarged to an extent you cannot
understand) is the difference between the power of the physical
hand and the power which lies in that hand when the body has
been cast aside . . .

And this brings in again another spiritual law which has
far-reaching results. You will remember that there have been
some who have passed through your lives who have possessed
what you regard as marvellous healing power in the physical
fingers and the electricity they are able to throw out.

Well, dear children, this lies within the reach of all. Many
there are—and again I think of the mothers—many there are
who have soothing, who have peace and healing in their touch.

Christ, of course, illustrated the power of healing in its
highest form; but I have told you before that being sons and
daughters of the Most High you are asked, you are entreated
by that which is Love itself to develop those same powers—
the powers which Christ showed for all time could be trans-
mitted through the physical covering if the heart and mind
were pure. Yes, that is the key, that is the solution of the
power: purity of heart and mind and the wish to serve.

I want to instil into your minds, if I can, that within,
entombed in some, imprisoned in many, fettered in varying
degrees in others, there is power, there is that marvellous,
controlling force—a gift direct from God—which is your own
possession, to be used when you are ready to be true to your
trust.

You see, dear children, where I am trying to lead you
in thought. The physical, to you, presents enormous barriers;
the body is like a high and impenetrable wall which lies be-

tween you and the garden of your desire—which is to be able to do and to think through the Spirit, in its sweet and precious liberty of action.

Yet, dear children, I want you to try and grasp that the body can be triumphed over, that although it may blunt those finer perceptions and feelings—the more sensitive side—yet in spite of this, in spite of that sense of restriction, if you have the courage, the faith and the patience, you can bring out those hidden powers of the Spirit for use among those with whom you come into contact . . .

Children, I know quite well that the outward demonstration of these gifts, in the way of impressing others, presents no temptation to you at all; but over and over again comes that deep longing to help, to lift up, to be able, really, to do something that is concrete—something which, in your own sight, will show you that you are getting a little nearer to the things which are of God . . .

I take you back to the illustration of the wireless. You may say that, in searching through your mind, you find nothing there to warrant the assumption that you possess this power. But although you cannot explain from whence it comes or how it is able to act, yet I can promise you that if only you will set your mind to the vibrations of holiness and of love you shall find, in a way you cannot grasp now, that the gift is there, that you can be used even as a channel to pour out power direct from the Spirit, that you can—by simple thinking, simple living, keeping as close as possible to the injunction of Love Divine—you can, even as Christ said, " follow " Him, not only through the dark valley of sorrow but up on to the heights, where He is able, through you, to send down a visible manifestation of that power of healing which is of the Spirit . . .

Children, there is so much to be said in regard to those laws which God instituted for the benefit of His children; but tonight I want to turn your attention to another aspect, which is in regard to the strangers who have gathered here and, in speaking, have brought in the names of many more who had not before passed through your physical minds.

Yes ! you have queried not only the reason but sometimes the advisability of such strangers demonstrating their presence in this way. It has seemed to you, perhaps, the introduction of names well known on earth savours a little of that deference to fame and popularity which is so common a characteristic amongst the majority.

Well, dear children, I can understand these thoughts; I can understand that what you would shrink from doing in your daily life naturally rouses a little doubt in regard to those uninvited guests at these evenings. Yet, dear children, when you come here it will all seem so plain and clear. It is the operation again of a spiritual law which, ignoring entirely the physical aspect of things, links up whom it will—links up those who are likely to be of use in the work which God has entrusted to those who will undertake it.

I want you to clear out of your mind such thoughts because they hamper those who wish to speak. You have been told that in the Spirit distinctions or differences of any kind —all those many man-created barriers—that those cease to exist. The one thing which separates is spiritual aspiration, and that divides only to the extent of the depth of the sleep of the Spirit within.

I put it that way, dear children, because I want you to realise that those who wish to rise—wish to work out the past—have every help it is possible to conceive; and the nearer we get to the Father so we see, so we understand, and so we long to succour.

By that same spiritual law, by that wish to climb, by that wish to know the Truth, your lives are weaved and interweaved again with many who are quite outside your range of thought. So, dear children, attune your thinking to this view, which is the view I am instructed to impress upon you: that common aim, unity of purpose, and the desire to serve, bridges all gaps. And, more than this, there are those drawn into these vibrations who, as yet, have been able to make but little progress, but, even so, are striving to work out the past . . .

So you see you get both sides of the picture; and it will comfort you to remember that not only are you linked to those who have done better than you have been able to do but also, by the same spiritual law—so entirely of love—you are bound by sympathy, by the wish to help, to those who are finding the struggle back into purity, into health of soul a difficult problem indeed.

On another occasion I will try and show you how you, and nature in all its forms, are, as it were, interlocked with the celestial beings who have been working for God since away back in that dim and distant past which you find it impossible to think about. I should like to explain that as all that has been, and is, is of the Father, so you and the messengers of Light, you and those disciples who were used to reveal Truth to the world—you and Divinity Itself—are linked, are interlocked in a way impossible to be broken or severed . . .

Yes, dear children, it is a little complicated just now, but as we go on so, fragment by fragment, you will get a little nearer to a conception of things as they are.

It all comes down to this—so simple and yet, in some cases, so difficult to put into practice: that by thinking of Christ, by holding on to the thought of His companionship you are setting into operation, in the most perfect way imaginable, not only the working but the life-giving power of those spiritual laws which, at this time, seem obscure indeed.

Everything created by the Perfect Mind is simplicity itself; and Christ, during His sojourn on earth, showed, in an indisputable way, how it was possible to make the communion between man and God complete—perfect in every sense there could be.

And if you would remind me that, even so, it led Him to the cross, then, my children, I would say at once that only through the death of the body can the glorious resurrection —that resurrection which is of so stupendous a nature—come to you or to any of the children of the earth—those children who, at one time or another, will realise the quest of the Spirit within . . .

And now, my children, I will leave you for a little while. Remember that this is an evening of work in a spiritual sense and, by sympathy and love, help those who wish to speak to you—those who wish to contribute something towards this gigantic task of revealing Truth to a half-listening world— the Truth which one day will have to be faced by all, faced and made their own possession in order that the Spirit may come into its own . . .

The Crucifixion and the Resurrection

WELL, my children, it is with great joy and with a sense of peace—the peace of the Spirit—that we meet together again. And I ask you, little ones of the Light—little ones who wish to be so faithful and so true—I ask you to come with me in thought and to consider a little more of those things which appertain to God; for, as you must understand, the things which are of God concern you vitally, inasmuch as you are of Him. So you see, dear children, that it is not wise; indeed it is the falsest of all theories to draw any dividing line between God and man.

Those who have wandered from His love are apt to erect many barriers—many obstacles so high, so broad, so deep that, from the earth point of view, it seems impossible that the Lord God Almighty could ever be reached by them. But I have told you before that though the children who wish to know Him not can separate themselves from Love Divine, yet Love Divine bridges all gulfs, and even those who spurn Him, with deliberate intent, are still companioned by the Christ whom they deny.

It seems to you sometimes that I strain your credulity almost to breaking point in regard to the compassionate understanding of the Father. But, dear children, when you come here you will find—with so much joy—that indeed I was able only to portray just a few glints of the glorious Light which His unbounded love represents. I want you more and more to allow the thought of Christ, of God, of the Great Father to penetrate deeper and deeper into your minds until it is linked up with the mind of the Spirit, which knows its God indeed.

Children, at this time you have been going over in your thoughts the nature of the gift which Christ gave on the Cross of Calvary; His sufferings and the dawn of that bright morning when death was vanquished for ever more.

And I am glad—speaking for my Master—I am glad that some of you have been able to extend your sympathy and understanding to those who loved Him so well; those who watched and waited; those who indeed passed through that which was worse than any physical death could be . . .

Children, I have tried to portray to you a little of the deep emotion which the earthly Presence of Our Lord inspired. But it is impossible for you to grasp more than a tithe of what this represented, because, to bring it home to you, you must indeed have seen Christ first—not only felt Him in your hearts and minds, but have seen Him—for the eyes, whether of the physical body or of the Spirit-body within, the eyes have a way of registering and of impressing the mind as nothing else can do. And, dear children, you are right in thinking that those who watched the maltreatment and waited through the long hours of agony, that these suffered as few can ever suffer again.

I am only bringing this in because it illustrates certain aspects of physical life; and while I am on the subject I would remind you of the women's part, both before and after the act of crucifixion had taken place.

You see, dear children, being women yourselves you can understand, in a certain measure, what it must have been to stand by helpless and to realise that help from any source was unobtainable, except by a miracle.

This is a point which has not been considered sufficiently. Those followers of Our Lord during His short mission upon earth had seen much, in regard to others, of power—coming they knew not whence—but bringing a result which was staggering to all. They knew that Our Lord, in this respect, was not as other men. I put it in this way because He was so intensely human—human in its best sense—and they could love Him and confide in Him, dear children, as you would a tried and trusted friend. Yet the power He possessed marked Him off from themselves, and so, right from the very beginning, in spite of the forewarning which had been given to them —given with that consideration which surpasses anything I can describe—forgetting the prophecies, those who loved Him waited minute by minute to see an exhibition of that power which He had shown so freely in regard to others . . .

Children, I must explain. My reason for referring to our

part is this: That as a test, it was the fiercest that has ever been put to man. I am speaking from experience. Cannot you imagine that our hearts and minds burned with a sense of injustice, burned with anger—yes, anger against those who, by trickery and devious means, had taken our Lord out of our midst; and, even as the psalmist of old, there were few who did not think it a fitting moment for the vengeance of the Most High to be hurled down upon those who had fallen so far.

Children, I tell you this because I want you to understand that we were just as you are today—full of those weaknesses and strengths which represent human nature before the greater understanding comes. As those moments dragged by so hope rose and fell again; so we prayed with faith and so we prayed in despair. And when it was o'er it was broken men and women who turned back towards the city, towards the life which went on just the same, but which had ended for us . . .

And the women suffered most—yes, I can say that the women suffered most, because of that capacity within—be they mother or not—that capacity for throwing their love over The Adored, even as a cloak of protection. To the women it was torture indeed. Not one of them who were His friends or companions would not willingly and gladly have laid down their life, as a mother would, to save that which meant so much to them . . . Agony upon agony, as the hours went on; and I am glad that my children can enter into something of the pangs which mother and maid experienced during that day, which seemed as years . . .

And when, dear children, we come to Christ's side we get at once His understanding way of looking into the hearts and minds of each one individually; and, because He was Christ and Love, so He came to her—(Mary Magdalene) who owed Him so much. And, dear children, when one has wandered very far isn't it to be expected that the thought of being safe home at last brings a greater sense of gratitude, because of the distance which lay between?

This woman had suffered much in the returning. That is another point for you to remember: Because Christ freed her of the demons with which she was possessed, it did not mean that she had no inclination to sin again. Habit is strong; the mind which has been bent one way instinctively swings back, however much it may have been adjusted. And I say that that woman suffered and strove and strove and suffered again, holding on by main force to the Love and the compassion of the One who had sought to save her.   And because she owed Him so much, because the love had a foundation of pain, of effort and of anguish, in proportion she suffered indeed . . .

And so Christ came to her, lifting her up above the darkness of despair, entrusting to her the greatest manifestation of God upon earth which has ever been vouchsafed to any one. Remember this always: That Christ, putting aside those physical standards, chose the one He knew to be the most suitable to which to show Himself—in His Divinity, in His exceeding love as well as power and strength . . .

Children, again I refer you to personal experience.   Cannot you imagine what it must have been to Mary to see The Beloved there, not only alive but, as it appeared to her, with full vitality and in perfect physical condition . . .

You see, dear children, that when one is immersed in grief, when one's thoughts are on the earth and, generally, what the earth covers so securely, it is not easy to turn the mind from that to the thought of life unbroken, life eternal. And she—just as so many before and since—she was, as it were, drugged by grief, and so Our Lord had to speak to her twice before she even found inclination to raise her eyes and to see the truth for herself.

This is a little thought I want to go out: I want those who have lost their dear ones to try and take in that this incident was not peculiar to Mary; was not confined to Christ.   Yes, using different words, may be, but if those who grieve could see with the eyes of the Spirit they would know that their loved ones were by their side asking the same question: " Why weepest thou ?"

This, dear children, is the first instinct, the first longing of those who have vacated the physical body; and, as you have been told before, the sufferings of those who are left behind have grievous effect on the one concerned.   You see, dear children, e'er the silver cord has been loosened; while they are, as it were, inhabitants neither of the world of the Spirit nor of the flesh, these who are passing on their way are held—yea, and are tortured by the cries of their loved ones who remain behind.

H

Their distress is twofold; and this is one of the many reasons why it is imperative that this Truth should be forced on the mind of doubting man. Their sufferings are twofold: First, because of the strangeness and, generally, the terribly unpreparedness of their condition; and then, accentuated in a way which only release from the physical can bring home, are their affections, are those links of love between themselves and those upon earth . . .

I put it to you like this: It is literal fact, and it happens all too often, that there by the empty shell the mourners, tortured in mind and heart, bewail the loss of the one so dear; and there again, close by, is the so-called " lost " one, seeking vainly, for the most part, to soothe and to console. I tell you, dear children—and in time to come you will see it for yourself—I tell you that there is no anguish to be compared to this, because not only are they enduring their own pangs of separation but, being free from the physical which protects, they take on the heart-broken conditions of the one who calls to them, it seems, in vain.

Children, as you have been told already, sometimes it is many days before the one released from the body is able to get free from the ties of that body. Where their loved ones go they follow; they cannot leave them through the long days or through the sleepless nights; and being so absorbed in what they see—so ignorant of spiritual conditions—we can comfort them but little.

Yes, dear children, it is a great, great responsibility; it is a responsibility that each one incurs when in grief self plays too big a part. Oh, I know that you will not misunderstand; you will not think that the great all-compassionate Father does not realise what this separation means to both.

From the very beginning, using every means Love could find, He has been seeking to force home the truth that where love is, death has to stand aside, where faith is nothing can intervene. And Christ, dear children, but emphasised what had been possible, and what will be possible, so long as this little world of yours goes on: If the children of the earth had trained themselves to use the mind of the Spirit, to look at things with the eyes of faith and understanding, and to free themselves of the many bonds of the earth, they too, e'er the third day had passed, could see their loved ones by their side.

This is not a gift reserved for the few; yet it remains for the individual to take up the attitude required—to get into touch with the things of the Spirit, so that Spirit can contact with Spirit, free and unfettered . . .

Many thousands—but you know it not—countless thousands, right down the ages, have known this by experience; have known that it was possible to stand free from the limitations of the physical body and to see—literally to see—something of the marvels of the Spirit-world which is all around them—close, closer than words can express.

Yet, dear children, as you know, Mary's statement was discredited, even as it would be today; and this is so indicative of the attitude of those who have not put themselves into suitable conditions to see for themselves. Mary's love—not her grief—but Mary's self-sacrificing, perfect love for the Master broke down all the barriers of the flesh; and, overjoyed, she ran to tell the good news to others: but they believed her not. And in the world today " the others " will doubt until they have seen for themselves; and then they too, with eagerness, will seek to pass on the good news: but, again, their listeners will doubt also, and much, much valuable time is wasted which cannot be regained.

Oh, my children, the resurrection and all the beauty surrounding it was never meant to apply only and solely to our Lord and Saviour ! His was the life of EXAMPLE, and His entreaty ever was that others should do the same, should follow in His steps; and, more than that, the disciples, as you have been told, performed greater miracles than Christ attempted Himself . . . So characteristic of the Divine Mind—so gloriously characteristic of His generosity, of that laying aside of power, of the wishing and the longing to pass it on to others; standing aside, watching, as a parent would, the efforts of His children and delighting in the good results which followed.

My children, underneath it all lies this great and important fact: The preparation, the attuning, the getting into touch with the things which are of God. And although the spotless purity of the Master seems so far from your own poor ideal, yet even so the Holy Spirit is able to be manifested through you. God delights to use His children to do what He, by a single thought, could force home upon the doubters and the unbelievers; yet He withholds His Hand, preferring to use those of His children who are willing to submit themselves to His guidance, who are willing to make the necessary effort, who are anxious to get a little nearer to Him in thought.

So, dear children, take heart and think not to yourselves "How much has yet to be done ", but rather say " By His Grace I will go forward, step by step, and even if those steps are small yet, because He is my Father, He will understand and He will help me to do better in the days to come."

That " understanding ", dear children, goes so deep that no words can be found to express it; yet the Spirit within is not content with merely resting on His Love, it wants to be up and doing, it wants to show that its love has some foundation beneath it.

You were told a little time ago—and I am glad that this message has lingered in your minds—you were reminded that Christ said to the one who wanted to do so much: " Lovest thou me ? " and then, as the affirmation came, so the words swiftly followed: " Feed my lambs, feed my sheep." In that simple incident there lies, in miniature, the story of the Life Beyond, which the emancipation from the body brings home so clearly and, sometimes, with such terrible remorse as well. Here in the Spirit we know that to love God is not enough; rather it is to do, in our small way, that work for which He has ever called for helpers: " Feed my lambs." Nothing for self, only the question put but to express the thought which was ever in His mind—Feed my lambs, feed my sheep.

And this goes on for ever, until the last straying one is gathered in. Work and service and effort; love translated into action; passive Christianity turned into active, vibrant effort. And when you come here you will see, in all its loveliness, what it means to work for God.

Charity

WELL, my children, I am very happy to be here again with you, and if some of you think that I have inclination to scold then I would banish that thought at once.

You see, my little ones, you are my children and your sorrows are my sorrows, your sadnesses my sadnesses too, and so if I begin to scold, then, also, I must scold myself as well.

My dear children, the whole trouble has come about because you understand so little about love; indeed, on going back on your lives, love is represented to you as something closely connected with disillusionment and disappointment and, in some cases, anguish too deep for words. Love has not been presented to any of you as it is God's will. Perhaps, Annie, I would exclude your early days, but no more.

It is a very terrible thing to us—who see on all sides such evidences of gigantic Love—to realise that those who are indeed of our heart have never been permitted, during their physical existence, to see even the outer garments of that which is glorious within. Therefore, dear ones, how can I blame you, how can I scold you because you fail to grasp my love, and, worst of all, that perfect Love which the Father has given to each one and which never, under any circumstances whatever, will be taken from you !

I know, dear children, it is like talking to you in an unknown language to dilate upon the Father's love for you, individually. Theoretically, you know it and admit it, but the facts of your physical experiences seem to show the other side of the shield so plainly that the imagination fails in the task of realising that that shield is bright and clear and shining if you had but the strength to turn it.

I want to get this quite clear; I want you to understand God's side as much as you can, and I want you to be able to speak to others, who have chosen the hard and rough road, with certainty and with conviction.

Love, dear children, is a very beautiful thing—it has so much power and strength and vitality in it. And those who have only been confronted with selfish love (I use that phrase in the earth sense but, of course, that word " love " is desecrated by such a connection) but those who have come only into touch with that twisted, malformed, hideous misrepresentation of love are to be pitied indeed—pitied with that complete understanding which turns the pity into the sympathy which is Divine.

My children, there is so much to be brought in in connection with love—of the brightening of life, of the sunshine and the flowers which are all allied to that condition—but I refrain. You have first to grasp this one important fact: That love knows no change, that it changes not when others alter, it retreats not one step when those who would come in between have been successful—in the sense that they have blocked out the memory of the love which is your own . . .

I feel, dear children, that in speaking thus perhaps I have overdrawn the picture. What has happened is simply this: That the enemies of the body, working on the mind, have, as it were, built up a little wall around some of my children, and this being of a resisting nature, unfortunately, kept out some of the love and comfort which we were endeavouring to get through to them. Yes, it is nothing more than that, and now I have dispelled that wall I can say, with so much happiness, that the only damage has been to that unity between mind and spirit, which is absolutely essential if happiness— relative happiness—is to be your own. I am glad we have worked through thus far, and I want you to understand this glorious fact: That because you are my children, because we have worked and suffered together for so long, there is nothing strong enough to do more than erect a temporary barrier between our love and understanding; and this love and understanding is going to expand, is going to assume such proportions that, in the near future, these enemies will retreat, knowing that we are stronger than them all.

My children, I've taken up a little time over the explanation, but, indirectly, it is part and parcel of the subject I wish to discuss with you this evening—which is in regard to the acquirement of that greatest gift of all which, for the want of a better name, has been given as " Charity."

If you turn to your Scriptures you will find that charity, or love—it matters not what you call it—you will find that this quality holds chief place. Other gifts are enumerated but they are all classed as secondary to that great gift of charity.

You will recollect that one inspired by God (Paul) said, in a most decisive way, that if he had all knowledge, all faith and yet had not charity he was as nothing. And that statement and its immense implication has caused considerable thought in the minds of students of the Holy Word, and so tonight I think I will give you, in miniature, the spiritual view and the interpretation which I ask you to put upon these words in future.

From the outside it would seem unjust that the acquirement of so much, so many gifts and qualities—all denoting effort and concentration—that these should be swept aside, should be powerless to stand alone in the absence of that one thing called " charity ". And I can understand that, to the reader, the thought must come that there is some discrepancy, some miscarriage of that perfect justice which all like to associate with the things which are of God . . .

Yet, dear children, looked at with the eyes of the Spirit it is absolutely clear, perfectly reasonable and, once the Life Beyond is understood, the only thing that could be . . .

I take you back to this: There have been many who have travelled far and wide, in a physical sense, exploring this little world of yours; and also, to a greater extent, there are those who have roamed from the east to the west and from the north to the south, mentally. I do not say " in imagination " because in this connection it is somewhat out of place, remembering the explanation I gave you of imagination a little while ago.

Children, in these travels much can be acquired, many useful tools, much that is gain both to themselves and to others. It is agreed that to travel is an education in itself; and whether that travelling is of the mind alone, or of the mind and body, it does not alter the truth of the statement that to travel is an education in itself.

Yet I must say this: That there is the education of the mind and there is the education of the soul, and they do not always march hand in hand. You see, dear children, when the body is laid aside, sympathy—that capacity for putting

yourself in the place of another, of, as it were, being able
to get inside the vibrations of their life and of their thought—
this is essential before you can be used to work for God in
a way which will count.

Do you understand ? Cannot you see what he who loved
God was trying to convey ? And I would like to add here
that those who speak under the inspiration of the Holy Spirit
are not able, always, to take in the full meaning of what they
prophecy or teach. The physical mind is the barrier. The
Spirit of God, using the instrument of the physical mind for
the time being, is able to push aside its borders and barriers
and to get through that which dawns upon the speaker but
gradually in the days to come. You will find this has been
worked out in a very comprehensive way in regard to these
sacred evenings—to The Message which I am trying to give;
to the Light of God which I am trying to reflect to those who
will pause and heed.

But let me get back. You see, when Paul said ". . . Though
I have the gift of prophecy . . . all knowledge . . . all faith,
and have not charity, I am nothing " he was referring to love
—that love which understands; that sympathy without which
love is but half itself; that ability to place one's self in the
position of others and, by that wide " charity ", not to judge
but to help them.

You have been told that the physical mind is laid aside
with the physical body; and some of those who have acquired
much learning during their earthly sojourn are appalled when
they come here to see the knowledge which must be their own
before they too can be used by God to help and to raise . . .

Dear children, it has been said by some that " life is what
you make it ", and I should like to say that this is true in a
far greater sense than the mind of man can grasp; but, on the
other hand, it is a very dangerous thing for anyone to say
who is without that precious protection of sympathy.

In the first place, life is indeed what each one has made
it. It is the Spirit's choice; it is the deep consideration of that
bigger, nobler self within, who lays down the path which
must be trod during the time the body is worn. And here,
dear children, I should like to tell you what is so common a
thing, and what you will find it rather hard to understand:

During the day many are hard-pressed by physical conditions, and the weariness grows so great that they pray God that their burdens may be taken from them; yet the weeks go on and, apparently, their prayers are unanswered.

Children, do you know what happens during the sleep state ? I tell it to you because it applies to you as well as to those harassed ones . . . The Spirit, being imbued with love for God, seeing the future—the glorious possibilities of that future—that spirit, free from the body which would retard, implores us and implores God that the burden should not be removed. My little children, if you could hear yourselves it would silence those questions of the physical mind for ever. It is as this: Free from the body, you limit us as to the help we are to give in the day to follow; and, as I have told you before, we dare not interfere with free-will, with the quest of the Spirit, with its aspirations to that which is of God.

This, dear children, is not fancy, it is fact: that not only are we commanded by you to stand aside, but also the Saviour, the Compassionate Father is asked to do so as well. Yet, dear children, I must add this: Because the Father is Love, Divine, unlimited, unceasing, there are times when He says to the strong spirit: " This is enough ", and He protects, He lifts out, ignoring—yes, sometimes, dear children, ignoring the bravery of that which is Divine within His children. The Father's heart is unable to watch them suffer so and, just as you would with your own, He takes on the burden Himself so that that which is so weak, and yet so strong, may take a well-earned rest.

That is one side of the statement that " life is what you make it ", and it is a beautiful thought—a thought which should hearten you in contemplating the sorrows of others— but only to the extent that you know the Spirit within will not be gainsayed, that the Spirit within defies suffering, sorrow and the blows of physical life, because it's love for God dominates it through and through.

Then, dear children, I turn to the earth aspect, which is unlovely, in many cases, because self obtrudes in a definite manner.

There are those who are well-placed—so far as material conditions are concerned—who are apt to dismiss, in a very careless way indeed, the troubles, the perplexities and the anxieties of others. The phrase comes up again and again:

" Life is what you make it ", and the inference is that these misfortunes are their own fault—are the result of something which is lacking in themselves.

And while, dear children, I have to admit that many misfortunes are self-inflicted—inflicted by that lesser self—yet I should be denying the working of the Spirit of God amongst humanity if I allowed you to think for one second that those who are in dire trouble, those who are experiencing the bitter pangs of want—if I allowed you to think that this is the result of their own weakness when I know that it is the direct result of their strength.

That is a point I want to drive home: Say not lightly—I speak to all—that this or that one's lot is self-created, in the sense that it is the harvest of the sowing of mistakes. It is a terrible thought to us that there should be quite a number who throw off responsibility, both of thought and of action, in this way.

This is what awaits them: When they come here they will have ample opportunity of proving the truth of the statement that life is what you make it; because, as I have tried to explain before, the long road of experience is not escaped by any, and those who have never worked until the body was aching and breaking, those who have not gone through the sharp pangs of physical suffering, those who have evaded those destructive enemies of poverty and partial starvation—these, when the body is laid aside, will have to come back and go through, with thoroughness indeed, each pang which these experiences bring. It is the only way of teaching the self-centred. It is not that earth-born craving to " let others go through what you have suffered yourself ", but it is the necessary preparation for progress, the only means for providing those essential tools of service, without which joy in the Spirit is incomplete indeed.

I want you to get this quite clear. In regard to sympathy, it should be developed with determination and concentration. The mere fact that, instinctively, you feel sympathetic over a certain case means, dear children, that before you took on the physical body you had passed through that same experience and now you know what it is like—the physical mind, to a certain extent, blurring the remembrance, it is true.

On the other hand, those who are unable to enter into

the lives of others shows quite clearly that these particular experiences have not yet been made their own, and they lie in front.

We have got a little away from Charity, you may think, but in order to express my meaning I had to take you a little afield and then to show you that, after all, we have come back to the point from which we started.

It is summed up in this: That " Exclusiveness " has got to go; either in this world, or in the many worlds beyond, that sense of exclusiveness has got to be lost, has got to be fought and killed.

You see, dear children, as you have been told before, in order to construct, in order to help, you must first be able to get inside the vibrations of the object. This applies, more than anything else, to the lives of your brothers and sisters who are going through their physical experiences; bound to the earth in many ways, yet the Spirit functioning always in the place where it belongs . . .

" Though I have all knowledge and have not charity I am nothing "; and when the body is laid aside this is worked out down to the last degree. In the measure that you have understanding and sympathy for others, so is your rate of progress; but if you have not that charity—that love—then indeed, in a spiritual sense, you are without anything with which to work.

Tonight then I want you to promise yourselves that, in addition to those deep feelings of sympathy which go out so readily to those in sore distress, you will try and extend that sympathy in regard to the opinions, the attitude of mind of those who are not quite in agreement with you.

This is my point—and when you are free it will seem so clear and simple: Children, there are many in your world who love God and who work for Christ; and because the human mind functions in different ways, so you get an enormous number of what you call " sects ", and each work for God in their own particular way; and, sad to say, amongst these sects the element of charity is, sometimes, missing in a very noticeable way.

Once you have seen the workings of God's Mind, as portrayed in the beauty of the spiritual conditions which are around you all, you will marvel that anything so trivial as a slight divergence of opinion could ever have been strong enough to erect barriers between children of the same Father, workers for the same Christ.

And yet it is so, and much sadness comes as a result, and the destructive forces of disharmony strike to the right and to the left.

I want you, dear children, to endeavour, in regard to this great Truth, to over-ride any little coldness or feelings of reserve which has sprung up between you and those others who have not yet been able to make this truth their own. It is difficult, I know. One's very loyalty—the remembrance of the effort, of the piecing together of the tiny fragments until a very respectable machine has been set into working order—all these thoughts are hard to fight against when, as it seems to you, others are disinclined to make very much effort even to find out whether your treasure is true or false.

Still, dear children, it is God's will—it is His most loving injunction that you should be united in your wish to serve, if not entirely united in the way in which you regard His truth.

You were told that exclusiveness in regard to faith had the effect of erecting formidable barriers, even when the body was laid aside, and I would remind you of the little incident of the worshippers who had, in the Spirit, built up a wall—even as of Babylonia—around them, shutting out their fellow creatures who also had passed out of physical life.

As you know, these were quite happy in their little centre of interest on earth; they were certain they were the only ones to be " saved ", and when they passed out, still holding tenaciously to the conviction that God had revealed Himself only to them, so they were prisoners indeed . . . Prisoners in a pleasant land because of their wish to do the right thing, but " prisoners ", shut off from the countless thousands who had long since left the plain and who were mounting and mounting towards the glories which have no end . . .

I bring in this little incident tonight as a warning to all who are exclusive in their attitude, be it towards their fellow creatures on earth who are less favourably placed than themselves, or be it in regard to their worship—their attitude towards God.

Over here, dear children, exclusiveness is unknown. In

this happy land of freedom there is neither " mine " nor " thine "—it is " ours ", and ours is God's; and we see so plainly that only by unity, only by the closest comradeship that could be conceived, is it possible to rout and despatch the destroying forces that would attack.

Oh, I beg all who read these records to take to heart my simple words; to be certain that in God's sight the wish to know Him, the wish to serve Him is all that He ever asks from anyone; and if they allow barriers or obstacles or divisions to be reared up between themselves and those other children of the Father, in that measure they are denying the Love which they wish to proclaim.

There is no getting away from facts. Underneath what I have said is the strong desire to impress upon all the absolute necessity of trying to understand the lives and points of view of others—literally to put themselves, mentally, in the place of the other—to consider their physical conditions, their burdens and their responsibilities, and to say to themselves: " How should I act if my life was the same ?" If that question is put and answered fairly, then condemnation would be withered down to its roots.

" Though I have all knowledge and have not charity, I am nothing " . . . When the body is laid aside the revelation will come of something of the gigantic meaning which charity represents—something of the love, something of that compassionate understanding—and with the tool of charity you shall work for God for evermore.

Now, dear children, I will leave you. I have spoken at length tonight because it was urgent that this particular statement should go out as soon as possible, in order to put the children of the earth a little more on their guard, in order to show them something of God's way and of that immutable rule which is in the Spirit—of co-operation, of comradeship, of fellowship one with the other . . . " And the greatest of these is love "—that love which some call charity, but which means just the same to those who have God in their hearts. And now I leave you.

Spirit Power

MY children, this is one of God's evenings, and I want you to attune yourselves to the things of the Spirit in every way you can. I want you to realise that the Holy Spirit is upon you all, and to make the thought your own that much has been vouchsafed unto you which has not come to the majority.

Into the Silence of the Spirit we enter; and the world and all those distracting thoughts connected with the earth—they must be banished beyond the portal.

Tonight, dear children, I have called you together for a special purpose, and I ask those who think they are strangers (Miss Owen and Miss Rowe) to lay desire at the Feet of the Master, and to listen with the mind of the Spirit to the little I am able to teach at this stage.

In the first place it would seem to you that, looking at things from a physical standpoint, you have much in common; but I want you to get away from those standards and to take it as literal fact that, in the Spirit, you—my little children—are linked to many; and the linking together is for one purpose and one purpose only: to rouse the dormant Spirit in slumbering humanity. Not, my little ones, merely to gather the flowers of remembrance and reunion yourselves—that is the personal privilege which comes to all who are willing to tread the steep and rugged road to God—but the main purpose is bigger, immeasurably, than that. You, the little children of the Light, (although perhaps it is but a glimmering which, as yet, has been made your own) you are entrusted with the Truth, with this revelation of Love Divine—and I speak most lovingly to you all. I say that you have been found worthy, in God's sight, to be used as tools; and could you but grasp what this privilege implies, then indeed would you kneel and thank the Giver of all good things . . .

This little life—so fleeting, so dwarfed, so in miniature

compared to the Great Life which flows on and on—this little life can, if you will, produce something which nothing else can make your own possession. It is for you to prove yourselves trusted children of the Father: to say to the world " We have nothing in common ", but to say to the children of the earth: " We have everything in common."

Humanity calls to humanity—those who have passed over and those who are yet unborn. Each are linked to the children of this little day. The " trinity " once more dominates and controls ! You must remember that those who have passed hence, who have wished to know the Father and His Love— they have retraced their steps; have, for the time, relinquished those glorious gifts and beauties which are their own; and taking but the power of Love as the instrument with which to work they have come back and, in humble places, amongst the suffering, the broken-hearted and those sore beset by the enemies of the body, so they have worked out, again and again, the deeds they did on earth . . .

And with the unborn this goes on in a way impossible to describe. Those in the Spirit—fettered to the Christ, seeing the glorious future in front—they too work amongst the sorrowful; go down into those planes which, as yet, are hidden from your physical minds, and, by patient understanding, have learnt their lessons, so that when the opportunity presents itself to take on the physical habitation, in their hands are the good gifts of the Spirit to lighten and to brighten the lives of others.

And thus it is, dear children, that there are those among you who call forth your love; who, as it were, open the gate between the earth and the Spirit: and, by their " understanding ", you will pass through and see the Light—the Light of Love which never fades, which never dies and which no suffering can quench. And that Light, shining through the darkness of the physical mind, rouses that which is of God within, when you, too, shall be torch-bearers to others, showing the lighted way, showing the safe and secure path, showing the glories which await all who have the courage to climb . . .

Yes, dear children, it is a great mission; it is a wondrous call; it is indeed a gift of the Holy Spirit—that comprehension of the meaning of Life, its purpose and the wonderful plans conceived and weaved by the Mind of Love.

My children, there is much we have to do together, and tonight is a night of work, not just as food for the physical mind but as manna for the soul. To you, little ones, I can talk, but there are many who are not ready yet and so the power of the Spirit—that marvellous, unlimited power, gifted to the children of the earth when they are ready to take it— has, for the time being, to be withheld lest it should be a danger indeed.

Oh ! my children, never be deceived. After the mutterings of the sky, after the physical demonstration of power, then came the small Voice—the hushed Voice of the Spirit— and that, that was God.

Children, I have something to say to you all, and tonight I am going to break through a custom of mine and speak direct to the two children I have gathered here. Therefore let not your thoughts go seeking others in this room. They are all here—those you love so well, those you wish to serve—but they have entreated me to take the leadership tonight, and this being God's will, I obey.

Yet there are things I would talk over with you e'er we bring in the personal again.

I want you to concentrate your thought on the marvellous power of the Spirit which dominates—though men think it not—this little world in which you dwell. " Body " you may be, Spirit you are; and this applies in that same proportion to everything in the world around.

Yes, dear children, although it may seem strange to you, even the pavements on which you walk are charged with Spirit power; and if you could see with the eyes of the Spirit you could read the life's history—nay, I speak not only of the little life of the earth, but the life's history of those who had worked upon it: the effort, the lack of effort; the striving, the weariness, the giving up, the despair; and, worse than that, the indifference, the ignoring of God, of His laws; the ignorance of their duty to others.

Yes, dear children, in a small space of the road or the pavement there is a volume of fact, an unending mass of information not only of the man who worked thereon, but of his life before he entered the physical body, and of those lives which have come into touch with his own.

And then, dear children, I take you on out of the " uninteresting " road, as it is sometimes called, to the green of the hills—if you will—or just to the little commons which are for those to play upon who have not gardens and green grasses of their own.

Yes, dear children, it has been noticed by many that in walking over the soft green grass refreshment both of mind and body, as well as of Spirit, comes as a natural result. Yet, as is so often the case, the human mind is content with the surface only, and very few remember to render thanks to the Creator for the benefits received.

My dear children, again I say to you: Could you look with the eyes of the Spirit you would see that above the green grass, a foot and sometimes more, there is Spirit-power—a gift from God to recharge His weary little ones as they go on their way. And should you ask me why it is that in spring-time the sense of refreshment is greater than later on, then I would remind you of those same spiritual laws, working so accurately, so beautifully for all.

Children, during the winter-time few there are who tread the soft green carpet nature provides, and thus it is that the grass is able to store its energy; it is able to lay up that which will be wanted in the days to come, that which will be called upon to an exceeding great extent.

My children, think you like this: During the winter-time, when nature, as it were, has closed its petals—shutting in the beauty and the sweetness that is a gift to all—then the human mind grows rather weary and that same vitality of the body is lowered to an appreciable extent. Yet when the sun shines, when the voice of Spring is heard echoing through the spaces until it reaches the listening ear of those on earth—when that call comes to be up and out, to feel God's sweet breeze, to breathe in the pure air, to expand the body and the mind in the sunshine—then you see the task which awaits the green grass beneath your feet. The children of the earth are badly in need of replenishing those forces, and so nature in spring-time gives and gives again.

And it would seem to you, dear children, quite reasonable that as the months pass on, and more and more go out into the open, so that power of replenishing grows somewhat less. And so it is not only nature's law but the law of the Spirit as

J

well that autumn comes—that time of re-harvesting, of drawing in fresh forces—necessary to nature in order to help man.

That brings me to man's part, which tonight I am anxious to impress on all. Has it not seemed, in regard to yourselves or those whose lives have touched your own, that winter has been long indeed, that spring—the spring of happiness—dallies by the way? Then, dear children, I would tell you, directed by my Master, that these also are the ones who are to be used for the replenishing of the spiritual strength of others; that that barren time—the time when no blossoms were to be seen, no birds heard singing in the air—that that time was the time of storing, was the time of gathering in those spiritual resources, without which indeed, when the brightness came, their powers would be soon depleted, their store exhausted. It is God's will that those so equipped—equipped by training I mean—shall be adequately equipped with the power of the Spirit—the power which does not fail and which changeth not, except to grow stronger, more dominant, more directly a tool to be used by the Most High.

Again I turn your attention to nature. Here and there, dear children, you see trees and shrubs which are, as you put it, " backward." And why is this? It is because something of the earth—some structure comes between them and the sun. And so it is with life. There are some who show no sign of bud and blossom, in a spiritual sense; but are these (as some would have us believe—yes, as some teach) are these to be rooted up and cast aside for ever more? Nay, this is our work, this is Christ's work: by effort to pull down those obstructions of the earth, to banish those walls of materialism and to let the sun of revelation shine upon them.

Yes, dear children, the trees are in a more helpless position; they are in shady places, put there by others; but here again you have your parallel, yet not to the very end.

I say there are many in the world today who, by their actions, by their callousness, by their spiritual indifference have indeed erected before the untutored a wall, which they call " reason "—the reasoning, the theories, the deductions which block out the Light of the Spirit. So the child—as the plant—is " backward "; yet this is the hope for all: The tree is the victim of the thoughtlessness of man; yet to the individual soul you can go, you can say with confidence, that walls

can be banished, that they, in their humble position—hemmed
in by a multitude of duties connected with the world—they, by
the power of the Holy Spirit, can be as beautiful, as fruitful
as the loveliest that can be imagined.

That is God's law. Ignoring conditions, trampling down
those physical restrictions, tearing aside those false obstructions you can go to these and you can say, with certainty,
that they in their squalor can be glorious indeed. And many
demonstrate this, in spite of teaching—or the absence of teaching—in spite of the lack of the helping hand.

Yes, the body may be worn and old, that garment of
flesh may be drab and, perhaps, unlovely to look upon; but
once the little physical cabin is laid aside, so they will emerge
into the glory which fades not, because God has said: Those
who seek to do my will, to them will I reveal that which is
of Myself . . .

Children, there is so much I want to teach you, so much
I want to instil, so much for you to learn, so much to do; and
yet, little ones of my heart, I should not be portraying the
Mind of the Divine if I did not tell you that by simple faith,
by the wish to serve, all those great gifts of the Spirit can and
will be your own . . .

Dedication, concentration, retreating into the Silence of
the Spirit, shutting out the world and its many voices and trying—ah ! yes, trying to reach that which is your own—the
Spirit of God, within and without. That is the way to unravel the
secrets of the Bright Spheres; that is the way to untie all those
many knots in the rope of physical knowledge; that is the way
to make Wisdom your own—the Wisdom of the Spirit which
shall permit you not only to enter into revelation yourself,
but to demonstrate that revelation to others.

There is no other way. Many have tried, many have got
through the first portal, and then, intoxicated by success, have
forgotten the quest—the quest of holiness, the quest which
demands consecration and devotion. Indeed they have gathered up gifts; but when they come here they will see that those
gifts were but misrepresentations of the real, but travesties of
the powers. In that day they will go back—yes, even to the
portal gate—and by service, by prayer, by faith make that
which God holds out to all, their own. Without service, prayer
and faith, the work that is done has no stamina, dear child-

ren; and that is the difference. Sometimes, from the outside, it would seem that the results are greater. But go back to nature—plodding nature, to the slowness of the growth—and then you will see how only the Spirit can emerge; and until the Spirit is free, in some measure, from self, from the world's way of thinking, so the work done passes away and the power has been wasted.

Children, I can't speak too seriously in regard to this (phenomena at seances). The power of the Holy Spirit is used extravagantly in order to demonstrate, not the Love of the Father, but rather the powers of the physical mind—those powers which walk hand in hand with popularity and success. This, dear children, has a harmful effect on that which is Divine within. Never think that Christ, the Great Understander, does not enter into the natural wishes of these, His little ones; but when they come here they will see, to their anguish, that the good gift, which is indeed of the Spirit, was not used to demonstrate the Divine but rather to catch the attention of the idle passer-by. Oh, think you not that I judge others; yet being a servant of the Most High I should be failing my mission if I did not seek to instil one little word of warning. When you come here, seeing things as they are, you will find it hard to forgive your lesser selves if that power was not used solely and only to bring the revelation of God's Love to suffering humanity.

Yes, the ways of the earth and the ways of the Spirit often run in opposite directions; and yet those on the Other Side are concentrating their powers in order to bring the greater vision to all who know the Truth. Yes, they know the Truth, but they understand it not: they take, but they are scarcely willing yet to give; they use it not for the furtherance of God's work, but rather only to comfort their own aching hearts.

Cannot you see the difference, and cannot you see the responsibility as well? Only Spirit can contact with Spirit; only the God within can reach out and find the Great God who made us all. Yet the things which stand for all time are passed over, and the pretty toy at hand—the poppy of consolation, striking in its brightness—satisfies, and they go no further.

Yes! the patience of God is infinite, but the patience of the Divine within you is another matter. And there are many who, when they are free, will be anguished indeed to see that they had the jewel of price in their hands, but they used it for their own adornment instead of holding it high so that the Light of the Sun might shine upon it and others might see.

My children, I hope I have not saddened you, because I know that in your hearts the wish to be used as God desires is foremost; and because of this a blessing—an unending blessing—rests upon you.

Now I have a personal word for my child whom you call " Louise ". (Miss Owen, Lord Northcliffe's private secretary for 20 years).

My child, you were directed here because there are those in the Spirit who wanted to seal the links between you and this great work. And I have been instructed to say tonight that if you keep the faith—in that higher, greater, nobler sense —then not only shall you reap on earth the joy which does not fade, but also those greater joys in the Spirit which no words can portray . . .

And I would underline what you have been told before: That not only has the story of your life run thus, but even before that body was your own, so the links were made, so I too was there and was shown at what hour your life would be intertwined with my children here. Yet, dear child, there is this to be said—and I want you to face it with that courage which is your own:

That faith untested is only half-faith; that love untried is not love indeed: that because you have accepted office under the Great Captain of us all, so you must arm yourself for war. Yes ! and remember that sometimes in your own ranks hidden enemies are to be found; sometimes even nearer still, in your own thoughts that which is not of God alone may seek to creep in; in your own heart there may come—ah ! it must be, if you are to prove yourself of God—there must come coldnesses and a sense of estrangement. Yet tonight I have been entrusted with this message to you: That e'er the enemy approaches, even as you hear it at the outer gate, commend yourself to God, and recall my words.

As in the Scriptures of old, God permitted, sometimes, that a warning should come to His faithful servants, so tonight I put you on your guard. Even as a soldier, armoured by truth, with the staff of faith (not a sword) in your hand, so indeed you shall battle for Christ, so indeed shall you conquer, if you remain true.

And I pray God with all my heart and soul that when the struggles come, so shall the Comforter come as well; so shall you look forward with calmness and resource, saying: " Christ goes in front and I will follow, where e'er it may be."

And then I have a word for my little child, Marjorie (Miss Rowe, Miss Owen's secretary) and it is true that I asked that she should be gathered in tonight . . .

Child, it may seem to you that the little boat of your life has passed over dangerous waters indeed. But I would have you know that when Christ is the Pilot—though storms may blow, though the forces of evil may seek to wreck—with Christ as the Pilot the rough waters are just as safe as the calm. Nay ! more than that. Have you not heard that when too pleasant the aspect, too still that which is beneath, so craft becomes becalmed and the harbour is not reached ? Yea ! that harbour which God has provided for all. And so tonight I would say that the boat which rides over the rough seas, being guided by Christ, reaches the safe harbour long e'er the other is half-way on its road.

Christ is here, and with His exquisite tenderness and understanding, bids me speak tonight with confidence and with sureness. So I tell you that the harbour is in sight, that the storms and the perils and the loneliness shall be forgotten, because God, using the tool of the loving hearts of others, works out His wonderful purpose, works out that which you, little Marjorie, came into the world to bring to pass . . . and that great response to the Divine within shall be fulfilled . . .

And now, dear children, I will not keep you much longer, but it has been ordained that I should tell you this tonight: That he whom Jesus loved, John by name, is here, and he tells me to say—to remind you of the Master's words: " If I will that he tarry till I come, what is that to thee ?" And, dear children, the beloved of God has tarried, and will tarry, till His Master comes. Here you get the explanation of his entry into the Bright Realms while still the physical body was worn: it was to prepare him so that when that tabernacle of flesh was laid aside, without interruption, he should carry on his work on earth for God.

And I must add that too often are the words of Christ misconstrued; yea, even John himself saw the danger of the statement—a statement which could be twisted by the enemies of the Light—and so thinking (and how human this is) to protect that which he loved so much, he added: Christ did not say I should not die; but, speaking to Peter said, " If I will that he tarry till I come, what is that to thee ? "

The laying aside of the physical garment—to one who knew God and the working of the Spirit—was, dear children, just as the throwing off of a heavy garb would be to you in your daily life; and he, recharged with power, with strength and with illumination—he tarried, and he tarries, till the Master comes.

No words can adequately express all that underlies this brief statement; yet I am constrained to tell you that there have been many who, voluntarily, out of love of God expressed to humanity, will, in turn, tarry on earth until the Master comes. Yet the preparation for this work must be got in first; and the understanding of what life—real life implies—this must be made your own; much must be seen and heard and understood in person if you too, choosing the harder, the greater and the nobler road, would tarry until the Master comes.

I send this word to Ralph: I tell him that the work he has been asked to undertake—that of penetrating into the Spheres of the Spirit—is essential if he would be numbered among this throng. This work on earth stands as the highest, because it is even as that of Christ Himself, in endeavour— Christ who works and walks among you, as in the days of old; Christ who bears your burdens, lifts you out of the pains of the body, soothes the mind, quietens the nerves. Yes ! this is the Master's work, this is the work which has been going on since creation started: that individual service, that personal, intimate companionship with the weakest and the frailest, as well as with the strongest and the purest.

The great army of God needs many to swell its ranks, to increase its power, to enlarge its scope of influence, to raise the broken-hearted and to protect the children. Therefore, my little ones, prepare yourselves—aye, and again I say prepare yourselves to work for God, with God; and, by His power, even to undertake those same miracles which Christ demonstrated personally upon earth. No barrier lies between you and them but the sleep of the Spirit. Awake then—yes, awake ! and take what is your own; accept the privilege, the honour which has been conferred upon you, and go forward, not only in courage, but in certainty of the promises of God . . .

And in His good time you shall see a glorious harvest indeed; you shall be amongst the gleaners, yet, as you glean, so you shall re-sow. And that goes on for ever and for ever. Because only by service can we contact with Christ, only by understanding can we help our fellow-beings, only by releasing the Spirit within can we demonstrate the glorious liberty of Spirit which is all around, which is charging us and the world in which we live, and which is an outward and definite expression (as near as we can ever reach) of the Holy Spirit which is the source, which is as a fountain sending out its beautiful waters everywhere, bringing life and hope and emancipation . . . The Holy Spirit which is upon you all tonight, cleansing your hearts, lifting up your thoughts, imbuing you with courage, and creating understanding, so that the illumination may come . . .

And thus I leave you. Send out thoughts of help to those who would speak, and remember that I have said this is an evening of work for God.

Holy War

MY children, we start a little tired tonight (8.30 p.m.) and
I must ask you to give out as much vitality as you can,
because there are several things about which I would speak
to you—and it would be a terrible waste of time and opportunity if God's purpose was not achieved. I think you understand ! I cannot make up for serious lack on the physical side
in a moment's space of time, yet in this room there is spiritual
power of an amazing kind—it is gifted to us without restriction—and drawing on that bountiful supply, so we go on and
so we conquer that which would hold us back.

My children, in regard to the campaign which is before
all those who wish to spread the Light, I have one or two
things to say, and I hope they will be helpful, not only to
the children of the inner circle of my love, but also to those
who would not class themselves as belonging to me at all, yet
know the truth in part, if not in full.

Before us all there is something which is in the nature of
a Holy War; and yet in using the word " war " I would not
have you gain a false impression.

In the world, right down the ages, there has been strife,
there has been bitterness indeed; and wars carried on in an
atmosphere of hatred are destructive in many ways, in addition
to those which are there for all to see. Yet, dear children, I
would have you remember that the most gigantic war which
could be conceived has been going on from the time when
humanity turned to the darkness away from the Light. This
war is a Holy War; this war is between those who would build
and those who would destroy: and this war must be waged
until the unity between Father-Spirit and child-Spirit is complete. It is to this Holy War that I would turn your attention.

You must remember, dear children, that ever since man
began to think for himself there have been those same great
souls who, in taking on their many experiences, have managed
to keep in touch with God; and these, oftimes solitary ones,

have ever fought against the multitude and, in some cases, have prevailed.

Religion, or religions, have survived many a shock and many a pitfall; and because in the world there are many expressions of religion it merely shows that the children of the earth, being children in a spiritual sense, have found it impossible to combine one with the other, in praising their Creator. I use the term " children " because if you watch the little ones at play you get illustrations again and again of what has been the case with those grown to man's and woman's estate. In the beginning the little ones play quite happily together, but as time goes on a clash of will and of desire is almost inevitable because of the different characters, the different temperaments possessed by the children. Most Mothers know that the one with the strongest will, the one with the most dominating desire gets the advantage for the time being; yet that advantage is, in reality, a disadvantage to the child himself, because next time he is not chosen as a playmate, as the love is absent which would make his presence welcome . . .

Children, carry that idea on a little further; expand it, put it into its right environment and you will find that it applies to those who, in the beginning, were linked together by their love for the Master. These are disunited now, not for a spiritual reason, but entirely for those same reasons of desire, of opinion and of power.

Yet I want you to take the spiritual point of view in regard to this; to recall my words as to " charity ", as to tolerance, as to the necessity for those who are linked to the things of God to stand shoulder to shoulder against the enemy which is attacking. When you all come here you will find no difficulty in sinking your differences in " service." That is the key which opens the door of Peace and of Unity between religion and religion upon your little earth.

Children, it has been said—and justly—that miniature wars—rather fierce battles—take place between those who call themselves Christians, those who are wishful to do God's work; and tonight I am anxious to impress upon you that in the future you are called upon to stand aside both from criticism and from estrangement in regard to those who view the Truth in a different way. It is most important that you should keep this thought ever in your mind: That this war is a Holy War; that it is not against those who wish to do the Master's work—even though they may be hindered sometimes by the shadows—but your war is against the destroyers—those who have banded themselves together to keep the Light from penetrating into the hearts and minds of God's children.

This then must be your attitude: That while you proclaim the Truth with all the force of which you are capable, yet ever you remember where your real enemies lie, and where your chief work has to be carried on.

Children, last week I reminded one (Miss Owen) that she was to go forward with the staff of faith, not with a sword; and tonight I want to enlarge upon that a little as we go along. I want you to realise that, in power, faith is far stronger than any sword could be; I want you to realise Who is directing you, and something of the army which is around you; I want you to watch your speech—to be careful that in trying to convince others you do not betray that which is of God within.

Look at the subject how you may, of necessity God's work must be done with His tools; and His tools, as you know, are Love and Service to others. Yes ! very often it is difficult to keep back the quick words and the quicker thoughts of criticism; but I want all those who read these records to have a clear statement as to the campaign which is before us and the methods which we intend to adopt, directed by the Spirit.

Children, in every-day life you will find—sometimes in the home and if not there, in a wider circle—those who are the Constructors and those who are the Despoilers. It is a curious thing, and it has been noted by many thoughtful people, that the fiercest criticism comes, as a rule, from those who have no desire, or aptitude, to build themselves.

Creative work is regarded, in the Spirit, as something precious; and I want to make it quite clear that when these artists—perhaps of trivial or mundane things—feel that they have failed to produce what was in their mind, and yet have done their best—I want these to understand that what appears as second-best on earth is not only classed but is turned into the very best in the Realms of the Spirit.

Children, you can all be artists; you can all create, if you will. And tonight there is a little point which it is necessary that I should drive home: In order to create, power is required; and that power (although you know it not) is indeed of the Spirit. Therefore, dear children, harvest those powers which are your own. Never allow yourselves to be a despoiler of the creation of another: be a builder yourself. Perhaps I have not made this quite plain; yet, dear children, I am trying to show you that criticism of the efforts of others is not only non-creative, but indeed is a diversion of the power which each one requires so badly in order to build themselves.

I take you from that thought to those many religions to which I have referred already. You see what I mean. Never say one word which is calculated to destroy the faith of another —nay, I go farther than that: which is calculated to destroy the carefully-built-up thoughts of another.

Yet you will say to me: " If I follow this plan how would anyone be convinced ?" It is a little difficult to the inexperienced, but the method itself is simple, as everything relating to God.

In regard to religious differences try and adopt this attitude: of seeking in each one those beliefs which are in harmony with your own. You will find, in the main, that however wide afield you may go that there is a God—a God who is good, who is worshipped and obeyed. Then, to come a little nearer home—and I am thinking of those many " sects " which we have talked a little about before—with these you have more in common. They believe in God the Father, they believe in the Saviour of the world and they believe in the power of the Holy Spirit.

You see, dear children, apart from anything else what an enormous lot you have in common with each other. All the essentials are there—the foundations are the same—and in talking to them bear in mind that it is directly playing into the hands of the shadows to enter into argument on those points on which you cannot agree. Rather, in conversation, go to the other extreme. You have got your fundamentals: talk about the ties which link you together; and if you pursue this course, dear children—I mean if you take the opposite attitude from that which is common today—if you discuss the things in which you are in agreement, leaving those many disputable points untouched, you will find that you are able to build up a friendship of opinion which, as you know each other better, will indeed grow stronger and more expressive of that brotherhood and sisterhood which should be between you all . . .

I want to labour this point a little; I want you to realise —all who read these records—I want all to realise that they, and we are as soldiers of Christ: not out to battle against our own kind but to battle against those terrific forces of evil which indeed tax all our resources; because in our own ranks there are those who as yet are but faint-hearted in their efforts . . .

Yes, dear children, when you are trying to show others the hope and the revelation which even now is being made your own, bear in mind always that in endeavouring to bring Light, indeed must you use only those weapons which are in perfect harmony with the Light of the World and the Love which He represents.

Never forget to be a builder; and never forget that in building you must start from the earth, or beneath it; and that you must commence with one brick at a time, and these must be added singly, with precision and with an eye to the future if your erection is going to be of utility in the days to come.

There are many thoughts which will arise from my words tonight, and I want the thinkers to, as it were, hand themselves over to the guidance of the Spirit, so that the messengers— working under the direction of God—may lead their thoughts into the channels which are of Him: on to that broad, un-bounded plane of realisation when they too will see the neces-sity of sinking their differences and of working and striving and battling together, so that Right may prevail and Love be established for all time.

And then, dear children, I have a few words to say to those who have been troubled by many doubts in regard to this further revelation of the Truth. There are those gathered into the outer circle of my love whose hearts and minds are devoted to the service of the Master; yet it has been their lot that many doubts and questionings have arisen in regard to the enormous responsibility attached to the handling and to the spreading of this Truth.

Children, for such as these I have a word of comfort and

I give it tonight by God's injunction: Those who are pure of heart and mind shall see that God's ways are not man's ways and that even the doubts of their mind shall be used for the furtherance of His great work. I tell them this: That because they have suffered and because they must suffer before this fuller revelation can become their own, so in turn, by the knowledge of the doubts and the questionings which assail the human mind, power shall be given to them to lend just the right influence at the right moment to dispel the misgivings of others.

I speak not of this little life; my vision is far far wider than that. I tell them that through the uncountable time to come indeed shall they see that God, taking the very doubts which assailed them—because their hearts and minds were pure—uses them for His unlimited purpose, turns that which might seem as loss into gain, into that which shall grow in strength and in beauty as the years go on. Yes! it is used again and again by the Father to bring Light to those who as yet wander in the twilight of understanding, sensing God and His purpose but not seeing face to face.

Then, dear children, tonight I must say another word or two in regard to Faith. Is it not true that all things which are worth having have to be striven for, have to be paid for by effort and by thought!

You, my little children—and many many others—could have been saved much suffering, many chills of the heart and mind if only you could have believed in the good intentions of the Father towards you, individually, during your daily life.

Yet, again, I have words of hope and cheer. I say that because there have been those among you who have desired that larger faith with all their hearts and yet have found that it escaped them—these shall see that God has used the waiting also in order to perfect the plan, to make more beautiful that which He has prepared with so much Love and understanding to be their own.

Yes! there are those who, if they could have believed in that which came only by the power of the Holy Spirit—if they could have believed much suffering, much much misunderstanding would have been avoided and the enemy despatched over the border never to return again. But I must convey the Father's Mind and the Father's view: Because the desire was there and yet the obstacles were too great, God will restore the years the locusts have eaten; and not only restore but show—yes ! lay it out before their very sight—what that time of waiting, of sadness, of unwilling doubt has produced in the garden of the mind, because—and only because—they wished with all their heart they could have done better, that they could have held on to faith undismayed, could have shown their faith without hesitation or misgiving.

Children, the things which are worth having have to be worked for, and they have got to be prized when they have been made your own. The plant of faith needs careful watching and much replenishing in the way of soil; it requires ever that the sunshine of God's Love should have an opportunity of shining directly upon it; that the pure fresh breeze of the Spirit should strengthen its stems: and then being watered by Service—by those waters which have been described as " Life-everlasting "—your beautiful plant should not only survive the experience of change of season but ever expand its branches, ever add new beauty to its blossoms, ever more send out sweeter and sweeter fragrance so that those who pass by are forced to stop and admire . . . Yes ! that faith shall be your own because the desire has been there, because the work and the effort has not been missing and because—though heart and mind fainted at the process—the patience held out until the Light was made your own.

And now, my children, I will leave you for a little while. There are messages which must be got in tonight and I call upon your attention and sympathy, which I know will be there for the use of those who speak.

Just one word for my little secretary (Dorrie), and Zodiac speaks to her direct because of this:

Child, never forget, although the strain of these evenings may be great, that this task will be shown to you in the days to come—nay ! not when physical life is laid aside but in the days to come—as the most important thing in your life: as a task so spiritual that indeed you will turn back and marvel that God was able to use you in such a measure and for such a great and glorious purpose. Think not lightly of it; and yet think not too seriously of the tax it entails . . . I see beyond the present; but your eyes are bound: yet trust in the Love of the Father and trust in my love as well.

Isolation

WELL, my children, it seemed a pity just at first to block out so much brightness, to veil from your eyes the radiance of the sun and the beauty which nature presents in such a delightful form at this season of the year. Yet, dear children, I must tell you that in this little room there is a loveliness which surpasses anything that nature can show. There is a Light—the Light of the Spirit—before which the sun, even in its zenith, would seem but as a candle shining against the light of day. In this room has been gathered, by those who love to assemble here, that which no tongue can tell—treasures from the Heavenly climes where all walk softly because Holiness is all around.

Think then to yourselves, my little ones, that you have not lost by forbidding the light of the physical world to shine upon you; for you are centred in that which knows no night, in that which indeed is an emanation of The Divine, of The Beloved, of the One you not only wish to serve, but the One whom you adore with all the force of which the Spirit within is capable . . .

Yes! it has seemed otherwise to some; it has seemed sometimes that the world, with its many irksome duties, with the toll taken on the physical body, has come in between; nay! more than that, has killed much of the love that they wish could still be there.

Well, my children, you know that I always face things squarely, and so tonight I am going to speak to you, just for a little, in regard to the plain of isolation over which every pilgrim must pass if they would reach the Promised Land.

I want you to look at things in a practical way: On the one hand, to forbid those bitter self-reproaches, that intense remorse, that personal loathing of self, because it fails so ignominiously to rise above its environment. Yes! to extricate yourself from that; and, also, to disown the notion which the shadows have tried, with great persistency, to force upon the minds of some of my children: That the distance between them and The Christ is so great that it can never be bridged; that it is no use continuing the task, no use trying to accomplish what is foreshadowed to failure !

Children, some of you who have read and studied the experiences of those whom you call " saints " have seen, with great dismay, that each one in turn passed over the desert-land; yes ! and that many were, as it were, bound and fettered for long periods of time to that condition which was as a wilderness indeed. Yet, dear children, in contemplating this you cannot ignore the fact that, in the end, the golden glory of revelation was made their own ! It is impossible to attain to so much in the way of spiritual progress without paying the price and, in some cases, the price is heavy indeed. Yet others have trod the self same path, and those whom you admire and revere so much—these too, my little ones, were forced again and again to ask themselves if love for The Master was dead for ever. These too became so isolated from the joys of life, and from those greater joys of communion with The Divine, that not only in a physical sense, but mentally and spiritually as well, the land was barren indeed.

I remind you of these incidents in the lives of others both as a warning and as a reassurance to you who also would take the steep, short road to God. Yet, dear children, you must admit that in one particular you are more favourably placed. You have those around you who can remind you that the bleakness, that the sunlessness of life's aspect is but a passing phase; is but a test—a most necessary test—to see if the physical will is indeed bound to that which is Divine within.

So long as the world goes on these battles between the physical and spiritual will continue and, in many cases, long after this world has ceased to be; yes ! under other conditions the battle will be waged until the enemy is overcome. But tonight, dear children, I want you, if you will, to listen to my words of love—yes ! to that love and understanding which escapes your comprehension altogether; I must say " altogether ", because the realisation which has penetrated into your minds is so infinitesimal, to me so unworthy of the name of love, that I say—perhaps with sadness—that your comprehension of my love and understanding, practically, does not

K

exist. Yet, dear children, one of these fine days I am going, in part, to force through some conception of the love I have for my own, and when that happy time comes, then—and then only—will you be able to grasp just a fragment of the love which the Saviour has for each one. At present that, too, is a closed book to you; but never mind ! books were made to be opened, and you have all Eternity before you in which to turn the pages; each page—nay ! each word being a definite, vivid expression of the Love the Father has for His children.

But let me get back. I would speak to you, dear children, about that very natural shrinking which you feel in regard to others going through the same experience   that of loneliness and, as it seems to you, isolation from the Divine Presence.

Well, dear children, it is something like this: You will remember when the children of Israel were on the point of leaving the wilderness, that messengers were sent in front to report on that which had been promised to be the possession of the faithful. You will recollect as well that there was one, and only one, who came back with a good report. That did not mean that Joshua had not suffered, it did not mean that the way he had taken had been freer from dangers, or that the view presented to him had been merely that of a sheltered corner, while the enemy lay hidden on either side.

Children, prospecting in that way would have had no value at all; and Joshua, having been trained, prepared and chosen as a suitable messenger, indeed went through as much or more than the others during his visit into the unknown land which lay beyond the confines of the wilderness.

I think you can see that this applies, without stretching any point at all, to the work which you have undertaken in the Name of the Saviour of mankind. Children, Joshua saw that before the Land of Promise could be made their own a struggle must take place; but he knew this also—the long sojourn in the wilderness, the gathering together of spiritual resources, the training, the discipline and the organisation— all in preparation for that great day when God should say: " Go forth and take that which I have given into your hand".

Children, I want you all to be as Joshua; I want you, in going on in front, not to allow the remembrance of your own suffering to be used by the shadows to keep back the spiritual progress of others—those others who, perhaps, if they knew all might hesitate to advance. I want you to reason thus with yourselves: To say " Hard though the road may have been, numerous the enemies, many, many the disappointments, yet here and now I can say I am safe and sound, because the protection was complete !" I want you to come back with a good report, dear children, weariness is so soon forgotten, and the pains of the body, and the vexations of the soul—why ! when they are passed, they are past; they are gone, and all the advantages lies in your own hands—the experience gained is a possession which no one can take from you . . .

Then hearken to the Spirit within, and do not think: " I hope they will not suffer as I have suffered "; or " I pray they will not be tested as severely as I have been tested !" Say to yourselves instead: " In spite of everything I am still captain of my soul, still following my great Leader on and on !"— and because that is the case with you so it shall be with them; and would you deny the brave pioneer Spirit that which will mean to it more than words can express—that which will be shown in most marvellous detail when the body is laid aside; that which will arm them with power, with joy and with a peace which nothing can destroy ? For the sake of suffering a little while on earth would you debar them from the great, immeasurable gain that is waiting for them just a span in front ?

Children, do not think that I cannot enter into that shrinking, which is growing in you, in seeing others suffer. It is, in the main, a Christ attribute, and it could be made solely an expression of the Christ Mind if only, if only you could take the broader view: not to stem your compassion but, instead of praying so often and so fervently that they may be spared, to turn your prayer into a strong spiritual force, voicing it thus: " God give them strength to go on and conquer !" You see the contrast ! The unwise parent, wishing to save her child everything that appertains to discomfort, prevents that child from following out the purpose for which the Spirit entered into the body—a loss so gigantic, so terrible that it takes much, much time and suffering to work out. Then there is the wise mother, who talks to her children and reasons with them; who tries to show them that by learning, by doing the little things which go against the grain, so they will grow up; and when they can prove that they are grown up, then liberty of action will be their own, and the restraining voice, the guiding hand will not be required, because they have entered into that condition when, uninstructed, they do that which is wise and follow that which is true . . .

I want you, dear children, to be brave for others. As you have found within yourselves sufficient courage to pursue the path with determination, is it quite kind to assume that others will not also be able to draw upon their spiritual resources in like manner ? Of course, you don't think of it like that; you only feel—your own wounds being unforgettable, at this stage—you only feel that you don't want them to go through what you have gone through; you want them to be happy; that their memories shall be sweeter and that joy shall not pass by on the other side ! . . . Yes, dear children, I know your thoughts through and through and I know you better than you know yourselves. I know it is easier for you to suffer pain than to witness others going through the same experience, and because that is so with you, cannot you expand the borders of your thought sufficiently to get a faint idea of the Father's feeling towards His little ones ?

You forget so often what it means to be the Source of Love, what it means to be the Father-Parent, from whom all parents draw their capacity to love; you forget that closest of all ties between you and the Father (far closer than physical parenthood could be) that you are of Him—that something of Himself is within each one . . .

Oh ! my children try and understand, try to look at things a little more from the Creator's point of view; try and understand how He feels when memories are too acute, how His Love suffers when you allow the darts of physical life to become embedded in your heart . . . Yes ! try and put yourselves in the Father's place !

This great work of ours is going forward; it is going to spread in a way you cannot grasp at this stage, and tonight I appeal to the strength in you—I appeal to you to be strong for others; because, if you are weak, then you are inflicting upon them the greatest injury that could be conceived.

They too must pass over dry places; they too must find

within themselves the will to go on, even though the consciousness of the Divine Presence may be absent. That is the greatest test of all—to feel that you have lost your Saviour; and
yet, dear children, the mere fact that it has come should
hearten you by the realisation that the next stage is the Land
of Revelation, where the sun never sets, where the most perfect
companionship can be found, where loneliness has no meaning, where Love rules, dominates and permeates everything
and everyone who is there.

The dry places then suggest hope, not despair; their very
dryness is a prophecy of the Living Water that is just in front;
their barrenness simply indicates that the flowers which never
fade lie just beyond the border. Out of the wilderness you
step into the Land of Promise, into the fulfilment of that which
you undertook away back in the dim and distant past, when
from God you set out to find God, through experience—to find
that which was your own, to link up the Divine within with
the All-Divine; to for ever demonstrate your sonship and your
daughtership with the Most High.

Yes ! as on a circle so the journey goes, but God is not
at the beginning and at the end only. As you have been told,
God is the Centre of your existence, and though you travel—
it seems to you—far, far from Him, yet at no time are you
farther from Him than another, because God is the Centre of
your life, and you cannot get away—you cannot separate yourselves from That from which you came . . .

Yes ! I know there are many who, it seems, indeed get
far away from Love; but children, they may turn from that
which is Light and Security and Peace, but the Father never
turns from them; and, if they would, if they had the strength,
by one effort of will they could make the contact between
themselves and The Divine complete.

You little know it, but a thought of Christ, nay ! a
thought which in any degree reflects The Christ—such as pity
or understanding or the wish to help others—these thoughts,
tiny though they may be, make the connection between you
and the Father-Spirit complete. Could you but see things as
they are, you would know that in that second, or minute, of
thought there is nothing which stands between you and the
Father; and I want you to apply this to those many who have
passed out of physical life who never knew the Saviour, who

indeed never knew God—yes! never knew God so far as the mind of the body was concerned. I tell you that not one thought of compassion, of kindliness or of the wish to serve others which passed through their minds did not make the contact between them and the Father-Spirit complete. Their ignorance of the existence of The Beloved made no difference at all. God knows who are His own; He knows the thoughts which belong to Him, and because He has the Father-Heart He is able to push aside the barriers of the physical and claim that which rightly belongs to Him.

When you come here, dear children, it will be a revelation to you to see God's attitude towards the so-called " heathen "; towards those of primitive races, those who understood but little, who were guided entirely by instinct . . . Yes! it will astonish you to see how these, passing through their physical experiences in an environment very detrimental to spiritual progress—so it would seem to you—to over-look what their lives worked out; what their sufferings, what their little acts of kindness did for the Spirit within; their love for their children; their care of the sick and the old; yes! and more than that: their helplessness, their inability to protect themselves from the fiercer kinds of nature, from the diseases of the body, from those deep anguishes of the heart which they did not understand, but dumbly endured . . .

Ah! dear children, all these things the Father has gathered up; all those unheeded, unnoted incidents which are taken as a matter of course in the lives of the so-called lower races. These are indeed turned by Love into good grain which shall feed the mill of the Spirit; and those which the world might mark off as " useless " well! when they come here they shall see that much, much has been harvested for them. They were sowing all the time but they knew it not, so Another reaped for them and put it all by so that when they were free they might have resources upon which to draw, and the power which those resources bring as a natural result.

Oh! dear children, more and more do I urge you to try and take the bigger view; to look beyond brief, shadowy to-day, and to be certain that the Promised Land is fair indeed; that it is worth a struggle; that it is worth the journey in order to reach it. Yes! it is worth many pangs and that is why there are those who, having finished their own earthly experi-

ence, are so anxious to come back and tread the path again
—or perhaps a little different one—with another. And you,
little children of my heart, you will want to do the same; you
will say: " Oh I remember how hard that seemed, how steep
that climb; let me help because I have been through it and I
understand !"

And that brings me to this: That in work of this kind—
indeed in any work that matters—it is absolutely necessary
that certain ones should go in front; that they should blaze
the trail for others, which means that the fiercest hardship
must be their own because they go forward not knowing where
the dangers lie; while others, seeing the warning posts here
and there, can take care, can be on their guard, can walk
warily until the dangerous place is passed. Yes ! it is
absolutely necessary that certain ones should go in front. Has
not your heart burned with love and admiration for the
hardened travellers on earth—for those who, guided by the
Spirit, went forward into the unknown and opened up vast
tracts whose existence had been unimagined before ? . . .

Children, when I speak to you thus all the entanglements
of the physical mind fall from you. It seems so clear; so
plain the meaning of God's purpose in regard to your lives.
And there is another thing you are apt to forget: The pioneers
—those who go into unexplored continents on earth, they
receive the first impression, they also reach the goal first, and
perhaps months, or years, pass before others are able to attain
to that same point. You see, dear children, that going in
front has its advantages and discomforts. Right down the
ages there have been some who have sought to penetrate into
the Unknown, and they reached, anyhow, the borders of the
Land of Promise, thus saving themselves much time when the
body was laid aside. Yes ! right down the ages this has been
so, although often it was done in secret because those who
were content with the valley objected to others climbing the
hill. So you see, dear children, that not only in the present
but in the past and in the future, there has been, and will be,
the hardy ones who, by their spiritual endeavours, will reach
the land of Light before those others who, as yet, have not
awakened to the necessity of going forward.

Nothing can take the prize from you. You may say to
yourselves: " But I am tired and would rest !" Yet, my little

ones, have you not noticed that when a child, resting on the grassy bank, sees another passing her—running along the road, the rest and the grassy bank loses its attractions; her weariness is forgotten; others have gone on in front and she must go as well . . .

I tell you all—and I know you through and through—that whatever the inducement, that however pleasant the prospect, the weariness of the road would not hold you back now; it would not be sufficient to allow you to witness others forging ahead while you were stranded by the wayside, cut off—except in imagination—from the glories which are in front. My children, that is the beauty of the things of the Spirit. Once you have felt the Hand of God you must go on; you must, anyhow, do the best you can to cover the ground; and though to you it may seem that you have left the toys of the world behind and you don't know how to make use of the gifts of the Spirit which have taken their place, yet, dear children, I am told to remind you that the barren aspect is, in itself, an indication of what lies just in front, though you realise it not. Gifts of the Spirit have been made your own; minds so buoyant will soon readjust themselves to the changed conditions, and once you understand how to make use of those gifts you will realise that indeed you have crossed the border, out of the wilderness into the Promised Land.

We have much to do in the days to come. Even from your standpoint the seeds are coming up in all directions; but the seeds which are hidden from your physical eyes are far, far more numerous, and many gardeners will be needed in order to protect and to train. Therefore, dear children, you see what your part must be: By the very depth and breadth of your own life's experience—and only by that—can you help others, can you be the one to see that the enemy does not draw too close; to take care that the Spirit—which can well be represented by the emerging of the green shoot through the earth—to take care when the unfoldment commences that not only shall the rain fall upon it, but the sun—the sun of God's Love. The rain is sacred; it is symbolical of life's experience; it is that which cleanses, and if sometimes it is over fierce and beats to the ground, yet without that rain the plant could not grow; and even if it, in its frailty, bends before the storm, so shall the warmth and power of God's Love raise it up,

again and again, until matured—yes! I say " matured " by
rain and by light, so it is firmly established for all time . . .

Remember, dear children, that you are as Joshuas, sent
to describe a Land which is waiting for the inhabitation of
all those who would show themselves children of The Divine.
So forget your wounds, throw aside memories which perhaps
are shadowed too much by the earth, and say, with faith,
that the Land of Promise is fair indeed; that it is worth a
struggle; that you are certain that, by God's grace, both hidden
and open enemies can be overcome, and that the encamp-
ment can move forward and take possession; pass out of the
wilderness into the Land which flows with milk and honey—
milk and honey, symbolical of that love and service which not
only admits you into the Promised Land, but also allows you
to remain in it for ever and for ever.

Be not discouraged over anything. If you could but see
it, you would know that you had cause for pure and unlimited
rejoicing; and never forget that whatever lies in front of any
pilgrim, Christ companions them all the way. Isolation and
loneliness are of the physical alone. When you come here
you will see that the protection was complete; that surrounding
you were a cloud of witnesses—yes! witnessing that they too
had taken the uphill path, that they too had entered into the
Promised Land; they who, by tribulation, have found that
security from tribulation which nothing can take away. These
walk with you, protecting, guiding, because your eyes are
bound; and these, in close communion with the Spirit within,
will lead you into the Land of your heart's desire—to the very
goal of the quest which you undertook.

And now I leave you. Keep your thoughts steady and
your will as closely as possible in touch with Christ because,
as always, we have work to do.

Failure

GOOD evening ! my children, and if I say in the beginning how happy I am to be with you all then indeed I should be understating the truth: I say tonight that God has been over-good to us all and that each one, as the days go on, shall feel that a blessing indeed rests upon them.

Tonight, gathering you into my love, I wish to speak to you about a very wide-spreading subject which concerns you all: I want to tell you a little about failure and success. I want you to consider these two conditions from the spiritual point of view; to banish from your minds the physical conception because it does not portray, even in a fragmentary way, that which is Truth indeed.

I speak to you all with most tender understanding of your lives, of your conditions, of your thoughts and aspirations . . .

To many that word FAILURE strikes an answering note in the mind connected with sorrow and disappointment. The course of your life has not run on smooth or easy lines and there has been that in it which has brought something like despair. That is the world's point of view; but God's point of view is so different, such a definite contradiction that indeed it needs pondering over in solitude and in quietness of Spirit.

Children, the word " failure " is used freely by those on the physical plane. The majority judge entirely by the outside presentation of any fact or subject; and if a man or a woman cannot show the possessions of the world—those decorative misconceptions of popularity and success—then there are many who say at once: " He is a failure !"—he has failed in that which he sought to accomplish.

I want you to go back on your own lives—on the memories. Many of them are tinged with bitterness and all with sorrow because—it seemed to you—that do what you may the conditions of physical life foiled you at every turn. Yes ! and it is quite easy to see that the judgment of others is correct from the world's point of view. Success has passed you by; others have reached that point to which you looked with such longing eyes—to which you devoted so much effort and so much consideration as well . . .

My little children, how I long for you to get the Christ view of lives like these; how I long for you to see with the eyes of the Spirit and to overlook the beauty and the power which you have been acquiring by " going without ", by laying aside the things of the world—perforce though it may be . . .

When you come here you will thank God for these so-called failures—thank God that this ambition, that that desire was not worked out as your fancy so ordained. You will look and you will see that God's ways are best—yes, are best.

There are many in this room tonight whom the world called failures: those who strove and yet as the years passed on had to look back and acknowledge that not one of their dreams had come true. Yet, dear children, have you not been told before that there is no dream—that has one thought of God in it—which is not worked out into actual fact in the Spirit !

I take you with me in thought and I ask you to turn those leaves of memory to where this went wrong and to where that went all awry; and tonight I am instructed to say that when you are free you will find that the failures were successes in a way which escapes your imagination altogether.

Yes, dear children, the world is very deceptive. Its conceptions are mounted on a false foundation—that of selfishness. And because the world sneers when this one or that loses those possessions which are so prized, loses that position which gave them power to control others—when the world sneers thank God, thank God because the Saviour's smile is yours for ever more.

Failure and success; humbleness and importance: and when the vision comes so you too, in looking out on life to those who have " failed ", will not only send out your compassion—as you do at this stage—but also the realisation of the part you have taken yourselves will come, bringing its comfort, bringing deliverance from those dark, questioning thoughts which now, it seems to you, stand between you and the bright Presence of the Divine . . .

Oh my children, cannot you grasp something of the glory of going without ? Cannot you grasp that those who are unprotected, from the world's point of view, are doubly, trebly protected by those whose power is as a sea compared to a little rivulet that wanders where it must ?

I speak in most understanding tones to those who've had to fight the battle of life seemingly alone; to those who have felt the lack of the strong protecting arm—those indeed who have had to fend for themselves, searching within for the resources which are lacking without; finding God only by treading the thorny path; understanding life only by going through the sad experiences of life. To these—to all so placed—I have a message of infinite hope and cheer: I tell them that indeed are they the beloved of the Lord; indeed do they love that which is Love itself; indeed have they willingly and voluntarily, in Spirit, laid aside the toys of the world, seeing the loveliness and the value of the gifts of God. That the Divine within —having vision seeing beyond this little day—is storing, is harvesting for the time of freedom, for the time when the physical body, having done its part, is laid aside and they, Spirit indeed, free from the world, free from its bondage, are centred in the Joy which has no end . . .

Children, though tribulation may have come close remember that the Master has said that tribulation can and will be overcome, because He has overcome the world. It is but of the earth. The physical mind suffers, it is true, but the Spirit within goes on, gaining new strength, enlarging its borders of usefulness, in touch with the Divine; and sorrow is unknown to that which is of God.

And then, dear children, I come to another point and that is the application of Faith; and again I ask you to look beneath the surface and to see the spiritual meaning—the purpose underneath.

There have been those in the world who have laid down that it is not wise to test faith too far; there have been those who—representing Faith itself, yet bound by the earth view— have put a bar across the free stream of the faith of others. and for this they will be anguished indeed when they see and know.

Children, I speak of the power of Spirit put into operation in any form. I speak of those who gathering up all their latent resources of faith have with trembling hands presented their gift on the altar of sacrifice, asking God to make perfect that which is imperfect; I speak of those who sore troubled by the body have gone in faith to God asking that He might heal them as He healed others in days long passed; I speak of those who taking their courage in both hands have lent themselves for use by those who have passed out of physical life—who have indeed handed over that tabernacle of the Spirit in trust to others so that God's will shall be done and His Love explained . . .

Children, I could enumerate instance after instance of those who, " fainthearted " though they might be, have yet found within themselves that strength which puts faith to the test. And I say now—under God's direction—that faith which is not put into action is not faith at all; faith which is of the mind is but an echo of the real—an echo of that which Christ has asked from you all . . .

And then I come again to the physical aspect. There are some who point out so readily that in this case and that faith has hardly been justified; indeed faith has produced nothing in a concrete form.

Oh blind and foolish ones ! Oh most ignorant mind of man ! Because no outward sign in physical semblance is there they say there is danger in exercising that which is of God within; they say: " Keep to the safe path; don't expect too much—don't expect anything lest disappointment should come !" Here you get the argument of that which is antagonistic to The Divine; here you get the most subtle argument of the evil one ! . . .

Children, this life of yours—so fleeting, so pressed in on either side by physical and material things—this life is but an echo of the real, but a materialisation of that which is Supreme, Divine, unending. And yet for the sake of that echo the gift of price is thrown aside.

Think it out ! Listen to my words for this is God's truth ! I say to you that one thought of faith, nay ! one wish to have more faith is producing that which can never pass away. Those who have gone in faith to be healed and have returned unhealed, these have built for themselves wonders

and beauties and power; and the healing which was not possible in the body—because they had taken on pain as part of
their experiences—that healing is transferred to the soul-body,
and that healing shall save them much suffering in the days to
come.

Think not of results in a physical sense. The body has
many enemies—it is but a garment which must be laid aside—
the mark of faith is on the soul, and that faith has cleansed,
that faith has restored, that faith has brought a strength which
nothing of the earth can take away.

Yes ! it has been said by those who should have known
better: " Wiser to keep on the lower plane; wiser to avoid the
risk of disappointment; wiser not to raise in the heart and
mind of others that which may not be fulfilled ".

Children, it is impossible to raise in the heart and mind
of anyone a thought of God which will not be fulfilled. So
I ask you to go over your mind and to think thus: " That
although my heart's desire may not be granted to me when
I wish it most, yet that heart's desire is being worked out in
the Spirit; it is but held for me until I am strong enough,
until I am wise enough to put it to its best use."

I want you to regard the showing of faith as something
so precious, something so God-like that indeed the pangs of
the physical mind are as nothing in comparison. I want you
to go to others and to say to all with confidence: " Have faith
in God; have faith in the answering of prayer; have faith in
the power of healing !" For indeed they, and you, shall see
that the faith and the prayer and the healing, all were preserved, all are in the Spirit, waiting—only waiting the appointed time for you to have and make your own.

Unanswered prayers ? Such a thing never has been and
never could be ! Even your faintest desire reaches the Mind
of Love; even those thoughts which are half of the world and
half of the Spirit find a response in the One who understands
you best—and never has one remained unanswered. Get beneath the surface; see the Spirit at work and know that God
is your Father and as your Father, tends and cares, supports
and guides His little children who, it seems to them, wander
alone on an unknown sea, guided by no compass but that of
a wavering faith. Yet because even that wavering faith is

there so the little craft of their life goes on its journey and finds God's harbour at last.

My children, faith is so precious; faith has such power that, of necessity, it must be worked for if it is to be made your own. You cannot see things thus, but we who are free we see the mighty, controlling, uplifting, directing force of faith; and because that one attribute is so charged with power then, dear children, of necessity, the task of acquiring it must be difficult, must be of rather a strenuous character.

The things which are worth having have to be earned; the things of little value, they come easily: but what can they bring you ? They are indeed as thistledown, alighting a little while and then taken on the breeze far out of reach are unregretted by those who wish to climb.

But faith is even as a strong staff—a staff which grows. Yes ! just a tiny reed, it may be, in the beginning; something you would protect, something you dare not lean upon for fear it should snap. Yet it can mature; it can grow so strong that indeed the whole weight of your physical life can rest upon it. But that staff can only grow by experience, only by testing its strength, only by patience and concentration. Yet in the end you have got that which can take you out of the valley up the steep hill-side, over rocks and boulders, over deep ravines—safe into the Father's Home . . . The trusted staff which has saved you not only from the perils of physical life but from those deep anguishes which await the immature soul when the body is laid aside; which awaits those who have chosen the easy path, those who have leant on the world, those who have not known that only Spirit can help Spirit, that only that which is of God can take you to God.

The staff of faith which never fails ! That staff is indeed gifted by Him to all when they have shown sufficient courage, when they have shown sufficient endurance to continue the uphill path.

To those who have started to climb with but a thin and weak staff to help them: to these I say that because within themselves the spiritual longing is so great, as they go on they shall see that, by the miracle of God's Love. that which was weak has been made strong; that which needed support shall indeed support them and others as well.

So, my children, I leave you with this thought in your minds: That the world's view and the construction put upon the outward and visible—these matter not, these are the things which pass away. You are sowing in the Spirit and in the Spirit the harvest is glorious indeed.

Keep the faith, dear children, keep the faith !—and remember all those who love you who are working for you, who are guiding every step: and have no fear, have no fear . . .

The Kingdom of God

MY children, we start a little over-weary tonight but—as you know and as I have shown you before, by God's direction—when the Spirit is in command that which is physical must stand aside. And tonight, because we have work to do, so we accomplish that which has been laid down. Send out your thoughts of strength, of faith and of certainty, and once more prove to yourself and to all who will heed, that the Spirit of God at work will not be gainsayed; that it is able to gather together the weakness and the weariness of the body and to demonstrate that because God wills, that it is as naught.

Tonight, my children, we have work to do; but I do not wish you to gather from this that you have slipped, even in the smallest degree, outside my loving care. I speak to all my children where'er they may be—whether their thoughts are lent to us tonight or whether the things of material life have for the moment distracted them from God's great purpose, His purpose in demonstrating His Love for humanity, and the perfect plan which evening by evening is being unfolded to you. Never think, dear children, because I place " the work " so high that it removes you into a lower strata because, as yet, you are bound to the earth, bound to that physical body which now and again—unwilling though you may be—comes between you and the realisation of the wonderful Heart and Mind of God. When you get a little further on you will see, with so much joy, that by concentrating on the furtherance of the work I did but honour you as Christ would have me do: I laid upon you the responsibility, and the responsibility brings privileges which no tongue can tell.

Tonight, dear children, heeding the request of one of my little ones (Miss Owen), I will attempt to tell you something about the Kingdom of God. Yet in the beginning you must know that physical language is totally inadequate to describe the things of the Spirit.

Many mistakes have been made, and will be made, in

L

regard to God the Father of mankind. In the first place I
must ask you to get right away from your idea of a monarch's
position. Of necessity you cannot think of kings without at
once surrounding them with pomp and splendour, with power
and much authority in regard to the lives of others.

Children, the position of a king of the earth and the
King of kings does not tally in any particular. And so, dear
children, I want you to banish from your minds that sense of
exclusiveness and the remembrance of all that furniture—
physical, mental and material—which shuts in those who have
been chosen to fill high places in a world which, in reality,
knows not its God.

Then, dear children, I want to say this: That the one who
put this question (Rev. H. R. L. Sheppard) that he, during
the sleep state, has wandered far and wide in the Realms of
the Spirit. In the Spirit he understands what constitutes the
Kingdom of God, and because it so arrested his attention
during those journeys (so soon forgotten) so the mind of the
body, catching a reflection of the greater mind of the Spirit,
sends out that query yet fears no answer can be given.

Children, many there are who have asked of us and
others: "Where is the Kingdom of God?" or " Of what is the
Kingdom of God?" and we—instructed by our Master—we
have taken them from beauty to greater beauty, from marvel
to greater marvel still, and at each point they have thought
or said: " Surely this is the Kingdom of God !" But we say:
" Not yet, not yet ". And so the quest continues and sometimes much experience has to be gone through before they
are in a suitable condition in which to grasp something of
the splendour. something of the beauty of the Infinite Mind
of Love . . .

Children, at this point I must try and explain that those
spheres or planes—which you refer to for the most part in a
figurative sense—that these, as some know well, are but conditions—conditions of holiness, or conditions which as yet
cannot be called holy because those who dwell therein turn
from the Light to the darkness, turn from freedom to a
hideous captivity indeed.

From time to time I have tried to explain to you that the
physical world and the spiritual world are undivided; that it
is impossible to say where one begins and the other ends.

Indeed they are so weaved together that in some cases the physical is directly a reflection of the spiritual, and in God's good time will be made the spiritual without any distinction whatever.

When those on earth—in order to convey degrees of progress—use such terms as the first, or fifth, or twelfth sphere they are trying to interpret in words what cannot be described in words at all. You see, dear children, we are all handicapped in the same way. There are " conditions " which we are most anxious to describe to you—to portray to you in imagery—so that some realisation of the Mind of God may be your own. And in order to do this we are forced to choose words and phrases which will convey something to your physical minds—something which you will recognise—and that is as far as we can go until spiritual sight is your own, when words are no longer necessary, their support no longer needed because (again in miniature) the eyes of the Spirit have seen something of the Glory of the Lord.

Dear children, I do not wish to destroy anything in regard to those planes and spheres which you have heard a little about. Such descriptions are essential and they give as fair a representation as it is possible to have while still bound by physical limitations. But there is one objection and this to us is of a somewhat serious character.

As it were, the inference creeps in that these various spheres and planes are separated one from the other; that there are spiritual distinctions just as on earth there are social distinctions; that those who are farther on are centred in such holy conditions that indeed space divides them from the child-like soul in those spheres which you grade as the " lowest "—that that void in between is there in very truth, as unbridgable as the gulf between a king of the earth and the beggar who creeps along the streets . . .

Children, I have had a little trouble here because this point is so important to impress upon you; and you know that when I am trying to break down barriers in the physical mind a certain amount of opposition (from the shadows) has always to be met and overcome. Still we go on.

Tonight it is my endeavour to show you that although those in the Spirit may be divided by conditions, separation—

as separation—does not and never has existed. Those who have learnt their lessons more quickly than others; those who have found within themselves resources, determination and will to find God; those whom you would describe as the " Angels of Light "—they indeed are but nearer in love and in patience and in understanding than the child of the earth, buried in materialism, buried in all those thoughts which block out purity and holiness and truth . . .

Cannot you see what I am trying to impress upon you: That the greater one's capacity for doing the will of Christ the nearer we grow to reflecting—in a fragmentary way—He who is Love itself. As we try to follow in His steps so also we try to do His work: we seek out those who have strayed; we travel far in thought in order to companion those who, it would seem to the world, are outcast from all that holiness represents.

Never think, dear children, that because you hear that this one or that one has penetrated into a higher and more glorious " sphere "—never think that he is separated from you or that you are divided from him. Still, as you must know, like calls to like; and sympathy of thought and aspiration dominates both the spiritual and physical worlds. And so it is that sometimes the children of the earth can be helped more easily by those (who have passed out of physical life) who as yet have not attained to those heights of spirituality to which your thoughts and hearts ever go out with such deep longing.

Children, in that last sentence you get the key to the whole so-called riddle of life and death; of physical and spiritual experience. If in your minds there is a desire for holy things there is that love and admiration for those who have got a little nearer towards the Christ-ideal than yourself have been able to reach. Then because those thoughts are in your mind, instinctively, without any barrier in between, those who are the most experienced in the Land of Light love to gather to your side as friends, as companions—not as dictators, not as directors in the earth sense—but as companions, as most understanding friends they come to you and they abide with you as long as the need and the desire remain.

You will see, dear children, what I am trying to convey. I am hampered tonight and always by the gigantic readjustment which has to take place in your physical minds when I attempt to describe that which is in the Mind of Love . . .

It would be incomplete if I did not draw your attention to another point which perhaps you may have forgotten: and that is the domination of the Spirit in physical life. In this material world of yours the Spirit of God dominates and controls. And although there may be those who refuse to recognise its guidance in their lives, yet even they when they are free from the body will look back and see that in spite of their destructive thoughts, in spite of their most destructive actions, the Spirit—if not able to hold its own—yet still controlled many of the events of their earthly experience.

You see, dear children, from this that I am trying to show you that this physical world of yours is not divided from any of those spheres or planes except, and only, by the thoughts of the individual concerned. It is strange to us that so many who read with delight and great devotion the sacred records of the sayings of Our Lord, can, at the same time, relegate the spheres of God as something which have to be waited for and which cannot be penetrated into so long as physical life remains. Tonight then, yet again, I ask them to reread those portions which relate to the Kingdom of God and to try and gather something of the inner meaning which The Master endeavoured to convey.

Children, in no instance will you find that the Kingdom of God is described as a place. Using various similies it is likened unto this and unto that; a condition is described—a mental and a physical condition—and anything which could be termed a " place " is rigidly excluded. You see, dear children, that it was impossible, as I have told you before, for The Beloved to speak to His listeners of things as they were. In the first place He was hampered, just as everyone has been hampered, by the lack of similarities in physical life and the inadequate nature of the words at His disposal. And I want you to remember also that although, in endeavouring to convey some impression to the physical mind, we liken the things of the Spirit to the things of the earth, yet always the things of the earth are but a crude manifestation of the things which are of God. The things of the Spirit get not their reflection in any particular from the things of the physical world; for there is nothing in your world which—being rightly interpreted—is not a crude reflection of one or other of the many marvels which are of the Spirit.

So, dear children, I come back, after going rather a long way round, to tell you—so far as it is possible for you to understand—where and what is the Kingdom of God.

Children, be careful in your thoughts regarding those many edifices which are in the world, constructed to symbolise the home of God. I speak with due consideration of every aspect of this great subject, and I see and I say that there is an element of danger in the importance attached to those edifices and their many requirements. Yet, dear children, I should not be portraying the truth if I did not explain that in those " houses of God "—so-called—if the hearts and the minds of those who worship therein are as sincere and as pure as may be—or, at any rate, if the wish is there to be sincere and pure—then those buildings, those walls do indeed contain a mighty force, a mighty power of the Spirit, which is used by God again and again in order to help those who as yet have not found that same strength within.

You see, dear children, it is rather a delicate subject; and yet viewed under the Light of the Spirit it is simplicity itself. As you know, in the Father's House—and the word should be " home "— are many mansions. And that means that being the Great Parent not only does He understand the individual heart and mind but also He has provided many channels through which His children may find Him, unimpeded by those distinctions of thinking which make such barriers upon earth. Therefore, dear children, it is quite easy for you to sympathise with all forms of worship of God. You look at things in the reasonable, commonsense way and you know that anything that is a help in raising the heart and mind to God—that anything which is able to do this is precious in the sight of the Father. Yet when you come here you will realise, dear children, that all unconsciously, at different stages of the earth journey, you took on this and that support, and as you grew stronger you were able to lay them aside and, finally, to walk in your own strength into the Father's Home.

It is in this connection that I would give one brief word of warning. Whatever the edifice may be, whatever the method of worshipping God, take care—take care that not only does God come first but that His second injunction is not overlooked: "Love your neighbour." Anything of the world, however beautiful it may be, however associated with holy memories and with sacred incidents—these things will be shown as obstacles between you and the One True Light if that injunction is overlooked.

You see, dear children, how I am trying to get things into their right perspective. These buildings, devoted to the honouring and the worshipping of God, are sacred in one sense and in one sense only: by the help they were able to give to the struggling soul; by the fact that they provided a vehicle through which this one and that one were able to find his God. but not more—not more ! Never deceive yourselves as to this. Beauty of raiment or ornament or architecture to the Mind of Love is as dust itself in comparison with the salvage of one poor soul. Yet forget not my words. Some there are who are helped by the outward semblance of beauty—it enables them to visualise the beauty of the Life Hereafter—and because of that it does its part; but again I say, not more than that in the sight of God.

Children, all unconsciously to yourselves I am getting you a little nearer to understanding something of the Kingdom of God.

I ask you once more to go back to your sacred Record— to the example of the Great Lover of all. Children, do you remember the incident when The Master bathed the feet of His tired disciples ? Keep that thought in your mind; and then recall my words in the beginning when I told you that a monarch of your world and the great Monarch of all were not alike in any particular.

You see, dear children, what I am trying to convey: That the Lord God Almighty, Creator of all things—that He who has not only created this little world of yours but holds uncountable worlds and states in the hollow of his Hand—His attitude is the same today as it was in the beginning and will be unto the end. The Father, the Christ, the Good Shepherd lays aside His glory and His power and tends the weary children of the earth, not as a concession to Love but as a demonstration of the Love which is yours and mine for ever more.

You see, dear children, when viewed from the earth's

standpoint and from the spiritual standpoint how different things are.

And now I bring you a little closer still to the Kingdom of God, and I ask our friend (Mr. Sheppard)—who is inspired with the desire to serve God to the best of his ability—I ask him to ponder over my words and to allow the Spirit within to decide as to whether or no what I teach portrays that which is Love Itself.

Children, the Kingdom of God is not in those distant heavens; the Kingdom of God is not reserved for those experienced travellers who, to you, seem to have worked through so much that you feel separated from them in every sense there could be. The Kingdom of God is not in any given place—not centred in any of those bright spheres which you long to hear more about—but the Kingdom of God is in the actual presence of those two or three who are gathered together in His Name. Yes! and in the heart of the humble worker—the one who does her best, unaware of the reward, unconscious of even the first threads of the pattern which she is working out in such beautiful design—there in the unselfish-heart, in the pure and simple thoughts, there is the Kingdom of God.

Children, within you all you have the Kingdom of God; within all those who have been created there is the Kingdom of God. But alas! in so many it is veiled and shrouded, so blocked in by the world that the owners perceive it not. Yet where the Holy Spirit has entered in there is the Kingdom of God, there is that which is sacred indeed—not built of stone or wood; the precious ornaments are missing; bareness and poverty often the surroundings—but where simple goodness reigns there is the Kingdom of God, and because it is His Kingdom, God indeed is centred in His own . . .

Children, I want you always to take that practical, commonsense view which, in its best sense, so nearly represents the spiritual, and I want you to think over the life of Christ on earth, to meditate on His holy teaching, to try and build up in your minds some conception of those gigantic truths which He sought to unveil to a world which understood Him not. I want you to balance all that with the little explanation I have given tonight and to for ever cast aside the idea of a monarch in an earthly sense; to remember that God wishes you to visualise Him in your daily life as the Friend in need, as the One who never fails, as a Companion as well as a Guide, to whom the word " dignity ", as you understand it, is unknown . . .

Once you see with the eyes of the Spirit the only dignity that has life in it is that of service; once the hearing is attuned to the Voice of the Spirit those things which represent power are seen for what they are—very often weapons used by the destructive forces not only to cause distress to others, but far more to damage that which is of God within.

So, dear children, I leave this thought with you, and I want you all to try and get something of the inner meaning which lies beneath; I want you to try and penetrate just one step into the Mind of Love and to think over His attitude towards His creation. I have told you before that the beauties of nature are but a pale expression of the beauties of the Spirit; I have told you that the most perfect rose which the world has ever shown is but a poor drab thing in comparison with the beauty of effort, with the beauty which is created and which will last for all time by simple thoughts of love and sympathy towards others.

Yes ! out of the endeavours, out of the thoughts of His children, God has built up the beauty of the so-called " spheres " of Light. That beauty is not far removed from you; it is in your presence now and has been and will be. Blind the physical eyes may be, but the Spirit within recognises that which is its own. So tonight I tell you that everywhere you go there is beauty, there is a definite expression not only of Spirit power but of the Holy Spirit itself. Ugliness is of the earth but beauty is of God, and so because there are portions of your little world which by their squalor and neglect are pitiful to look upon, so the Father has surrounded that which is of the earth with the beauty which is of the Spirit.

My children, we have had several little things to contend with tonight, but as you know it has never been my rule to give way. Once you acknowledge that that which is antagonistic to God is strong enough to divert you from your purpose, then indeed are you striking at Love Itself. And so I bid my children go on; and you shall find that we have done better than you imagined and that those concerned contributed their part, though nerves may have suffered a little in the process.

My children, I leave you now for a little while, but only for a little while. The personal messages must stand aside tonight because I am anxious to leave upon your minds a deeper impression of the wonderful thoughts which are in the Mind of Love for His little children, who, as yet, understand Him not at all . . . And now I go.

The Holy Spirit

GOOD evening! my children, and it is with great joy that we meet together in this way. Yet I have a few instructions to give you and I ask you all to think with the mind of the Spirit alone tonight for indeed we are on holy ground. I entreat you to still both your thoughts and nerves—which are of the physical—and to enter with me into the courtyards of the Lord.

Children, tonight, when your minds are lingering on the outward manifestation of the Holy Spirit, I think it an opportune time to tell you just a little—I can do no more because as yet your understanding blocks the way—but I would tell you just a little about the gift of the Holy Spirit, which has been man's from the day of creation and will be for ever and for ever.

Keep this thought in your minds: That the bestowal of the Holy Spirit on those who had been prepared by The Master to do His work—that that was but an outward and visible manifestation of what had been and what would be the free gift of all. With the Great Parent there are no distinctions, no divisions—no " sheep and goats " in any sense whatever. It is the Father and His little ones; the Saviour and His children, which He loves and cherishes for ever more.

Oh ! listen to me and try and learn and understand ! God is your Father and the best gifts are for all His children alike; yet, as would seem reasonable, there are some who are not ready for them, many who would not prize them, others who indeed would use them for most destructive work. So, dear children, you can gather how it was, and why it was, that those who had followed Our Lord, those who had listened and tried to learn—ah ! remember that: tried to learn in spite of physical disabilities and the limitations of the physical mind—these, dear children, because they had prepared themselves were suitable vessels to receive this most Holy gift, to be good stewards of that which had been placed within their hands: power unlimited. And remember that when this power comes there are those—yes, there are those who would divert it from its sacred purpose; there are those enemies, those dwelling in the darkness who because of their own captivity seek to enchain others. So it is a double responsibility, and so it is that the heart and the mind must be prepared by sorrow by those deep anguishes of the mind, that the things of the world must be thrown aside, that those encroaching desires must be torn out of the mind, lest when the gift is bestowed destruction itself takes place.

Oh ! my children, cannot you grasp something of what I would convey ? There is this gift direct from God making communion between the two worlds complete, unbroken; there is that power which can help others, which can console the sorrowful, which can relieve physical suffering—there on all sides lies this gift from God. But man, alas ! is not ready for it and so the years go by and barrier after barrier rises up between the children of the earth and the Glory of God—the glory of that profound Love which knows no limitations and which puts no limitations to the progress, to the power of you and of me.

It is, dear children, a subject on which I can take you but a little way, yet I would explain to the stranger present (Rev. Hugh Allen)—ah ! stranger so he seems, but brother and friend of mine—I would explain that the gift of the Holy Spirit, bestowed in those long past days, productive of so much—the gift which indirectly altered the whole history of the world—that that gift in exactly the same proportion is waiting for humanity to accept today. Yet while man bars the possibility so the gift remains ungathered; while the physical mind denies the manifestation of the Holy Spirit in daily life, so that which is of God remains unused, untried . . .

Cannot you see the responsibility which lies with each one ? Cannot you see how this attitude of thought grieves that which is Love Itself ? Cannot you see how it is keeping back the spiritual progress of the world ? Yes ! and this will be so until there are those strong enough in faith, pure enough in heart, valiant enough in Spirit to proclaim God's Truth; who will go back on their sacred records and read with the mind of the Spirit the simple teaching—the direct teaching of The Master Himself.

The Master said that to those who loved Him He would manifest Himself; and, dear children, right down the ages there have been those—who have suffered much for His sake—who have not only sensed The Master but have heard Him and seen Him in their actual presence. Again I say to you listen not to the voice of the unbeliever. " Imagination ", " delirium " these are the explanations that they give; but to the faithful those with the prepared mind to whom the vision has come, they know—they know that The Master has not only spoken to them, not only companioned them but out of His great Love He has shown Himself in that guise which they, bound by the physical, could recognise.

My children, I reminded you before that Christ said to His disciples—to those who loved Him: I go away. For a little while ye shall not see me, but again in a little while ye shall see me. And, as some have already been told, during those long years of trial, of work and so-called persecution Christ fulfilled His promise again and again. Oh ! my children, get back to the realisation of the Father's Heart. Does it sound possible to you that He who led them out of their homely ways, who took them away from their kind, who forsaw the path they must tread—is it possible that the Great Lover of all would withhold the joy and the reassurance of His Presence from those so sore beset on every side ? The Master promised, and the Master came again and again and supped with them, comforted them and directed them on their way; and under His protecting wing those few men were able to show to an ever-growing world the beauty of the Fatherhood of God.

My children, have I not told you before that in the Father's sight there is no difference whatever between His children. Some are younger than others in experience and so require more care, more watchfulness, more understanding than those who are linked to Him—who instinctively know how to protect that which is of God within from the enemies who would destroy. And so I say to you tonight—directed by The Beloved—that the same privileges, the same gifts which were bestowed on those simple men of old can be yours, can be possessed by anyone who will take the rough hillside. who will ignore the physical, who will steel their hearts to suffer. The gift of the Holy Spirit and all it means, the gift of seeing Christ while yet bound by the physical, this waits—waits for man to claim as his own !

Children, when you come here you will marvel, as we have marvelled, that so much has been done by conscientious people, by those who think they are dominated by motives which are both practical and sincere—what these worthy people have done in the way of erecting barriers between themselves and the God they would worship. Yes ! unconsciously, those who are out to strike Love itself have been listened to— and why is this ? Because that mind of the body, pursuing its endless course, as it goes gathers unto itself more furniture, and more and more, and so the owner, forging through the knowledge of the world, all unwittingly has built up an impenetrable barrier between himself and the wisdom of the Spirit.

Cannot you see that by choosing the complicated, by allowing yourselves to be emersed in the " thinking " of the world, as a natural result the thoughts which belong to God get crowded out ? You cannot serve God and mammon, and in regard to " thinking " this is driven home with most terrible force. The way to God is hard but it is simple; it is steep but it is direct, and all that anyone is asked to do is just those two things: Love God, and seek to serve your neighbour. If only those gifted with the powers of physical thinking could hold that thought in their mind how much they could have done for the world, how much they could have taught to a spiritually ignorant people, how much nearer they could have drawn humanity to the Fount of Wisdom, Who lives but to pour out on His children the knowledge of the things of the Spirit—the Truth, unbound, unimprisoned by all that physical thinking which in itself is a denial of faith. If only they could remember Christ's own words: Unless you become as a little child you can in no way enter into the Kingdom of God—that " Kingdom " which is not in spheres far distant, that Kingdom which is centred within. You cannot come into your own because the door of the Kingdom is locked and barred, for there are those thoughts which are centred all round it which forbid an entrance.

Get back to the child's attitude of faith; keep to the simple paths of thinking, and by concentrating on God that wider knowledge of the things of the Sprit, of the wonderful laws which govern your life and mine, the unravelling of the secrets of the earth—these and many, many more which as yet you understand not—these shall be made your own if only you will approach God as He has directed.

Oh ! children, think it out alone, think it out in silence, think it out when you are closest in touch with God and try and realise that between you and the gift of the Holy Spirit there is nothing but your doubts, your unpreparedness, your immaturity. If only you could realise the significance of these gifts I should not have to ask you to prepare and yet prepare still more; if you could only grasp just one degree of the joy—the inexplicable joy—which this close communion with the Divine brings of necessity, then you would not rest, nothing would hold you back—the things of the world, the pangs of the body and the thoughts of others would be taken just as an added impetus to spur you on . . .

And then there is one other point which I should like to bring in tonight, and that is in regard to us. As you know well, there are countless millions who have " come back ", as you would say, to this little world of yours in order to help their brothers and sisters, in order to bring them into that same sweet peace which is their own.

Now, dear children, there have been some who ignorant of spiritual laws, have exclaimed: " Oh why bring them back; let them rest; let them be at peace !" Well, dear children, in their minds is a very definite misunderstanding of the Mind of Love. I ask you to consider this in a practical way. Once more, is it reasonable that the Father would allow one of His children to be deprived of that which was their own because they wished to help their loved ones on earth, who as yet do not understand the meaning of physical life ? I put it to yourselves—to those who have children: I ask them would they—with all their limitations, with that strange travesty of love which is only possible while bound by the body—I ask them if they would treat a child in such a way ?

Children, in everything I want you to put these things to the test. In reading your Scriptures I want you to stop and question: " Is this according to the highest standard of Love ?" and if there is anything in those records which fails to come up to that, then you may know that the minds of those who put the words together were responsible and that God, in great or little measure, has been misrepresented.

I come back to my point. Is it reasonable that those who out of love both for you and for the Saviour of mankind—is it reasonable that they should be separated from their conditions of joy, earned by the experiences of physical life ? When we come here in this way we bring our gifts with us, and that is why, if you could see with the eyes of the Spirit, you would know that in this room, everywhere—every inch, as you measure space—there is the beauty, there is the power, there is the glory which is of God. Blind though the physical eyes may be the Spirit within is responding to the Spirit which is everywhere, within and without, and when that which is within links itself up with the Divine the unity is complete.

So, my children, I entreat you when you hear such foolish things said that you will answer with faith: " My loved ones bring with them their beautiful conditions !" And more than that: each act of service done to another enhances that beauty; each time we are able to strengthen you—to keep you firm to your purpose—so added power is our own. The Father gives through many channels. Sometimes it may be that the power, coming from on High—coming from the One who is all Holiness, all power, all Love—charges many as it passes from one to the other; and when you upon earth are conscious of that indwelling Spirit so its course is not ended. Out again go the rays of power and, dear children, could you see things as they are it would appear to you as vibrations of light, exquisite in beauty and colour, which indeed vibrate in ever-increasing circles and expanding force—on, on until at last it reaches again the Source, when, recharged, it is sent on its journey once more . . .

I am talking to you of things which are beyond your ken, yet I must prepare your minds ever more assiduously than before. I am impelled to try and implant therein some conception of those wonderful powers, those mighty spiritual laws which are in evidence on every side; yet I am held by lack of illustration and by lack of understanding in minds so anxious to learn and yet still held by physical conceptions.

Still, dear children, let me get back to simple things for they are the greatest and the grandest. I tell you that you cannot think one thought of sympathy or of real love without actually sending out from yourself those waves of light. And then from that I ask you to think of what real service creates— real love for God, the wish to do His will and the wish to help others for His sake and their own. Try, dear children, from the remembrance of this simple thought, to magnify and to magnify and to gain some understanding of this mighty force of the Spirit which is at your disposal, used by you unconsciously, unheeded, and yet for all that doing its work, doing God's work—creating fresh strength which shall help the weaker ones on.

And then one last thought, and I speak to my friend and brother (Mr. Allen). I ask him, in God's Name, to try and follow me in thought in what I have to say.

In these conditions where holiness abounds the things which are of the earth must not penetrate, yet I would tell him this: That the things of the Spirit over-rule and control the things which are of the world. I tell him that " duty " lies nearest to God; that should two paths lie before him then not only the spiritual point of view but the most practical as well is always to follow the road where he feels closest in touch with his Master. If only the majority could realise this then decisions or indecisions would fall from them. The test of every question, every decision, every opportunity is: " Does this bring me closer in touch with the things of the Spirit ?" That is the path ! Duty to this one, duty to that one stands aside; God comes first, and by ministering to the God within so the plan of one's life works out—as I have said—not only best spiritually but best practically in its highest sense.

There is much which lies before you, much that would seem in the nature of tests; but I say to you that God is able only to test the strong because the weak would fall or fail under it. Cannot you see to what I'm leading your thoughts ? —that the hard road, that the road which brings enemies to be encountered, that the road which is steep is the road to God; and because there may be much to contend with so God sends down His power, recharging and recharging again, even as to the disciples of old, so indeed, in His good time, those who are valiant shall find recompense, shall find the joy which can never fade in that perfect companionship, in that perfect unity with The Divine.

M

Oh ! let not your heart be sad.   Joy is in front, and in the measure that the Light shines upon you so the joy of the Spirit shall be your own; and in comparison the joy of the earth will be as the light of physical day compared to the unending Light of the glory of God.

And now I go.   Children, I want you all to give out sympathy and welcome; I want you to put out of your minds the personal and to lend yourselves as instruments of God because tonight there are those who would come, and by coming they demonstrate in your midst the power of the Holy Spirit and the unlimited grace of God.

Holy Communion

WELL, dear children, after a little absence we meet together again in this way; and I want you for a moment to consider with me something of the significance of those few words " in this way ".

To those who know but little of the power of the Spirit—of the unbounded Love of God—such gatherings are dismissed as of little importance; indeed by the ignorant as something which savours of a folly too deep to be condemned in mere words. Yet to the few—and mark you, dear children, that from the beginning of the spiritual history of mankind it has always been the few—to the few who have listened, who have waited for God's Voice, the answer has come. Yes! " in this way " has a meaning which can never be grasped until the body is laid aside, and then only in part. When that freedom is your own you will come back—as you put it—and you will see that where the wish to serve God holds true, where two or three assemble together in His Name to get direct instruction from the great world of the Spirit, there is the power—when you come back you will marvel at the complicacy and yet the simplicity of the method, of those spiritual laws which operate so truly, so harmoniously, making the communion between those living under physical conditions and those who are free, untrammelled by the earth and all it means . . .

Children, there have been some of you when you have climbed the steps to the altar which represents Holiness to the world at large—when you, and many, have felt it a privilege indeed to kneel and to receive that evidence, that physical evidence of Christ in your life, Christ in your heart and mind. Could the eyes of the Spirit see things as they are then you would be enthralled by the beauty represented; and I would have you understand this—that however the priest, so-called, may fail in representing his Master the blessing is the same if only your heart and mind wish to be linked to Him. Never think that with the things of the Spirit the things of the world

can overrule them; never think that because one here and
there fails in his or her duty that the Father cannot brush
aside those obstacles and stretch out the Hand of Love and
bestow upon His children the gift direct.   Many there are,
thank God ! who can enter into this spiritual communion—
this wonderful privilege which they, by reason of their office,
are used to dispense; many indeed represent their Master as
nearly as a child can represent his Father; and if you could
view things with the eyes of the Spirit you would know that
Christ keeps step with the one who gives, and Christ Himself
strengthens and purifies the heart and mind both of the giver
and the receiver, and so the blessing is two-fold in power and
in beauty.

Children, I do not use language which is flowery to describe such scenes as these; I must leave it to your imagination—that imagination which has its foundation in the Spirit—
leave it to you individually to build up some idea of the wonder, of the purity, of the exquisite loveliness of the conditions
round the altar of God when those who love Him gather there.
Yet, lest a false impression should be left on any mind, I
would remind you most earnestly that the altar—whether it
be consecrated or not, whether it be new or old, whether it
be fine or poor in quality and in decoration—that that altar
to the Mind of Love is as nothing, nothing except that it has
the power, the influence to draw the thoughts of His little
children closer to Him . . .

Again I come back to this little gathering here—to the
many gatherings all over the world brought into being by the
wish to find God and to obey His wishes.   Let not physical
conceptions have an entry.   Howe'er it be, whatever the circumstances and conditions, where two or three gather together
in His Name, there is the blessing definite, tangible, sure and
unbreakable.   Yet, dear children, by reason of the fact that
this direct communion with those in the Spirit requires much
preparation, much discipline, many bitter lessons learnt—by
this fact so is it possible that the power of God can not only
be demonstrated but is attracted in greater force, because that
which was necessary from the individual has been forthcoming
and the Father only waits to give and to give again.

There are some who have not studied this question—who
have not thought it worthy of consideration, who challenge

the statement that in gatherings of this kind the power of God is there in a more definite form than in the large and splendid churches which have been built in honour of His Name. Yes! this has been challenged by many and tonight I want to give a plain and direct explanation as to the why and the wherefore of this fact.

Here I draw your attention to a point which is evident to all those who are used to this particular form of service. You have noticed that apparently under similar conditions the power cannot be drawn upon to the same extent; that it is more difficult to separate those in the physical from physical things; that the world in a material sense obtrudes and the mind, alas! is too easily distracted from the sacredness of the communion which is taking place.

Again you have your simple answer. The necessary effort, the indispensable concentration and consecration has been absent, or has been delayed by those things of the earth which the shadows use to come between God and His little children.

Yes! dear children, and my words—spoken with so much love and understanding, spoken with that sympathy, with that inner consciousness of your lives and of the conditions which surround them—these words are given tonight with double emphasis to you and to the world at large: I say—by God's direction—that the power drawn together in this way to be used in an unlimited measure, depends solely and entirely upon the hearts and minds of those concerned. And remember that here it is that " the past " comes in; here it is that those foundations which have taken long to bring together, which have been built stone by stone with weariness, with dejection and with something well nigh despair—here the past takes its rightful place, and on that past—on that slowly accumulated foundation of endurance—so the present power is established for ever more.

To those strangers who have questioned the feasibility of this I say: Is it not a God-like truth that suffering, that work, that determination should have the power to build up the necessary holiness which is essential before those in the Spirit, who are of the Spirit, can come and speak to you as comrades and as friends. Again I say that this gift is not reserved for the few, but alas and alas! it is the few only who will submit themselves to the necessary discipline, to the necessary preparation for what is indeed God's work; because the gift can come only to those who strive to be free from that which would hold them back.

My children, I have talked somewhat at length on that little phrase " meeting together in this way ", but I want you to think it over, I want you to be certain that your Heavenly Father understands completely how it is that sometimes the physical body comes in between; how it is that the things of the earth make barriers over which His children try to step, sometimes in vain. And while I am speaking thus I want you to consider this point in a reasonable way; I want you to look at things in that practical spiritual way which always brings back into their right position—into their right perspective as well, those aspects which before looked all awry.

Talking among yourselves you admit that these experiences are " tests " but even so do not appreciate that if these tugs of the physical were absent the whole battlefield of your life, of necessity, would be changed. I have told you before that only by struggle, that only by fighting against the enemies of God can you attain.

You see, dear children, instead of viewing your minds and your desires alternately with loathing and with sadness, if you could get the true view—the spiritual view—you would see at once that these so-called enemies, by God's grace, can be shown a little further on as true friends indeed because, and only because you tried to get free from them—you wished to be linked solely and only to the things which are of God. Without these encounters—and you have noticed again and again that many seem to escape them—without these encounters you could get but a little way out of the valley, and the hillside, with its beauty and power and promise, would be denied to you for many many a long experience to come. Those who seem to escape such struggles they, dear children, have not evaded them but they are reserved for the by-and-bye. Drifting along with the tide in the comfort and ease provided, the boat of their life is not set in the direction of the Golden Shore but rather towards those many byways which lead nowhere, and when their length has been traversed out must come the oars and the boat must be rowed back by the sweat of the brow and by that deeper anguish of heart and mind.

The long journey of experience is the same for all, but free-will is man's gift, and until the Spirit within gains a semblance of freedom so the physical controls and so these issues are postponed and postponed again. Yet have I not said that the easy road contains more suffering because of its length than the short steep hillside ? Have I not said that to those with courage the helpers not only come, but using that courage—that wish " to do " as direct power, by the grace of God, again and again they can help and protect them from the deep and dreadful ravines which each pilgrim has to get over if he would follow the Voice to the heights beyond.

You see, dear children, that enemies in number or enemies in force do not denote (as so many of my children think) that heart-breaking lack of spirituality in themselves; rather to the experienced soldier the fiercest tussles come. He that has braved much in the past has—all unconsciously, perhaps— built up within certain reserves and certain resources without which he would not dare to face those enemies of Christ which seek to bar the way.

Oh ! take heart all of you and yet beware of that subtle influence which has been given ground among you—the influence of self-despair. I mean the despair over the weaker self, which you think is a direct indication from the greater self of how big your failure has been. The greater self knows what lies in front; that greater self is not appalled by the enemies of the Light, but it is hindered in its progress when the physical mind abuses and listens to those who are out to destroy. Therefore, dear children, it is quite consistent to say: Be of good cheer, and yet be on your guard against the enemy which is within the gate. Those nervous thoughts, those destructive senses which so often are in evidence— these and these only are the obstacles which have to be overcome; and if you could leave things with God more freely He could control them every time in a way so reassuring that very soon they would cease to exist at all. It is not only urgent, it is imperative that the chosen workers of the Most High should be free—free to take up their task not only as duty but as the greatest joy their life could hold. And that, dear children, is what God means. It is against the Mind of Love that this gathering together should represent to some of you (medium and note-taker) dismay; that it should present fears of any kind. God has given you a gift which you understand not, yet in the giving and the bestowing He knew that the sense of responsibility and the strain must come, but only for a while—mark you that—only for a while ! Once you can hand over yourselves to Him so the joy and the peace will come, so those nervous apprehensions will depart and so you will feel the protection all around. Have no fears for the future, yet be on your guard !—remember that, dear children.

And now I come to the second half of what I wish to speak to you about tonight, and that is in regard to old ties, old friends.

Many have found that friendship is not understood by the majority; that very often it is regarded as one of the diversions of a busy or easy life; and so friendship has rather lost its high and beautiful position in their estimation.

Well, dear children, I would like you to think a little about Christ's attitude towards friendship and the pinnacle on which He placed it; and then to remember this: That in addressing the faithful—again " the few "—Christ said " Ye are my friends !" and then with that wonderful understanding of the human mind He added that all those who did His will were His friends.

It is rather a wonderful thought—when you come here you will see that it is the most wonderful thought there could be ! We all know that Christ is our Friend, yet completion being in the Perfect Mind, Christ said: " Ye are my friends." I think that puts a different interpretation upon the friendship which Christ has for all. When you are thinking of an ideal of One who is all tender, all love, all kindness, it is not difficult for you to understand that He is the universal Friend, because Love is so inclusive; yet because He is the Friend of all it does not include the fact that you are His friend as well. I think you see the point. But Christ made the statement, clear and direct, that all those who wished to do His will (which, remember, is following the direction of the Divinity within) that each one was His friend.

From that thought I take you on to another. In your world it has been said that old friends are best, and some people have interpreted that as barring out those who are new acquaintances in their earthly life. But that, dear children, is entirely the physical view, which concentrated on the world ignores or forgets those deep abiding ties of the Spirit. Yet the saying, dear children, is perfectly correct when viewed in the spiritual way. Once more I ask you to remember what I have told you about that long " past " before you entered into physical life. In that long past those ties were made and perhaps many years go by on earth before—working out the pattern—you are linked together. Yet remember this: that sympathy, that mutual interests, that that understanding of each other's point of view—that this but signifies that the tie was made long long ago; and again you have the echo " old friends are best !"

I want you all—all who read these records—to think on this with the mind of the Spirit, to apply it to everyone who has passed through your lives. You may be old or you may be young, but when two are drawn together by mutual sympathies and, above all, by mutual aspirations, then you may be certain that the tie between you is ancient indeed. The linking has been delayed, may be, because with each one certain experiences had to be worked through first, certain lessons learnt and made their own. The preparation was indeed of God so that when the two lives met there should be that in each mind which should be able to recognise the affinity in the other . . .

Oh, my children, never be deceived by the earth view, which is surface indeed. There are those who are coming into your lives who have been linked to you, and you to them, through aeons and aeons of time, yet from the earth standpoint you are as strangers. I speak not only of those who have passed out of physical life but also of those still in the flesh, and I entreat you to bar them not; to remember that I have said " old friends, old ties are best " and it is God's will that your lives at this stage should be intertwined one with the other—it is part of the pattern, part of the plan.

And then I bring you back once more to the remembrance of Christ's definition of a friend and, above all, to that most glorious privilege which He has bestowed upon us—His friendship—not His Kingship over us but His friendship with us; yet so characteristically He adds " Ye are my friends !" " My friends "—think of it, dear children—to be deemed worthy of being a friend to the Crucified, to that which is Love itself ! Try and gather in something of the wonderful meaning underlying that phrase—not the condescension, that is not God's way, condescension between the Father and His children never has existed and never will, it is of the earth and not of the Spirit—but the gracious promise and invitation, first to be our Friend, and then that divinely-human longing of His that we should be His friends as well . . .

Yes, dear children, each evening as we go on we learn a little more, we gather in just a fragment of the Perfect Mind; yet this should tell you, for the comfort of your heart and mind, that only by what you provide yourselves could I or anyone speak to you in this way. God gives a thousandfold to our one, but if that one portion is absent so He, with sadness, cannot give of all that much which He longs shall be our own, because the mind of the body refuses it and free-will cannot be gainsayed.

And now, my children, I am going to leave you, but I want my little secretary to be certain that the power is all around her tonight; and if I spoke rather quickly in the beginning then because of this and the strain entailed, so is the love and the recompense there to help her on her way.

Power

MY little children, all of you here, be heartened—all the dear ones who have been gathered into my love take comfort, for the dawn is at hand ! Take comfort in the thought that you have listened to the Voice of the Spirit; that you have been asked to take the rough hill path so that others may follow on, may emancipate their real selves, may be free from the earth and all it represents . . . My children, rejoice— rejoice that God is able to use you; rejoice that the Father is able to use the minds and bodies of His little children.

Tonight, meeting together in this sweet way, there is much to talk over, and I want you all to concentrate on the object which we have in view—that is the breaking down of the barriers between the world of the flesh and the world of the Spirit. I want you to lay aside desire—those natural wishes in regard to your dear ones—and to offer up your hearts and minds as a contribution to this most important task of pushing aside that which intervenes between you and what is your right—communion with God and those gathered together under His Love. Those who are working—it is true, under slightly different conditions—but working with you and you with them to proclaim God's Love to a blinded world, to a world immersed in its own pursuits, chained by its possessions, imprisoned by the many destructive desires of the flesh . . .

Oh ! my children, thank God indeed that you can put these things in their place; thank God that that most terrible awakening, when free from the body, shall be taken from you—that the remorse which burns and burns will be, in great measure, saved you when you walk in the Gardens of the Lord . . .

Tonight, dear children, I want to speak to you about POWER—power in its physical sense, and that great and mighty power which is a gift direct from the Most High.

173

In your little world physical manifestations of power are on every side. Machinery, you think, has come into its own. All those many inventions of the mind of man stagger the majority by their scope and their conception. Yes! dear children, but have you not thought of this: That in regard to motive power, as man learns more so he lays aside the cumbersome parts; that as the inventive side—the inspirational side—of the physical mind gains its freedom so man sees that the greatest results can be brought about by the simplest mechanism.

Is there not a lesson in this? Go back on the history of the past. Each invention was greeted as astonishing evidence of the power of physical thought—yes! and with apprehension too, for man saw (or thought he saw) danger lying side by side with that which he had brought into being . . .

And then the next stage—the getting used to what was marvellous once on a time; and then the mind of man seeking fresh fields to conquer, striving and struggling to express something of the knowledge cabined within that which you call the " sub-conscious " mind.

Yes! all around you are evidences of this. Daily fresh news comes—may be from afar, may be close at hand—of the domination, of the controlling power of the mind of man . . .

Ah! dear children, in this simple illustration lies a tremendous lesson for us all. It symbolises in detail the spiritual processes of man; and I want you to come with me in thought while I attempt to show the parallel.

Is it not true that those who gather unto themselves the tools of the mind pass through many stages, adding and adding to their knowledge; and when they have drawn in all that the world can teach then the Spirit within wakes up and takes control? If this does not happen during the physical stages it must take place when that obstructing body is laid aside. Think of it how you may, the man who seeks but to make his own the knowledge of the world, irrespective of the wisdom of the Spirit, in time must retrace his steps, throwing off this, casting aside that, until he comes back again to simple things and simple faith . . .

Yes! in illustration today you have it worked out in a crude form. The more man knows the more he finds he can dispense with; and sometimes he is staggered by the simplicity of the greatest inventions of all.

That is the lesson which all must learn. Just as I described to you that " Evolution " was based on " Involution " so indeed, dear children, you will find with the journey of the Spirit that much furniture, much that impeded was gathered as it went through its varied experiences; but as it learnt, as it got free, as it responded to its God, so this and that was laid aside. And you can tell the experienced soul by its simplicity —yes ! by its faith and trust in God as its Father.

The knowledge of the world, good as it may be—and I have told you often that it plays its part in the training and in the disciplining of the physical will—good as it may be there is something which is infinitely better: the wisdom of the Spirit which brings peace, which brings not only knowledge but revelation of the purpose of your lives.

Oh ! my children, be not deceived. Power there may be in the physical world of a kind which is stupendous to the mind of man; but in that same physical world there are resources untouched, there are gifts, there are powers waiting to be used in the service of mankind. And, dear children, only those who are faithful and true, only those who are humble and pure, only those who put others first and self last can be trusted with the things which are of God . . .

Yes ! indeed these gifts have mighty power, and because this power is so great the shadows, playing on the physical mind of those who would make them their own, seek to induce them to put them to a use God never intended and suffering comes inevitably as a result during the earth life and greater suffering when the soul is free—when the soul stands by its Christ and sees what has been done . . .

My children, the highest only is for you. Those gifts which even daily are being made more nearly your own—these gifts must be guarded as holy indeed. That which surrounds them is as straw to be thrown aside; that which can protect them comes from within and not from without.

Hearken you then to my words of warning, given with love, with a complete understanding of your lives, of your aims and your desires—listen to my words of warning: Keep to the simple path, keep to the straight clean path which leads to God. Never mind the intellectualities of physical life. In God's sight these are as nothing; and when you are free you will find indeed that they but burlesqued the knowledge which was made your own as you followed the Voice of God and found Him.

The warning is two-fold, and the warning is for now and all time: Keep free from everything which comes between you and Christ. Remember that in Christ there is power, there is opportunity, there is a revelation which can never be fathomed. Yea! I go farther than that—I say that in the name of Christ alone there is a power which can dominate and control the fiercest forces of darkness there may be. Pride —that consciousness of self and of mental advancement—all these are the subtle temptations of those who are out to destroy; and, dear children, must be faced as such.

Ponder o'er my words. Without Christ you would not have the power to raise your hand; without Christ no thought could flit through your mind! Think of the world's conception of power and then remember that without Christ this little world could not be. Until man knows his Source, until those governed by their physical minds can realise to Whom they belong, so the road goes on and on, so dissatisfaction and sadness keep step with them, so they wander round the mountain and the heights are never reached.

Cannot you see how I long for my children—how I long for all those bound by physical thinking—to be free. Waste, waste, waste !—seeking for what can never be attained, they turn their back on The Promise and so—although God's Love never changes and never fails—they shut themselves off from the brightness which is their own.

Yes ! think of the power of the Spirit, the power of the Name of Christ, the power of the protecting care of The Father. In the simple narrative which His disciples—those who loved Him put together with much care and thought, in that simple narrative you have all you require to reach the highest . . . " let not your hearts be troubled for I will send you a Comforter ". Those words ring out again and again: " I will send you a Comforter "—the Comforter which shall give you all knowledge, all joy, all peace; and the power of The Comforter is in your presence tonight. Gather unto yourselves that which is so freely offered, and thank God that as little children—children in simplicity—you can come, you can ask and you can receive . . .

Remember there will be others who will try and lead you into complicated paths of thought, but tonight I tell you for your guidance that the Word of God, given in those days of old: " Love God and your neighbour " are all that is necessary to give you your hearts desire when the body is laid aside and you receive, consciously, the blessing of Christ . . .

Keep this thought fixed firmly in your mind—humility simplicity, faith and trust in God . . .

And now, my children, I will leave you for a little while; but there is one who would speak—a stranger to you all—yet one whose memory has been loved for many a long day and year, and it is God's will that tonight he should push aside the centuries and address you as brother and friend . . .

Keep the peace, hold on to holiness and indeed God's blessing on this evening shall be shown to you all . . .

(Stephen speaks)

Dear friends and comrades in Christ, indeed only by the grace of God could I demonstrate my presence here tonight and the influence I have been allowed to have upon your lives . . .

Speaking of those ancient records (Bible) brings in my name, for there—so lovingly narrated—my little part, so short, so brief, is enshrined in a setting of which it was altogether unworthy . . . They called me Stephen, and many a young heart has thrilled at the story of the boy who was honoured in dying for his Master.

Tonight I want to speak to you about that marvellous privilege which was my own. Young as I was the protection which was all around me was amazing in its completeness; and truth to tell, dear friends, I did but little—everything was given to me; and during that last incident which has been held up as heroic, well ! there was nothing heroic in it at all. My love for Him who gave me so much—the joy and the peace and the happiness which filled my soul—ah ! that was a million times stronger than any pangs of the physical could be. I saw Christ ! I saw that which was worth ten thousand deaths to reach; I saw—in miniature it is true—the reflected glory of God, and then was centred in the Light which never fades . . .

Oh ! my dear friends and comrades, never think again that Stephen was great, that Stephen did aught but the merest to express his love; and as a lesson to all I would tell you that it was far easier to " die " for my blessed Master than it was to live for Him after that physical death had taken place. Then my struggles began, then I realised the inner truth of that saying: " Live for Christ—live and demonstrate your love for Him . . ."

You who know that " death " does not divide, you who know that the physical experience is not interfered with— you can enter into the meaning underlying my words: that I found it far harder to live for Christ than to die for Him in those days of old.

I want you all to think of me with love, but for ever to turn your mind from that trivial incident; to try instead to enter into my thoughts and feelings as I watched others— bound by the body, surrounded by enemies, hemmed in on every side—as I watched and worked with them through their long experiences which they, out of greater love, had taken on in their Master's Name.

You see, dear friends, the spiritual view ! Yet I would not underestimate the value of the little story as narrated by those who loved me. Again and again it has inspired the young, it has been used as the turning point when danger lay close at hand. Again and again the story of the boy has en- thused not only the young but the old, and because of this it has done its part. But to live for Christ is the test, and that is the message I have been asked to give tonight: to turn your thoughts ever from the dramatic to the prosaic; to influence you to see things as they are—that the life of work, of laying aside self in its many deceptive forms—that the life of effort and of consecration is indeed the Christ life, indeed it ex- presses the ideal. And, thank God, after my body was laid aside so He permitted me, so He helped me, so He helps me now to live the life which expresses something of the Christ Ideal . . .

This is my message to the world—one day to be given

out broadcast, one day to be read, one day to be listened to as Truth: That though to die for Christ may be sweet, to live for Him is His desire; though to demonstrate in definite action your faith by so-called martyrdom has its part in influencing the minds of others, it is the life which is the test; it was the life of The Master that has held Him in the hearts of His children and will for ever and for ever . . . Live for Christ, dear friends and comrades, live for Christ.

And now, Farewell !

N

Spiritual History

MY children, tonight, as always, we have much to talk over and I want you—again as always—to do your part, to send out into this little room thoughts of love—yes! and of true desire that you may be used by the Father in making the conditions perfect in every sense there could be.

You know, dear children, that every day brings its tasks, and every day seems to bring its burden too; but there are some who forget this simple fact: that because of the work and the burden, so every day brings the protecting care of the Father.

You see, dear children, that in taking one side only you have got a story which is incomplete. There are many who on rising in the morning feel a shrinking—yes, it is akin to pain itself—a shrinking from what lies in front during the hours which are associated with work. Nay! dear children, I am speaking not of those who turn instinctively from labour; I am speaking of the vast majority, for, sad to say, the vast majority are engaged on those tasks which, as they think, are the least congenial to them. But doesn't this fact explain itself? Cannot you see beneath the surface? Is it not possible to grasp that there must be something of God which lies hidden under the ugly aspect which is presented to you?

Oh! my children, though I have tried to teach you much yet still you have much to learn—not as you think of the unpleasant side of physical life but, thank God, of the beauty, of the brightness, of the steady flow of the Spirit-life which ever daily is growing stronger, more dominant until, in a little time to come, it will entirely overrule that which still remains allied to the world and to physical things.

My children, these few words in commencement are entirely of sympathy and not of censure. It is impossible to go out into the streets of any large city and not be appalled by the sadness, by the disappointments which earthly life seem to hold for all; and the chill comes. Yes ! perhaps over one's own condition, but still more so does the chill come on looking at what represents greyness, hopelessness and that deep despair—despair over tomorrow and all the tomorrows to come . . .

I wish, dear children, that it were possible to take from your eyes the physical bandage and to allow you to see with that sight which is God's free gift to all, which would have been in the possession of humanity long since had not the children of the earth turned from the things of God and all they represent. Yes ! dear children, the eyes of the Spirit see far indeed, and what to you represents sadness, literally is worked out in definite form as beauty—and believe me I do not use language which is figurative merely when I tell you that that beauty lies all around the sufferers in concrete, tangible form.

A little while the earthly experience goes on. To those so bound by " time " it seems long indeed; yet one day, thank God ! you will see with me and you will realise with amazement how little was asked and how much was given in return !

And now, dear children, I want to speak to you about a very large and important subject. I use the word "important " in its spiritual sense, because what I am about to say is of first importance in regard to the progress of the soul—to the getting free from those things which are as chains, fettering and torturing while they are borne.

Children, I have told you before—or I have indicated it in outline—that the spiritual history of your little world has been divided (I use the word in the earth sense) has been divided into three periods or eras. I have given you to understand that in the first God was represented as a mighty King, full of power; one who gave many injunctions and who expected to be obeyed. Then, dear children, as the mind of man grew a little more tutored—a little more prepared for a further expansion of the Truth, God came as Christ, and as " Christ " the whole aspect of the Fatherhood of God was changed for evermore.

Children, there are few, in reading the old Records, who do not at once see that although God was regarded as King and Ruler, yet again and again His Love and care was shown towards His children, in spite of many failings, many treacheries, much forgetfulness of the past and the protection vouchsafed to them.

I put that in because I want to underline tonight what I told you before: that Christ as Christ—tender, understanding, everything that represents Perfect Love—that Christ and God the Ruler were the same.

And then, dear children, I want to speak to you a little about the third era, about this time of revelation, this period which already we have entered upon, when the Spirit—that which some of you designate as the " Holy Ghost "—is being, and will be demonstrated again and again on earth amongst those children who are wishful to find the Light.

Children, as I speak thus, it seems to me that perhaps in spite of my warning words I have, as it were, separated one period from the other; but, as you must know, each and all form one perfect whole, and when Christ came God the Father, or the Ruler, was not lost but was shown by example as representing Love Itself. So, dear children, I would remind you that the power of the Holy Spirit has been in operation right from the beginning of time, right from the beginning of creation. Through the ages here and there, sometimes in noticeable numbers, there have been those who have allied themselves to God, and these have manifested and demonstrated that the power of the Holy Spirit was the gift of all, and not reserved for any portion of the history of mankind; that it was there, waiting to be taken up when there were those who were willing to accept the responsibility . . .

Children, I want you to go back on your sacred Records again and again. I want you to re-read some of those older portions of the Scriptures because therein is prophecy, there—involved in strange language it is true—but there is the Truth preserved and handed down from generation to generation, notwithstanding the fact that that same Truth has suffered from the conceptions, or the misconceptions, of those who were the custodians of the Holy Word. God said that in the days to come He would make a new covenant; that His words should be written on the hearts and minds of those who loved Him, and there should be none who would teach the other but all would get the Truth direct from Him . . .

Now, dear children, I have put the statement in somewhat different words from those which were used, but the meaning is perfectly clear to all who read with a wish to understand. And here I must ask you to try and allow yourselves a little more latitude in regard to quotations from those Records which were prepared by man in the days of long ago. Some of my children are really distressed when I, or those who speak to you in this way, swerve a hair's breadth from what you call the " correct text ". Well, dear children, as I think you will understand, that attitude is entirely physical and associated only with the limitations of the physical mind. In reading the Holy Word get down to the meaning; once that meaning is enshrined in your heart and mind then you are at liberty to clothe it in any language you think most adequate to express that which God wishes to teach.

Now, dear children, when Christ came that new covenant was given; and I want you in thinking over this to try and remember the gigantic change which came over religious thought. Slowly, it is true, but even as a mighty ocean covering that which was dry and barren land, so the teachings of Christ, so the interpretation of the Truth imparted by those who followed, swept over engulfing all.

And then, dear children, I remind you of those who were closest to the Master during His earthly life. The majority, as you know full well, were as little children in regard to spiritual things; and yet, so marvellously, so astoundingly to all who listened, the power came which enabled them to speak without preparation—to speak the Truth which God had implanted in their hearts and minds . . .

You see, dear children, to what I am trying to lead you. Over and over again there have been those who love God who have been able to use this same gift, who have been able to demonstrate in a definite form that He had written the Truth on their hearts and minds. The prophecy has been fulfilled in a way impossible to exaggerate; yet there is one terrific obstacle to be overcome—the obstacle of the physical mind, which by reason of its very limitations relies upon itself alone. You see, dear children, that although it may seem to you rather a cruel fact that the physical mind, itself so limited, should be punished by its limitations, yet does it not show you that God, being God, has provided something which is greater and stronger and better ? . . . (interrupted by faintness of medium).

In regard to those trained by The Master, you will remember with what faith they followed the instruction given and how each time they waited (as God promised in the days of old) for His Word to be written on their heart and mind before speaking His Truth.

Then we come to the phrase: " They shall not teach each other." Children, it is hardly necessary for me to point out that for a long time to come man will not be sufficiently in touch with his God to be able to get the Word direct. And so I bring you round—after taking a very circuitous course—to those who are the missioners of God, whatever their particular creed, however they represent their Master—to all those who have God in their heart—and tonight I wish to say to them just a word which will be interpreted, I hope, as understanding a little of the disappointments and discouragements connected with a life devoted to the spiritual education of others . . . (unable to proceed owing to faintness of medium).

My children, I am going to close this evening and I ask you if you will meet together tomorrow night so that we may continue. There are conditions tonight against which it is hard to work; and although I seem to leave you with sadness, yet I would ask you to have faith in the thought that we shall meet together again in happiness, and that all will be as God intends . . .

Rest in peace and commend yourselves to the great Father-Heart, who understands all things and how it is that sometimes it is difficult to disentangle yourselves from the physical when it is a little troublesome. Just leave everything definitely and personally in the Hands of the Father, not forgetting what has been, but saying to yourselves, in faith and trust, that God will provide . . .

We are indeed bound together by such close ties that when the body is laid aside it will be found by all that, in reality, the physical was powerless to come in between . . .

Oh ! I thank God ever and ever for my little children; I thank God that He has permitted me to guard and guide and care for them ! And here and now I say to you all that my love for you and your love for me, by God's grace, passes all expression in words, because through the long years we have worked and we have suffered together, and because where love is only perfect understanding has a place . . . Yes ! I thank God for His over-seeing care; and in His Hands everything is safe, and all, all is well ! . . . Goodnight ! my children.

*   *   *

MY children, I thank you all for obeying my request, and I thank you too for many thoughts of help, all of which have been used to their utmost; and these prayers shall be shown to you in the happy days to come as producing power of so great a character that indeed you will marvel at God's Love.

Children, it seems to you somewhat strange that more help is not forthcoming when there are those among you who are willing to submit themselves to the guidance of the Spirit.

Well, dear children, these thoughts arise merely because you are still bound by the physical aspect of things. Tonight I will tell you that had it not been for this work for God— which my child had taken on in the Spirit—had it not been that the severity of the experiences she has gone through were for work for God, then I tell you quite frankly it would have been impossible to keep the enemies of the physical at bay in the way we have done.

" But " you exclaim, " see how pressing they are !" Yes, but again I repeat that had it not been for this work my child, and your child, would not be in the physical body at this stage.

You see, dear children, how wonderful are God's laws ! Some there are, swayed by the world and its conceptions, who have urged and entreated—nay, who have commanded that this precious communion should be abandoned because of the strain entailed on the one so used. Yes ! they knew it not, but they were being used by those destroyers who have not allowed one avenue of attack to be overlooked.

In this there is a lesson for all. Thousands who are working for God are also harassed by the enemies of the flesh, yet they work on—not in spite of these enemies but because the work they do comes under the heading of Service, and so in a gigantic way they are protected from that which would strike them to the earth itself.

On all sides there is suffering, yet again and again it is noticed that the weakest survive when the strong of body pass out. This is experienced in a way so revealing that I gladly bring it in this evening.

You know, dear children, that among your own friends there are those who strive and strive, who again and again return to face the enemy and prevail in a way which cannot be rightly estimated until spiritual sight is your own. These, dear children, because of the strength of the Spirit within call to their side those who fight for them, those who are indeed of God and these bring His protection with them . . .

It was necessary to give this little explanation, and now I pass on to the subject we were discussing last night.

Children, in regard to the custodians of the Truth, I have something to say, and I hope those who read these records will try and realise that I am seeking to portray a little of the Father-Mind towards these who have voluntarily sought to represent Him during their daily life.

You see, dear children, that in many cases—nay, in all cases—the Spirit is far and away more ambitious, more spiritually ambitious than the most ambitious physical mind could be; and so right through the ages there have been those who, anyhow, have set out to do their Master's Will. Some, perhaps, have found that the enemy was too strong, that the world drew so close that it could not be fenced off as effectively as they hoped . . . Children, God understands all hearts, and as God judges not so I entreat those who will listen to judge not these themselves.

And then, dear children, I turn your attention to all those earnest ones whom you have met and whom, in many cases, you have loved as well. These indeed represent the Truth not only to the best of their ability but in a way which has brought God's blessing upon them. To such as these I speak—and there are many in this room tonight. I speak also to those still bound by physical restrictions, still hampered a little by the body which (against their will, perhaps) sometimes makes barriers between them and all they wish to be.

When they come here all will be so clear and they will

find that because the wish held good to be true to God so indeed God has worked out that wish in fact, to remain for ever more.

In regard to those who listen to them: well, dear children, teaching spiritual things is not an easy task. Unconsciously or consciously the physical mind has built up certain conceptions of the Truth, and if anyone seeks to interfere with or to broaden the boundaries of their thought, they are met at once with a veiled or definite hostility which so often does its destructive work. I mean, dear children, that the one who would teach, that the one who has vision of something of the magnitude of God's Love, that he is checked and he retreats back into his shell, keeping his gift to himself.

Then, dear children, that other aspect has to be met and faced. Some there are who cannot portray either the story of Christ's life on earth, or the wonderful teaching He gave so simply, so beautifully for use in all ages, for all times. They have not the faculty; and there are countless numbers today who, because the shepherd is inarticulate, so they stray.

Children, I am fully aware of the responsibility of this remark, yet even in your little experience you know that this is so; and tonight I must say that those who gather together to worship God, to hear His Word—that these have a right to expect that the interpretation of the Word should be given in a way which will reach their hearts and minds.

Now, dear children, we have got to keep our balance of thought. Most of those whom you have loved so much have possessed that gift—the gift of portraying Christ, the gift of opening the door of revelation—perhaps in varying degrees, but believe me it is something when anyone has the perception and the strength to open that door, even if it be but an inch.

Children, the gift of speech is a weapon—it is a tool which cannot be overestimated because of its influence on the minds and characters of others; and when you are free you will see that the foundation of that gift was solely and entirely the power of the Spirit.

Now mark you, dear children, I am fully conscious that there are many who possess eloquence—who indeed are rich in expression, whose words throb with life and meaning—and some of these use it not for God's work. Yet remember

" service " has many branches and channels, and the one who uses his gift of speech towards the betterment of the world, towards the righting of a wrong, he indeed is using that gift as God intended. But those who desecrate the gift—ah ! these are building up for themselves much sorrow and much suffering when they come here and see the purpose of the bestowal. They sought not to uplift but rather to drag down that which was truth and holiness and purity and faith.

Yet, dear children, forget not my previous words—that all the various attributes and abilities of the mind are indeed but manifestations of the Holy Spirit, and as such should be treated as sacred indeed . . .

I come back to the sheep who have a shepherd to guide them and yet that shepherd finds it almost impossible to put into words the way they should go. To those shepherds I speak with so much love and understanding, and I tell them that if they would put even half the reliance on the spiritual mind which they place so readily on the physical, indeed they would find that the Holy Spirit—the gift of language—could be used by them with the liberty of an unlimited Source.

And then, dear children, I want to speak to you about those edifices which are held in such high estimation by all, not only you who love your churches but even by the spectator who has no personal interest in the Faith they represent.

Well, dear children, I have something to say to you which perhaps will come as a surprise, and yet being your most loving teacher—not your schoolmaster, remember that— but being your most loving teacher I am anxious that you should get the spiritual view of as many things as is possible.

There are in your little country buildings and ruins which in your eyes are regarded as sacred trusts; and while I can enter fully into your attitude towards that which stands for so much in religious life, yet, dear children, it is my duty to tell you that sometimes you err a little in regard to this.

Yes ! there are those, on passing through precincts which are hallowed by memories, who have felt that indeed they were on sacred ground—and so they were, but not for the reason that they think.

Children, has it ever occurred to you to pause and think —when examining the old and lofty walls, when in mind measuring the girth of the great columns which support those roofs of workmanship both beautiful and rare—has it ever occurred to you to think of those who put the stones together ? Yes ! I know that he (or they) who designed that edifice which brings such joy to the senses—I know that he gets full measure of rightful recognition—but tonight I want you to think a little about the workers—about the humble workers who put it together with so much labour, so much weariness, so much heartbreak and despair. For, dear children, in the days when those magnificent edifices were built labour was not as it is today. In those times of long ago the life of a man who was a toiler was reckoned but lightly indeed. I do not speak without due consideration when I say that many of those buildings which you revere so much contain in the very stones themselves stories of hardship entirely beyond your imagination.

So, dear children, you will see to what I am leading your thoughts. Those buildings are indeed hallowed by time, hallowed by the prayers which have risen from them, hallowed by the sacrifices, by the devotional thoughts, the aims and the aspirations of those who worshipped therein, but most of all —yes ! most of all by the labour, by the suffering exacted from those humble, forgotten, unnoticed workers who indeed have enshrined, not their names but their lives in the stones which remain . . .

Oh ! dear children, try ever and ever again to get Christ's view of human life. I do not say turn from your admiration of that which is old and rare, but I ask you to give your attention to what is far older and far more precious than anything the material world can produce. Yes, on all sides you have examples: in the cradle where the baby lies, in the man, in the woman, in the child who plays so carelessly by the wayside— ah ! these, dear children, are old and precious indeed ! Physical standards have no place, but the Spirit within each one has toiled and worked and suffered right down through the swelling waves of time, long, long before the oldest erection ever found a place . . .

Keep your vision clear; but before you can have a clear vision there must be that readjustment of values so that you may understand how God regards things, so that you may understand the spiritual aspect of life—that which God has sought to reveal since creation began.

You see, dear children, I am taking nothing away but I am turning your attention to what is infinitely greater in value, infinitely older in history, that which cannot pass away: the journey of the individual soul, the quest of the Spirit—that which is within you, which is within me, which is within the beggar in the gutter, that which is in the tiny babe who has experienced but one hour of physical life.

My children, as we go on we have much to talk over together, and I am instructed by our Master to tell you tonight that in His sight the things of the earth are indeed as dust, which as time goes on, inevitably, must be blown away; and that His jewels—that which He holds most precious of all— are His children, and it is these which He watches ever and ever to guard and to protect.

I think there are some of my children who will be able to take from these few words just the little hint I am anxious to convey. Yes ! love the house of God but remember that your greater love belongs to humanity; that those who passed with you up the long aisles were infinitely greater in import- ance than the treasures which you admired so much. And because of this I led my children away from the big and the grand (Canterbury Cathedral) I took them into the humble village church, and there from the lips of one who had simple faith they heard God's message direct. Cannot you see the beauty of simplicity more and more ! There in the little church, free from all that adornment which forms an essential part of worship to some—there in his poverty of attire he showed the richness of his mind and the power of the Spirit at work.

Children, search how you may you cannot find a grander or a greater subject than the Love the Father has for His little children, who understand Him not. Right from the heart he spoke, striving with might and main to get his message home; and there are those of you who can witness to the fact that the message went home in very truth.

Yes ! keep your vision clear, but remember that before this clear vision can be your own there must be a mighty readjustment of values, there must be that inner conception of things spiritual and things physical without which indeed Christ's view is veiled . . .

Children, there is one other little point in connection with this. I want you to realise that the things of the world are so dependent upon man; I want you to see for yourselves that however ancient an erection may be that it is within the power of those who possess it to destroy it or to entirely alter its character.

Yes ! and in this there lies a lesson which shows you that the things of the earth are impermanent while the things of the Spirit remain for ever more. In your own brief experience you have seen what was once an old ruin restored; yet the word " restored " is incorrect for many reasons, because that which is of the earth, which has crumbled away, is not brought together again but something which bears a resemblance to it is put in its place—nothing more.

When you are building character, when you are training the thought of the young you are indeed putting together something which can never pass away. " Oh ", but you say, " people forget so soon !" Again you are thinking only with the physical mind, while I am speaking of the mind of the Spirit; and I say that not one thought planted in the mind of another, not one pure thought created shall ever pass away.

In the hands of each one of you there lies a power greater than possessed by any Pharoah in the days of old; in your hands lie also the capacity to leave your mark, not in the confines of the earth, but indeed in the Realms of the Spirit— to leave that which will be remembered long after this little earth has passed away.

Little children, keep yourselves from idols, but read not into this anything but the Hand of protection. So easily the physical mind fastens on this and clings to that while all the time the real treasure—that which is of infinite value—is over-looked. God understands the human heart and mind; but the next stage, dear children, is this, and it is of so gigantic a character that I am evermore anxious to prepare you evening by evening as we meet together in this sweet way . . . God understands the human heart and mind and He waits—yes ! with unending patience He waits for His little children to understand a little more of what is in the Father Heart and Mind.

Oh ! keep this thought ever before you—that because you are His children you have a right to understand what is in the Mind of God. Then you will be able to do, dear children, what has never been excelled by anyone: you will be able to, instinctively, whatever subject comes under your consideration—you will be able to see it in its spiritual sense, you will be able to see beneath the physical aspect the Mind of God at work.

Yes ! keep your vision clear . . . (words missed) . . . but remember that until your conception of values is brought into harmony with the Christ view then indeed you travel on a circle, returning to the point from which you started without having explored any of those beauties which lie above and beyond you, as well as around you everywhere in the physical world . . .

My children, I am pleased with you all tonight, and tell my little secretary (Dorrie) that I counted her here as well.

My child (Margaret) I want to say a word to you which will comfort and reassure you as to your part.

The thought has come to you that you are not being used to supply the missing vitality in the one (medium) you love so well, and that thought I intend to answer once and for all time.

God knows how to use His own, and again and again from you has been taken for her that which only you could give; and you have been told that when it is a question of service a hundred-fold is given in return. Thank God, dear child, that He can use you so easily and so effectively, thank God that you belong to Him in every sense there could be.

And now I speak to my other child (Mrs. Moyes).

Annie, sometimes it seems to you that your place is a little on the outside because neither the writing nor the speech is through you; but God looks at things in a way so entirely different from the physical. I put it thus because you argue within yourself that " facts are facts."

Well, dear child, when you come here you will find that physical " facts " are not facts at all; and that is a little point which I pass on to all my children hoping it will help them in their upward climb. You see, the only things which are real, which are permanent, which will remain are those connected with the Spirit—those which are engraved in the Spirit World itself. Fear not, and have courage over everything. Is it not feasible, Annie, to you that after so long a journey, after so many encounters the victory must be great indeed ?

And now. dear children, I leave you for a little while, but I do not intend to tax the strength of my child for too long a period tonight, and yet it is essential that those appointed to speak at this stage should not be held back.

Ask God to help and strengthen you so that you may help and strengthen the one who is used.

Thought

GOOD evening ! my children, and I hope tonight that you feel as closely in touch with me as possible. Of course you argue among yourselves that Zodiac, having passed through so many experiences, having lived in a time altogether different from your own, having—as you put it—allied himself to Christ right down the ages, that it is hardly to be expected that he should not be influenced by the tremendous gap which obviously lies between his view point and your own.

Well, dear children, I have to go back again and again on these little points because it is necessary for many reasons hidden from you at this stage—it is necessary that you should be able to come to me even as a child to its trusted Mother and to feel that there are no barriers in between us at all.

Has it not occurred to you that The Master would hardly have sent me into your midst if I had been so ill-equipped to understand my children's point of view ? Has it not occurred to you as well that it would be a tremendous waste of time and of effort to have linked myself to you in this sweet way if I were not able to say at the same time: " There are no barriers, there are no obstacles of the mind or body which are strong enough to intervene between me and my children."

Now, little ones, I do not want you to make any reservations. I am not only speaking to you here but I am speaking with added emphasis to all those who, week by week, read these records—records of communion between those who are free and those who for a little while are bound to physical life. I say, with no qualification whatever, that I understand each point of view entirely; and more than that, their lives—long before they took on a body of flesh—their lives were laid out before me down to the minutest detail, and there are some in the happy days to come who will be able to go back on the past and mentally put a finger on this incident and on that and to recognise that, by the grace of God, I was there and I was used by my Master to divert that life into its right and finest channel.

Children, there are some amongst the younger ones who still think: " Ah ! yes ! Zodiac is more in touch with those who are farther on, those who have suffered much, those who by self-discipline have brought the physical will (for the most part) into harmony with God."

Again, dear children, you are wrong. Those who as yet are finding the road both long and steep—these of necessity need my ever guiding, watchful care; and so I ask them to take me into their thoughts in as companionable a way as can be conceived, for only by this close contact can I protect them, can I lift them out of the passing clouds which the shadows bring along in order to cast a shade on the brightness of the Love the Father has for all His children.

Well, little ones, tonight we are met together for a variety of reasons and as we go on those reasons will be shown to you, and I think you will agree that in themselves they constitute a memorable evening . . . Yes, the peace of God is here, His angels are protecting you all, and around them is a rainbow of Light which is coloured in a way I scarce can explain because, dear children, the colours of your world are not a true parallel of the colours which run through the worlds of the Spirit—which indeed are part of their composition, if I may use that word in a spiritual sense. Think then to yourselves " All, all is well !"—and the Voice of the Spirit shall be heard out of the Silence proclaiming that which is of God, that which belongs to the Life Everlasting—to all that Eternity which cannot be fathomed by any mind except that of its Creator.

Tonight then, dear children, in quietness and peace we will consider one or two points which so often cause discussion among those who, necessarily, are limited by the physical mind and still more so by the viewpoint of the world.

In the days of old there was much prophesying, there was much fore-telling of events, and it was the custom then (long since died out, alas !) for the people—the masses to congregate together or to approach the great teachers of their time and to ask in faith for direction. And, dear children, the one chosen by God to demonstrate His purpose—as far as might be— always rose to the occasion, and guidance of a gigantic charac-

O

ter was not only forthcoming but was followed without questioning by those who asked.

Dear children, that is a point which many are apt to overlook; indeed those fast rising doubts make it difficult for them
to see beyond the concrete, beyond the present and to place
their faith in any future whatever. Yet I would ask you to
consider this in a spiritual way. Again and again there have
been those crises in the history of nations which indeed have
caused a thrill of fear to run through the hearts of all. But
when brought face to face with a catastrophe which seems
imminent then humanity as a whole discovers that also it is
Spirit. Yes, that in that intricate physical organism there is,
mysteriously hidden, something within which can not only
seek its God but which is driven to do so by its necessity.

Oh, dear children, if only these half-awakened children
could realise the power which is within their reach they would
be able to alter entirely the trend of thought, and thereby the
history of the world. Yes ! it is a gigantic truth. Over and
over again you have seen, even within your own short experience, that prayer—concentrated prayer—is a mighty force,
that it has had the power to stem the tide of evil, that it has
had the power to lighten the weight of physical affliction, that
it has had the power to regenerate the Spirit of God within the
individual, even if it be but for a short period that the awakening lasts.

My children, those of you who love your country, those of
you who with bigger view can extend that love to humanity—
I appeal to you all to forever spread this truth: That concentrated, earnest prayer is unlimited in its power and effect.

On all sides you hear rumours of war; nay, I speak not
only of those battles between man and man but I refer to war
in its wider aspect—to all those contentious questions which
are being raised everywhere, in every country and which, for
the most part, are ignored as something too unpleasant, too
uncomfortable to be heeded . . .

Children, tonight I make a pronouncement which is rather
serious in its inner meaning: I tell you all that these disturbances of thought, this hatred one for the other, those many
desires for power, for influence, for the prize of controlling
others—that all these emotions are stirred into active being
by those who are determined that evil shall overcome good . . .

Of course, dear children, that is impossible, as you know. All that the strongest evil can do is to delay the working out of the great good which God intends, and which God has laid down shall be the gift of man. Yes! dear children, we have got to face this matter both frankly and sanely, and I want you by your thoughts to try and steady others. When you hear of a world war, when there are those who whisper sinister things as to the " punishment " which must overtake both the sinful and the followers of Christ who now inhabit this little plane—when this talk goes round argue not against it but rather tell them the remedy, the remedy which is prayer !

Children, right through the ages there have been scourges, there have been destructions to life and property which have been grievous to witness—and it must be so. It must be so for this great spiritual reason—that when things go well, when the conditions of physical life improve beyond a certain measure, then instead of the heart and mind of the individual being raised to God in thanks the heart and mind of the individual turns to the things of the earth and binds and rebinds itself to the chains of the flesh and all that it represents . . .

So sad is history in one sense, so sad to think that man— a child of God—that man could be so blind. Yet, dear children, again and again that journey of obstruction is shortened by one of those so-called catastrophes which, by the very nature of its horror, brings man back to his soul's quest, insofar as it awakens within the voice of conscience, the voice which says: " Take care !"

Tonight, dear children, I want to leave in your minds no sense of uneasiness as to what lies in front of your little world, but rather to show you, as far as I am able, that it is within the capacity of each and everyone not only to save themselves but also to save the generations which are to come.

Thought, dear children, has such building power; thought when rightly directed—by which I mean directed to Light and not to darkness—that power of thought is not only used to help the ones concerned but even as a harvest is stored to be called upon in time of need.

Oh, my children, let not your vision be darkened by anything which is of the earth, but also let not the earth stand between you and the great hunger of the Spirit within; that hunger, that longing, that striving, that intense desire is indeed of God—and indeed must be forthcoming if humanity is to make any great stride towards the wonderful goal which lies in front—the goal which must be reached by every one.

Tonight then, dear children, I ask you to be on your guard still more closely over the thoughts which find a holding in the physical mind. This is of the utmost importance for it means that one day when you need that bulwark of spiritual thought—one day a brick here and there will be missing, and through the apertures the darts which cause so much pain to the heart and mind—through the apertures those darts will be sent, and while we can heal the wounds, yet because that bulwark was of your own building we cannot prevent them from striking the physical heart and mind.

Yes ! the power of thought is a subject to which there is no end; it is a subject which has had a certain amount of attention upon earth, but in proportion to its value it has been neglected indeed.

Children—I speak to you all—one day you will have to recognise that thoughts are things; one day you will have to contemplate how those thoughts—which were of you and yet not of you—how these were used to divert your heart's desire from finding its rightful resting place in your arms . . .

The Spirit discriminates, it is true; but the physical mind, so careless, so unused to be on its guard—the physical mind has the power, not to wreck the plan but indeed to mar some of its beautiful outlines, some of that exquisite design to which the Spirit gave the greatest prayer and thought.

Children, I divide the Spirit from the physical mind, and if you could see things as they are you would know that you were not dual but that in each one there is a trinity, separate yet making a complete whole—body, soul and Spirit !

The physical mind, as it were, has its eyes focussed on the present—on the bright, big colours, unable to get any true vision of detail in its real sense. The physical mind—blunted by the body, immersed in interests which for the most part are of a transitory character—the physical mind functions on its own, because freewill cannot be interfered with and as yet the Spirit is buried beneath the things of the world . . .

That, dear children, is a rough outline of those who as

yet have not found their God, and of course it varies in degree, but in the main, that is how the physical—the body is represented.

And then you come to the soul; and to use an illustration in rather a free way, the soul is like a garment upon which much has to be drawn and worked. Yes ! worked in with a minuteness of detail which is beyond your understanding. Now, dear children, 1 used the word " drawn " and it is something like this: The events of your physical life, the incidents and the experiences which the Spirit intends that it will go through—these are, as it were, drawn in faint outline on that which represents the soul. Yet, as you will perceive, it is but an outline merely, and the going over even of that outline has to be done while the physical experiences take place in their sequence.

Here we bring in that subject of " fate ", we bring in that gigantic hypothesis that as life on earth is planned it is no use resisting the tide which takes you on.

That, dear children, I will explain, but first of all think of it like this: On the one side there is the physical mind—limited, in some cases literally crippled by the obstructions which it has gathered to itself. On the other you have the Spirit—that which is all pure, that which is of God Himself; and between the physical and the spiritual the struggle goes on. On the one hand the Spirit is striving that that outline shall be traced in with the precision which it intended, that the weaving in of this and of that shall be in harmony, that the bright colours shall blend with those which are less bright, that even the darkest shall contribute their beauty to that which will remain for all time. Yes, fighting and struggling it does what many will never understand until the mind of the body is laid aside. Over and over again the situation, as it were, is saved; some devastating, destructive work is averted and, moreover, the Spirit sends back the physical mind over the same ground again and again until that part of the tracery is true to the great design.

Children, you see the " trinity "—and I would not have you think that the soul is represented by a garment merely, although that word " garment " expresses both the physical body and the soul body as nearly as is possible.

Now, dear children, listen to me ! Those who are seeking to find The Master, those who have found Him and yet at times drift a little away—these unconsciously have handed over the domination of their destinies to the Spirit, while the physical mind has lost what it once held so rigidly.

You see what I am trying to teach: that apart from anything else the wish to find Christ immediately reverses the balance of power, and though the physical mind may err on this and on that, although its treacheries may be many, yet because that deep decision of the physical will has been made so the Spirit is able to make good that which otherwise might have marred—might have hindered the beauty which was in the process of execution . . .

Children, I want you to get this clear in your mind. Sooner or later that garment which the soul body represents has to be finished according to the Spirit's desire, and I ask you to think it over and to reason it out within yourselves: Isn't it wiser to try more and more to help the Spirit by your thoughts ? Isn't it only practical to so hold the reins of the physical mind that the tracing of the outline can be done once and for all with no retracing to make that which is ugly straight and neat ?

By " thought " you can not only complete the outline of the design but you can fill it in in a way no words can describe. Children, I would tell you that there have been those who have done even better than the Spirit set out to accomplish during the earthly stages. To you this sounds impossible, I know. Have I not said that the Spirit is ambitious indeed ? Yes, but you forgot one great important fact: That ambitious for advancement though the individual Spirit may be, the Eternal Father is more ambitious still; and so it has happened that there have been those who on gaining release from the body have seen with thankfulness indeed that not only was their life worked through to design, not only was the harmony maintained, but, by the grace of God, they did better even than the Spirit's quest when it entered on its physical experiences.

Children, I come back to this: That when some of you long to lay aside the little cabin of the flesh—which holds you so fast, which is so irksome, so cumbersome in use—that when you are free that soul body, which is a direct result of the

physical experience, must be worn by you until by processes
of refinement again that soul body is discarded for something
which is so closely allied to the Spirit that there is no distinction except in the degree of representing Christ.

Oh ! children, if only those in authority would speak, if
only those who have the care of the masses could find within
themselves the spiritual strength to tell them what they are
doing and what lies in front ! Yes, it is easy for some to talk
of great catastrophes overcoming this little world, but to go
back to hard bed-rock fact, the greatest catastrophe of all is
going on in the individual life, in the individual soul, while
the Spirit is tortured indeed . . .

Only by getting down to the individual, only by breaking
up those obstacles which obscure his vision, only by teaching
him how to hold on to God can catastrophes in bulk be
averted.

You see, my little ones, that indeed the greatest tragedy
is at it concerns the children who stray. Let not any think
that judgment comes in here, but oh ! the pity, oh ! the waste,
oh ! the unnecessary suffering which man is piling up for
himself when the way into happiness and peace lies open to
him.

Children, a great responsibility lies on those who refuse
to penetrate into Truth, a great responsibility lies on all who
have it in their power, in their capacity to teach and train
the untutored minds of the majority. Yet, dear children, let
not your hearts be sad, for again and again when the need
has come there has been found those who could lead, those
who could do God's work and save His people. These crises
come as an inevitable result of careless thought and careless
living. Therefore we come back to our starting point: I entreat you all to give full value, full importance to those
thoughts which flit through the physical mind, sometimes remaining, building up character or destroying that foundation
which already has been commenced . . .

My children, I seem to you very serious tonight, and so
I am, but not in the way you think. The seriousness of it all
is that there is so much reckless waste of opportunity, so much
unnecessary toil, so much that could be dispensed with in the
way of grief, of pain and of mental suffering. Human nature

cannot be hurried but it can be steadied, and the only steady-
ing process which is possible is by the prayers and thoughts
of those who know their God. Yes, think it over and try and
put yourselves into that attitude of mind when the Father can
not only use those thoughts to strengthen and purify yourself,
but in an unlimited measure can use them to drag out of the
mire, out of the darkness of misunderstanding those who are
linked to you by the closest tie there could be—those who are
your brothers and sisters, those whom God calls His children
although as yet they know Him not.

And now, my children, I will leave you, yet keep in mind
ever during this short time we are together the importance of
thought—the power it has to contribute or to take away.

                    *   *   *   *

THOUGHT

(Extract from Instruction given by Zodiac on April 30, 1922.)

The first point tonight which I will deal with is that of
the effect of thought. Thought, as you know, is the background and basis of all action. That is why the physical mind
needs to be strictly looked after. But carry this on to a further stage—that of creating the garment of the soul, which it
does in a literal sense, as well as in a figurative sense. You
must try to visualise thought as something quite definite—not
as an intellectual quality only. Thought has form and colour
and individuality, so much so that once the physical body is
discarded it is—for the want of a better word—materialised
into the next body in which the Spirit carries on its evolution.
There you see what an important part thought plays. I have
said that in form, in colour and in individuality thought is
materialised; therefore the next citadel of the Spirit is being
built by you and by us every minute and every day of our
existence. Beauty of any kind, action, conception of merely
physical ideas are at once shown in the new body. On the
other hand, the thoughts of self and the darkness of the physical mind is also portrayed in all its sadness. I wish I could
show you, as I see it, one of those spiritual bodies which have
just been adopted by the newcomer. They present a curious
appearance. It is as though, in some cases, a beautiful scheme
of things had gone wrong at a crucial point, thus marring its
perfection. That is often so, and when the stranger sees what

represents the marring he is grief-striken indeed. It is not a
matter for over anxiety, however, because once it is seen
where the weak part lies, that can soon be built up by the
owner, because—remembering all the other beauty produced
—it means that he possesses a strong will and has overcome
much . . . That is rather a hard thought for you to take in—
I see that at once; but you must remember that I am speaking
of the covering of the Spirit and not the Spirit itself. Just as
you would imagine, the bodies assumed after the earth body
can be quickly changed and changed again, but each one bears
and retains all the characteristics which you associate with
those you love. You must remember that the physical body
you know so well was not created by physical birth alone—
its individuality was perpetrated long before that—and that
body is discarded when finished with, just as the previous
bodies have been discarded and as future ones will be also.
It is seldom that perfection is reached with any particular
body. As a rule the occupier progresses to a certain extent
and then, before all the resources of that body are completely
exhausted, another is assumed. There are no gaps or waiting
spaces here. It is as though you on earth, when a coat was
getting worn, provided another before the old one fell to
pieces.

Another point is this. How often it is forgotten on your
side that action is subservient to thought. The physical mind
and the practical side of human nature assumes an importance
altogether beyond its merit. The world judges by action and
not by thought, and so you on your side take this view almost
entirely. Here everything is reversed. Action is recognised as
only the outward and visible sign of thought and like all
physical things is soon merged and forgotten in the past. The
life of the thought behind the action, however, is much longer,
but that life is not for ever, otherwise it would be a very hopeless thing altogether. The life of that thought only lasts so
long as is necessary for it to be either worked out by the Spirit
or merged into the Spirit, when it no longer has a separate
existence. Until either one or other of these things happen
that thought is as definite and as separate as human beings
are definite and separate from each other. There is no vague-
ness at all about them; as I said before, they have their own
individuality. Thought, then, is one of the most beautiful or

most dangerous things to indulge in, and it literally means that what each one sows has to be reaped in time with sorrow or with joy—the choice remains open to all.

Although I have spoken rather seriously on the question of thought, I do not want to create a wrong impression in your minds. There are many thoughts of a trivial and entirely physical nature that really do not emanate from the person concerned at all—they are the reflections from others either in your world or in the world just outside the earth plane. They, as it were have no roots at all; and it is only when those thoughts are welcomed and voluntarily taken in by the individual that they become attached or personal. The mere fact that some thoughts are unwelcome, or are distasteful shows that they are not your own thoughts at all, and never can become your own thoughts, unless you are very much off your guard. I tell you this because so many people are troubled by thoughts which are not of a spiritual character at all—almost the reverse it would seem. They are troubled by them and search through their own characters to find out what is in it that has attracted them—they cause sorrow often and distress always. These thoughts are but tests which have to be endured in order to prove the metal of those so attacked. If the pure were never assailed by thoughts not wholly pure, they would be untried and, therefore, not in a position to claim their purity entirely as their own. It is the same with everything of a like nature; the mere fact of possessing a quality in an advanced stage means that that quality has to be tested and retested over and over again, in order to grow still stronger. And it is only by using the antithesis of that quality that the test can be satisfactorily carried out.

I want you all to think over this and apply it generally. It is exactly the same with bad temper—or rather I should say—good temper, and with patience, especially with patience. Could you see what patience looks like here you would think that nothing less than equal beauty could come close to it. But how is patience gained ? The answer is obvious to you all— it is gained by much vexation and much trying of that patience by others. In colour it is lavender—that I mention because at the beginning I told you that thought, besides other things, had colour . . .

Heredity

WELL, my children, I want to say first of all that it is wise when commencing these little gatherings to dismiss all thoughts of failure as connected with the body, and to place your entire assurance upon God. Now, little ones, it may have seemed to you that events have not justified the trust which you endeavoured to place on the power of the Spirit, so I would once more draw your attention to things as they are and not to things as they are worked out on the physical plane.

My exhorting you to have perfect faith in God that the physical might be overcome brought not only protection to my child, but indeed another brick was added to your own spiritual resources, and although you knew it not the evening in question did its work—its great and important work for the Spirit enshrined within each one.

Ah ! yes, I know to you the physical plays so great a part; that which is evidenced before your sight takes first place, and it is not easy to say when a breakdown occurs: " This is success !" Yet I bid you take my words to heart for indeed you shall see in the days to come how the gathering together of spiritual resources in this way not only left its mark upon you but upon the world as well (and in this case I speak of the physical aspect of the world)—it shall leave its mark, for the time is coming when those whom the Holy Spirit has touched shall go back on their tracks and they shall read and learn the lesson which lies there.

Can you not see that if this work had been carried on under favourable conditions, its value would have been infinitely less ? Because of the strain entailed, because of the wish to lay self aside so that which has come through by God's grace—that truth shall live for ever more and it shall leave its mark on the physical world in the measure that the world can understand.

And now my children there is another point on which I

wish to speak and that is in regard to the use of these records. There are those who have been diffident as to the free use of the truths which I have sought to teach; they are held back by many reasons, some of which have their connection with the earth and some which are entirely of the Spirit.

Well, dear children, as I have told you before, when you are free you will find that " mine " and " thine " do not exist; you will find with so much joy that each and everyone gladly —oh ! so gladly shares their treasure, be it great or small, with those who are willing to take. And why is this ? Because they see in all its magnificent detail that everything belongs to God, and that He—the Great Possessor—lives but to scatter on all His gifts with a generosity which never fails, with a lavishness you cannot understand until the mind of the body is laid aside.

Yet, dear children, I would not have you think that I ignore those rules which have been brought into being by man as a protection. You see, dear children, that when what you call " the law " says " Thous shalt not " not only does it protect the owner but still more so does it protect those who as yet are easily swayed by the forces of darkness, easily influenced to betray that greater self, to gather that which they have not sown, to harvest that which anoher has worked and toiled to produce . . .

Keep your minds at a level poise. The laws of the earth framed by man, for the most part do valuable work in protecting the immature, the soul which as yet has not learnt its lessons.

So, dear children, I am not ignoring that it wouldn't be wise to do away with that which comes under a very comprehensive heading—which restricts man from using that which has been produced by the mind of another.

Yet, dear children, in our case it has no application at all and so tonight I make it quite clear that the truths I seek to convey, that the unfoldment of faith which has been entrusted to me by The Master—that these words are open to all, and indeed I entreat those who have God in their hearts to make the fullest possible use they can of that which is given to the world only and solely by the power of the Holy Spirit. And, dear children, there is one thing more I would add in this con-

nection: That neither I nor my child need recognition, yet for
the sake of the Spirit within the one who speaks I would remind him that a word of thanks is due to God Himself—for
His grace, for His understanding of the needs of humanity, for
His great great Heart where those who are as little children in
spiritual understanding are concerned.

" Render thanks to God and speak so far as you can these
words of truth, this fuller revelation of the gift which is man's
own, this exposition of the great Love which the Father has
for those who as yet understand Him not." That is my message to those who have asked and also to those who have won-
dered mentally how far they were at liberty to use these records.

And now, dear children, I come to the subject of what
my little ones are pleased to call " the instruction "—and oh !
my children, could you but look into my heart and mind you
would see that your loving thoughts over my simple words
have indeed been a gift which cannot be priced and which
will be held by me for ever and for ever . . .

Children, tonight I want to speak to you about that which
has caused much discussion amongst the busy minds of men;
yes ! and thought of a comprehensive nature, in the physical
sense, has been given to it as well. As usual it is not my
intention to destroy but rather, if I can, to turn the attention
of those who will listen to the great spiritual meaning which
lies beneath the physical fact. I am referring to the subject of
Heredity.

It is curious to us that the majority are content to rest, as
it were, on their laurels, and not to pursue this question (or
the many which arise from it) to its ultimate conclusion. Still,
dear children, you will see at once when you are free that
although man traversed in thought half the journey, according
to physical standards, on this subject and on that—you will
find when you are free that after all it was but a bare inch of
the ground which was covered—so vast is wisdom, so limited
is knowledge; so spacious, so far-reaching the realms of the
Spirit, so narrow, so shut in the field of the physical mind.

Children, in regard to the inheritance of characteristics
and to the inheritance of physical disabilities, I would ask you
to look at the question in this way:

True it is that in families certain qualities apparently are handed on from father to son or from mother to daughter—although it has been found that more often the characteristics of the father are evidenced in the daughter and those of the mother in the son, in varying degrees. And then we come to that very sad aspect in regard to disease, in regard to those many weaknesses to which the flesh is prone; and I want you to give me your full attention while I try to put in language which will be understood the spiritual aspect, the great unpenetrated truth which lies underneath it all. And here, dear children, I bring in also that oft discussed, oft abused theory of Predestination which, as it were, throws a slight shade over the more important topic under discussion.

You see, dear children, that in order to show you things as they are I must lift your minds completely out of the physical representation and plant them, so far as I am able, in the great world of the Spirit, where Truth is born and where Truth persists in spite of the wrecking thoughts of those on earth.

Children, I have told you that the lives you lead in this little world—that the experiences you undergo were decided upon by the indwelling Spirit which is of God and which God has gifted to you. Yet have I not said as well that " like attracts like "—that those with mutual sympathies are drawn together and, again, those with distorted tastes have allied themselves to those who have chosen the same precarious path ?

Now look you, dear children—on the one hand you have the physical aspect and on the other you have that which is of God. The Spirit imbued with strength according to its emancipation—and only according to that emancipation—the Spirit takes on that which will help it most, that which will contribute further to the freeing of itself from what is antagonistic to God. Remembering what I have told you regarding the long journey of the Spirit—the taking on of experiences and, alas ! too often the turning to darkness out of Light—remembering this it is not difficult for you to imagine that although the Spirit is pure, untouched by so-called sin, yet during its journey much that is of a cumbersome nature has been gathered to it; in some cases to the extent that that which is of God is suffocated—strangled by the adverse influences of those who are out to wreck.

So, dear children, bearing in mind the freedom or the

captivity of the Spirit, it is not difficult for you to understand that experiences are taken on according to the ambition of that which is in the process of evolution. You see, dear children, this accounts for much. Those who love God consciously come into this earthly life—this short period of trying and of testing, and out of the greatness of their love they choose indeed the hard, rough road, bringing but few supports to help them on their way. And thus it is that sometimes the body into which they enter is seriously hampered by weakness, by lack of power to function as God intended.

Now wait awhile. There are many causes which contribute to the weakness of the body. Some there are who today are paying a heavy price for the disregard of nature's laws by those who were before them. Others, dear children—and forget it not—others are suffering from the same motive which inspired themselves. Those who were before them, through whose bodies directly or indirectly they came—these in many cases were heroic souls, and they chose those experiences which indeed left their mark upon the physical tabernacle which was worn.

I want you to consider this in its spiritual aspect. I deny not that the weakness in the one body is reproduced—sometimes in most terrible form—in those which follow after; yet, dear children, I ask you: Does not this truth throw the bright Light of God's Love over those who suffer, over those who indeed have paid a great price for the inestimable privilege of going through their earth's experience—the privilege which brings them what nothing else can do, for those experiences force on the spiritual progress in a way no words can express.

And then we turn to the sadder side—to the so-called inheritance of undersirable characteristics, and here it is that you get the working out of " attraction ". Those who are bent on denying the God-head within, they during the sleep state mingle and have companionship with those who are like minded who have passed out of physical life or who are waiting the opportunity of coming into the flesh.

You see, dear children, that " influence " is a far, far bigger thing than man has ever taken into account. Just as those who have led a wayward life on earth pass out with their lessons unlearnt, so there are those who down the countless aeons of time likewise have not learnt their lessons, and it makes no difference whether the physical experience has been carried through or not. Like attracts like and that is the tragedy which all have to face.

But, dear children, you will say to me: " How is it that sometimes from the most degraded a pure flower springs ?"

Well, this is so easily explained when you have seen something of the Love of God, something of that love which many of His children are able to show towards others.

In cases such as these the Spirit imbued with strength, deliberately chooses an environment which is agony indeed; chooses it because by example—by showing purity where only impurity is found, by throwing out love where hatred holds chief place, the Spirit is able to demonstrate God in their midst . . .

Children, I want to take you a little further still; I want you to consider the theory of Heredity not merely from the physical side but to penetrate through that into the spiritual, and I want you each one to answer this question for yourself:

In regard to the inheritance of characteristics, is it not logical that the Great Source, the Great Parent of all must be taken into consideration ? That man evades, and because he evades God his theories remain theories and as facts they cannot stand. Go back to the Source of this life and that. In each one there is Spirit—that which is even as God, part of Himself; and so tonight I proclaim that because the weakest and the frailest has the inheritance of God within, God shall prevail !

Yes, dear children, the significance of this is far reaching. Even in your day experiments valuable to the individual have been made. It has been found that a child taken from those who are bound most closely to the things of the earth—to so-called vice, to all those disabilities of the flesh—that it is possible to take a child and in the right environment for the most part to overcome, or keep back that which it would seem was its natural inheritance. Nay ! I forget not that again and again the experiment has failed and the child has reverted to type, but for each one who has strayed there are hundreds who have struggled on with many backward thoughts may be—but yet have kept themselves free from those lower strata of evil which otherwise would have sucked them in.

This tonight is my message of hope, my message of faith for all: I say that the weakest and the most degraded can be reclaimed, can be set on a sure foundation of spirituality because of those inherited characteristics from their Divine Parent, which nothing can destroy, which are there in the individual, crushed down by the forces of evil perhaps, but which sooner or later shall and will assert themselves once more.

Children, never listen to those who class this one and that as " hopeless ". From the physical standpoint they may be, but in the Spirit that word is unknown. There are conditions which have been hinted at during these sacred evenings which are indeed of darkness, which in comparison to " evil " as you know it, are as an inky night to the twilight before the dawn; yet never has it been said—never would it be allowed that the weakest, that those sunk into the innermost depths would not in time by the grace of God, be gathered into the Light which never fades, gathered into that sonship and daughtership with their Mother and Father God; because the inheritance is there, because they come from Him, and nothing which emanated from that which is all-power, all-thought, all-Love—nothing which emanated from the Source of Holiness can do aught but return to its Source at last . . .

Children, you will see how those ideas which come under the heading of Heredity and also of Predestination—how in some cases they reflect half-truths, and again how misleading they are when looked at under the light which shines from God's Love. Yes ! as I have said, the Spirit within has chosen the path that it will tread; it has chosen the path from that early beginning which your minds cannot grasp, and it will choose its own path right through the unfolding Eternity which is the gift of all. Yet looked at with spiritual sight, how plain it all seems, how magnificent is the generosity of the Father !

Oh, my children, in taking these thoughts of the earth, these many theories and deductions which man has laboured to produce, remember this: That it is not God's will that you should stop half way, yet again and again those bound by physical thinking do that, and there the weakness lies. I ask them but to carry on their deductions until the end of the chain is reached; I ask them not to limit the inheritance of the

P

individual to those who have trodden the earthly way; I ask them to get back link by link to the One who created, to the One who thought out everything; to not only give God His due but to recognise that which is hidden underneath—that which indeed shall prevail because God has promised it, be-caused God would never consent to the final dissolution of that which was and is Himself . . .

Children, rejoice !—rejoice for many things; rejoice that there were those who suffered aforetime, and because the blows of life fell thick and fast you, in turn, are bearing part of the burden—not of their burden, but because the tie be-tween you was so strong, because the love for God was in your heart, you were attracted to those who were strong in Spirit, and you have borne your burden too.

And then, dear children, I would draw the attention of the many readers outside this little circle to the incredible folly of those class distinctions which play so large a part in this little earth life. When you come here not only will the folly be apparent, but the humiliation will be great as well. Those who have chosen the easy path—they indeed will see with shame that the despised, that those reckoned of no account were the strong souls, were the pure souls, were the souls who had seen God face to face, and because of that were struggling and striving to express in a fragmentary way something of the beauty of the Divine Mind.

Remember this and let it curb your judgment, remember that the deep decision of the Spirit is responsible for the en-vironment in which each one is placed, and it must be appar-ent in certain conditions temptation is rife indeed. Therefore judge not when the forces of evil sometimes overcome those whose lives are sordid and free from joy, those who are hemmed in by the many horrors of physical life, those who walk side by side with poverty and with care. Judge not these, dear children, because in time to come you will see that all the while they were Christ's friends and that He calls them thus. And again I say judge not those who surrounded with the beauties of the world, with a multitude of comfort yet wilfully seek that which is of darkness and repudiate the God within. I say judge not these but pray for them instead, for great, great will be their affliction when this brief sojourn is ended and they see the wrecking work that was done.

Oh ! compassion for all, understanding for all as far as may be, helping by prayer and thought and action ! This is the gospel of Christ, this is the truth He taught, this is what He waits for those who love Him to adopt . . . Prayer, faith and trust, and above all the deep conviction that the spiritual inheritance of man shall prevail; that the earth's standards shall be brushed aside because they are of the earth and not of God; and in the future, purification for the individual, perfect unity with Love, all working with their Maker in restoring those others who likewise missed the path which led into light and joy and peace.

And now, dear children, I leave you. If there are any loose threads which you require to be fastened securely then as time goes on I will come back to the subject and all will be as God intends. It is not wise to unveil too much at once of the treasure which is waiting for you all, because the physical mind must be trained—must be brought along so that, in its degree, it can keep pace with the mind of the Spirit, neither hindering it nor forestalling it in a false way but just fitting into its little niche, contributing its part to the great grand quest which lies before it—the quest which ever daily is becoming clearer, the clouds passing beyond the horizon leaving the view beautiful in prospect and the path free from those obstructions which would hold you back . . . And now I go.

Divine Justice

MY little children, it is indeed with joy that we meet, and I want you in future to try and exclude every other thought but gladness in connection with this sweet communion—to realise that the long period of physical strain has been lifted, by God's will, and that because the work was continued in spite of the complaints of the body, so, as always, in His good time that which would bar was taken away.

To you all as the days go on an added sense of refreshment and strength will come. I speak to all without exception: I say whatever the days have to hold that sense of inward spiritual refreshment shall gain strength, and according to the will of each one it shall grow and grow. Oh! my children, I wish with all my heart that you could see something of the power which you draw together by meeting in this way, by laying desire aside, by asking not for this one or for that and by excluding the physical things of the world although these concern you so nearly . . . I wish, dear children you could witness some of the beauty and the power; and yet again I say that because you cannot and because the realisation entirely escapes your physical mind, so you shall see that God's ways are best.

Yes! in this room tonight are gathered together many who inhabited the far parts of your little world, and a still greater number who have come from those regions of the Spirit which indeed are holy and full of peace. Therefore, dear children, resign yourselves into their care and with assurance show your faith in the goodness of God, giving out your share towards the harmonising of these conditions which are as nearly perfect as may be.

Tonight, dear children, I am going to attempt to talk to you about a subject which is not only beyond your comprehension but which is beyond the comprehension of your guide and those who are gathered here. This may sound strange to you but my brief word of explanation will make the matter clear.

I have told you that however we strive, however near we may attain to what represents to you "the ideal", however much we love our Master individually, yet we cannot fathom or attempt to fathom the Love which He has for the children He has created. We are limited, dear children, in this respect because the Mind of Love is too vast altogether, too comprehensive to be grasped or understood by any. Yet, dear children, evening by evening it has been my privilege to try and unfold just a little inch or two of that wonder and glory which I have seen. I have talked to you of God's attitude towards those on earth and it has amazed you, yet tonight, dear children, I must underline what is fact: that there is more difference between my conception of the Father-Heart and what it really contains than there is between your conception and mine. No words could express it and I do not attempt to explain to you further than this: That what we have witnessed through the ages of that gigantic Love has staggered us by its unlimited nature, yet I am bound to say that in comparison with the Heart of God the view permitted to us is limited indeed. As we go on day by day year by year so, as it were, the curtain is drawn back and we are allowed to see and to understand a little more of the Eternal Love of the Father, and this goes on for ever and for ever . . .

Tonight, dear children, having prepared your minds a little I am going to put into the language of the world something concerning that which has been called Divine Justice . . . Children, remember my previous words, remember that I am attempting to portray what is beyond my own understanding because of its infinity, yet listen to me and learn just a little more about the One who loves you best.

In your world, dear children, " justice " is applied in many different ways and in regard to many dissimilar things but tonight I want to take you a little further on out of the physical standpoint and to place you on the threshold of things as they are.

First of all I would speak to you about that quality which immediately flashes through the mind in connection with Justice—I mean Mercy. Well, dear children, the mercy of the world has got a little twisted from mercy as we see it in

the Spirit. Nay, think not that I am criticising that which is
essentially a spiritual attribute, but you will see my point as
we go along.

In speaking of mercy how often this attitude is adopted:
That to receive mercy is a great concession, is an act of generosity which by its unusual nature attracts the attention of all.

And then, dear children, that word comes up so frequent-
ly in worshipping God, and I want you not to eliminate it
because that is impossible, but rather to give it its right interpretation. Again and again the children of the earth—for the
most part those who seek to do God's will—approach the
Father entreating that His " mercy " may be extended to them.

Well, dear children, that is man's idea of God but in
reality God looks upon you and me in a totally different light.
In one sense His mercy is around you all the time—I mean
that His Love is for ever fighting with the greater self within
so that the real you, the Spirit imprisoned by the flesh, may
not suffer by the lack of mercy shown by the physical mind.
Over and over again, by His grace, by His merciful Love the
battle goes to the Spirit, and the physical, for the time being,
is overcome. Because of the mercy which is a phase of the
great Love He represents, because of His mercy you, dear
children, and I as well indeed have reason to thank God—
to thank Him that it has been extended to us; but when it
comes to the attitude of conciliation, when you approach im-
ploring that His Face may not be turned from you, then indeed it is misunderstanding Love in a terrible and destructive
way.

Oh ! think you not that the Father does not understand
that during the years the physical mind has been trained by
others to regard Him as its Judge, to approach His altar asking
and yet hardly expecting that He will listen to the petitions
made, because of the unworthiness of the petitioner. God
understands how it is that this attitude has come into being,
how it is that man, even with the best motive there may be,
unconsciously has discredited his Father by imagining that He
was like unto himself. Many there are who can reflect something of the Christ Mind, but God is not reflected in man's
image of Him as concerning matters of this kind.

You see, dear children, that you have a lot to learn;
you see also that it is impossible to learn unless there are

those who are willing to go through the necessary lessons themselves in order to teach you and others something of the nature of the Father-Mind.   Tonight I want you to for ever put away the thought that God extends mercy to His children as an act of grace in the spirit of condescension, for such is impossible to the Father-Mind.   Yet I go back on my previous thought and I say that you can think and dwell and ponder on His merciful intervention between the physical and the spiritual self; but when it is a matter between the Father-Heart and the erring child, that word " mercy " is swept out of being by His enveloping Love and understanding.

Now, dear children, we come back to Justice, and I had to build up in your minds some conception of Mercy first, otherwise it would be impossible for you to gain even a little of the inner meaning of the Justice which is being defined.

Continuing on my remarks of last week I want you to consider just for a moment that big question opened up by the choice of the Spirit of the environment in which it will go through its earthly experiences.

Now, dear children, on all sides even with your limited knowledge you see those you love placed in conditions which, as you put it, are the very worst there could be considering the temperament of the one concerned.   And how often is it that it appears to the physical mind and the physical sight that one is " sacrificed " for the other; that in a family there is one who bears the brunt, one who is looked upon as the proper person to take the rough and the difficult and to make it smooth for others; and in spite of wishing to believe in God's love, again and again the mind exclaims against the " in-justice " of physical life.

Yes ! dear children, from your standpoint injustice is flagrant indeed; but I want you tonight to try and get a little higher up and, as it were, to stand on the side of the hill and look down on physical life, when from the little distance you have attained things will be seen in their right perspective; and as your mind is able to traverse farther up the hill of understanding so your view will be broadened and the perspective at each point will be seen to be better still.

First of all, dear children, we will take facts as they stand. I would not attempt to deny that in a way too gigantic to be

put into words some apparently suffer sorely for the weakness
for the omissions of those to whom they are linked during their
daily life. Yet, dear children, a fact is not a fact when viewed
purely from the physical standpoint; a fact is only a true fact
when God's part has been taken into consideration when, as
a rule, the whole prospect is changed.

Children, I go back to the choice of the courageous Spirit
and I say that not only has that Spirit shown heroism but it
has shown a practical commonsense which cannot be excelled
in physical life. Here you get the thing in its true proportions.
I grant you that the going may be hard, that the sensitive mind
and the shrinking heart may be lacerated again and again, but
for every barb that finds a resting place so is God compensat-
ing in a way you can never grasp until spiritual sight is your
own.

Children, look at it like this: I have told you before that
it is impossible for one to injure another without that injury
having to be made good; I have told you that it is a spiritual
law that you cannot think one good thought in connection
with another without the fruits of that good thought being
gathered to yourself. Look at it in God's way and when, as
is often the case, you are brought up with something like
horror against ingrained selfishness, that consideration only
of individual comfort and desire—when you see examples like
this then, dear children, thank God that indeed their responsibility is not your own; thank God and pray that the Light
may come to them ere too late . . . Too late in the sense that
the accumulated burden is so heavy that much suffering and
effort must be forthcoming before they are free to walk with
happiness in the Gardens of the Lord . . .

Oh ! my children, for ever remember the shortness of this
little earth life, and when there are those who make you suffer
—sometimes unconsciously and sometimes with intent—then
take it in the spiritual way and be glad that when you
step free there will be that less to make good on your own
account; remember that although the pangs of the physical
heart and mind may seem terrible to bear during the earth
stages yet, in a way so wonderfully kind, those pangs instan-
taneously are turned into power and beauty and holiness. Holiness—that is a big word to use but suffering is so cleansing;
suffering can do for you in a short time what nothing else can

accomplish, and when you stand free from the body you will thank God with a gratitude too great, too deep for words that He gave you sufficient vision to take on experiences which wounded your heart and mind during the earth life which then has passed through its course.

One step nearer to understanding, one step nearer to a conception of Divine Justice !—and dear children, particularly would I bring this to your attention: That because God has such a magnificent conception of Justice it does not mean that the men and women of the world should leave things to Him entirely without contributing their part. Tonight I speak with double emphasis about those vast ranges of " service "—the care of the delicate young, the thought and the provision made not only to cure the many diseases to which the body is prone, but also the preventive measures which indeed are of the Spirit, because those who work in this way are joining hands with Love so that suffering shall be abated.

Children, I told you once before that in regard to the care of the body—that which is the temple of the soul—three things were necessary in order that those on earth should work in harmony with those in the Spirit deputed by God to help them on their way. Yes ! three factors are necessary to keep the physical tabernacle in as fit a condition as may be; yet, dear children, not forgetting what I said last week about those deep decisions of the Spirit in regard to the pains which assail the flesh.

Children. within the reach of all those who live in what are called civilised countries there is at hand: First God, then the Spirit within, and then the use of those tools of service which have been provided in such an adequate way (doctors and nurses). You see, dear children, I am not excluding any-thing of the world which is of a helpful character but I ask you to keep things in their proper place. When the body is assailed by enemies remember this: First the Great Healer, your Creator; then that Spirit within which is all-strength, all-power because it is of God; and then. dear children, to use with commonsense and, I would add, with temperance as well. that which has been provided by the concentration of man on the various methods and means of succouring the physical body.

You will say that I have got a little far from Divine

Justice but not so, not so ! There are those today, very many, who have found within themselves sufficient spiritual resources to put faith to the test, to approach their Maker with trust and to ask Him to heal that which is hurtful and harmful where the body is concerned.

Now, dear children, such as these have many criticisers and, for the most part, those criticisers are not in touch with God so far as faith is concerned. I know only too well that " mistakes " have been made—I use the word in the earth sense—mistakes have been made because such as these have excluded that which science has to contribute; and have I not said that the ideal is the combination of the three, keeping each in the place I have stated ?

Yet, dear children, back again we come to the justice which is Divine. Those who try so earnestly to keep their minds on a high level, those who by prayer and preparation endeavour to keep in direct touch with the Great Healer, these are building up for themselves spiritual resources which indeed will be valuable when they are free. They bring their gain during physical life in the sense that for the most part sadness is kept at bay, and love for God brings sunshine into lives which otherwise would be grey. And when those who tried conscientiously to put faith to the test—even though they ignored the gifts of the mind which God has given to His children—in the measure that these were sincere so they shall find hereafter that the cure which was not possible in the physical has been carried out in the " body " of the soul.

God's justice never fails ! In the big things there it is seen in all its glory; in the tiniest detail, in the wish for faith— in that raising of the mind hoping for faith—still more is the wonder shown because to the Father nothing is insignificant, nothing is of little importance because the thought was directed to Him, and this being so the effect of that thought shall last for ever.

Children there is one other aspect in regard to this particular phase of thinking. There have been those who have found it essential to go directly against the advice of medical science—there have been occasions when the conditions of their life made it absolutely impossible to follow out what was a direct command. Yes ! in your own little family circle you have had it worked out in detail; how one—my child—

listened to the Voice of the Spirit and found not the physical disaster which was prophesied but sufficient physical resources to carry on her life of work. (6 months' war work on the land).

Divine justice again ! You see, dear children, that man overlooks one great fact—he does not take into consideration God's mighty plan, God's overseeing care. And so to those who have put faith to the test—to these I say that in their physical life as concerning the body and its equipment faith indeed has its place, but confuse it not, let it not lie amongst the other toys and tools upon the ground, but rather regard it as a star—the star which reflects God's Love, that star which not only shines during the earth journey but when you are free will be seen in all its magnificent glory, calling you on and on to those heights which have no end . . .

Children, there are many other aspects of Divine Justice. Those who have undertaken the care of the sick if their wish to serve is true and clean, then indeed is God able to use them to show that kind of mercy which He delights in the most.

Think you like this. There in your public buildings and still more pathetic in the little homes you have those tortured by diseases which indeed drain the physical, and also the spiritual resources so far as the earth view is concerned. Then you have the healers: First, God, the Great Healer of all, then the guides and helpers—those who imbued with a love of service willingly, oh ! so willingly come back to this little earth and labour thereon; and then again you have in the physical world the doctors and the nurses, the mothers and the sisters and the prayers of the friends outside . . .

Don't you see the magnificent justice of God ? How the one who suffers, ignorant of the spiritual laws which are working so harmoniously—that the sufferer lying there in its helplessness by the very fact that it does suffer is able to contribute to the spiritual resources of countless others, ah ! yes ! and forget not the wonderful gain to the individual, because pain is so hard to bear. Then trace back the sources: remember those who are far distant, unable to render help in physical form—remember that these by their thoughts, by their prayers are helping the sufferer, helping those who are tending the sufferer; and again in turn, by their wish to help, they are helping themselves as well.

Mighty is the Mind of God, gigantic in its conceptions, merciful in a way we cannot understand, because He takes that which is brought into being by the evil and uses it as a stream of unending blessing to others . . .

You see, dear children, to what I am turning your thoughts. I stated before, and I do so again tonight in a most emphatic way—I say that in regard to the diseases of the body, when man puts God first so he will see results altogether unimaginable in proportion to those which are brought about by the application only of the science which is of the earth. Good that may be, yet by putting it first he is arresting —yes ! arresting that greater good which is his desire . . .

Oh ! children there is so much to learn ! Tonight I have been able to touch only upon a little phase here and there, yet I hope I've left on your minds the conviction that those apparent " injustices " are not only examples of justice but indeed are demonstrations of that generosity, that mercy, that Love which cannot be exaggerated because they are of God.

And so, dear children, passing on from one subject to another I ask you to consider those whom you grade as the " Insane ". Yes ! and this phase of illness is perhaps one of the worst which can be experienced.

Now, briefly, these complaints of the mind can be divided and placed under three headings: Those who have taken on as part of their physical experiences a mind which is not, as you would say, true to balance. Then there are a vast number who by their own heedlessness, by their own disregard of the warning voice have brought upon themselves an imprisonment which it pitiful indeed. And then there are those others which I would class all together—the ones who have found the road of life too steep and the ones who by " accident " or by the carelessness of others have damaged that delicate fabric which you call the brain.

Children, in your own experiences you have known those —lovely in character and in thought—whose minds have been clouded, who indeed have suffered grievously from complications of the physical body which have had a direct and disastrous effect upon the mind, and you have said: " Oh, the pity of it !" and again the thought has come " the injustice of it that one so sweet, so attached to the things of the Spirit should be overtaken by such a fate . . .

Children, there have been one or two such as these who have come back to you and have told you of the beauty and the power which is now their own.

And then I pass on to those we have put under the second heading—the many who quite unconscious of the risk which they run, seek not to control either the desires or the thoughts of the mind. As wilful children they run into danger by ignoring the greater self within, they allow the things of the earth—its trivial mundane details—to obsess them to the exclusion of everything else.

Now, mark you there are countless thousands of such as these in the world today. What have they done ? So natural a process ! Because they gave way to their lesser selves during the many years which have passed so when the test comes there are no resources on which to fall back. The Spirit within has been suffocated by self, and in time of illness these pray not to their God, but rather listen and invite those voices from the darker realms—those who at last are able to dominate them in every sense there could be during the years of physical life which remain. Sad indeed is their plight, and there are many such as these out of the physical world as well. We do not call them " insane " because we see and know that they have handed over themselves to the control of those who are the enemies of the Light !

You see, dear children. I do not wish to overdraw the picture but in this lies a warning for all. The enemies of the physical are many and the pains and the conditions of the body have their effect on the physical mind; but God the Great Healer is accessible to all and if those who are inclined to err in this way would remember to hold on to that Anchor He could not only steady them but lead them out of danger into safety and security, because there, in their own hands, the future lies ! Only by their damaging thoughts have they brought upon themselves that which fills others with horror and dismay . . .

And then, dear children, we come to those who by so-called accident, by war and pestilence have found themselves still in the body but with a mind that does not respond as in the days of old.

Children, restorative work is going on apace, and again I bring you back to the thought of God. You will find that those who tried to keep in touch with goodness, who had ideals—even if these were only of a kind—that these, in time, are restored. Again you have the demonstration of spiritual law. Those resources of character, that bending and blending of the will to right—that has not passed away, but the damage has been done to the physical organ; yet habit is strong and under certain conditions great cures have come to pass. The Spirit within has linked itself to the Great Spirit world without, and though the physical mind be unconscious, the good work goes on apace.

In all these examples you have Divine Justice shown in detail, and more than that: you have it outlined before you that on all sides there are resources of an unlimited character, yet because of the " disability " or the pain experienced so in that spiritual self the harvest is stored . . .

Oh ! my children, think this over and remember the responsibility of the lesser self towards the greater self; yet think not because God is the Creator you must approach Him and ask for " Mercy " to avert that which earthly justice bestows. Remember that God regards you as something precious, something that is treasure indeed, and that on all sides help is provided—that everywhere, in every phase of life you may explore, running through every act, through every incident is that deep strong river of His Love.

Divine Justice !—which to us is interpreted thus: The great Father-Heart, pouring out Love unlimited on all His children, fighting for them so that they may have the great gifts which He intends shall be their own; wrestling with the physical mind so that that same physical mind may show something of mercy towards the Spirit within . . .

And now, dear children, I will go, but oh ! let not my words be brushed lightly aside. See in your lives, in the trend of events the Guiding Hand of God and rest you content, worrying not over what the future holds and covering the past with the leaves of forgetfulness; because once the body is laid aside that " past " will bear a totally different representation to you. God directs and God guides in a way no words can explain when those of His children even barely wish that the Spirit should take first place; therefore, worry, anticipation or foreboding is totally out of place. Anticipate that God will provide not only the things of your material life but also those great contributing gifts which are necessary for the harmony of the Spirit with that which is Love Divine . . . And now I go.

Telepathy

WELL, dear children, once again the time has come round and we meet together to still more closely bind ourselves to the things of the Spirit and also, as it were, to cement once more the tie of love there is between us. And, dear children, I want you in thinking over your few possessions to try and remember to count us in these as well, because when you come here you will see so clearly that however many jewels a person may possess, if the jewel of love is absent then by its very absence all the others are but lifeless stones.

It is a point which I cannot over emphasise. I know full well that you have said together that it is far easier to love those who come to you in this way than it is to love those who walk with you in physical life. You say that, dear children, but so often when the warring things of the daily round come a little too close you forget that very love which you have professed, and which in a way you cannot understand now goes far deeper than the physical and is beautiful and strong in the Spirit.

Yes! it's a little confusing when you are dealing with two worlds. You want to be centred entirely in the one which calls you in a way that never will be resisted in the days to come—for there your sympathies lie; but perforce practical life in the physical body goes on and much disharmony and fret of nerves come as a consequence.

You say you are so " out of your element ", and so you are! Oh! dear children, cannot you understand when this and that goes rather hard that your Heavenly Father is not unmindful of the position of things; cannot you realise that there must be always those who live in the world who are yet not of the world, and because the sense of loneliness and unfamiliarity is all around you should rejoice for in itself that is an indication where your real self dwells, where it functions and where is its rightful Home . . . Children of the Light

yet doomed, as it seems, to live in darkness or in half-light,
and you long for the Door to be opened and to be free of all
those obstacles which hinder your progress towards your soul's
desire.

My children, I understand all this and much more which
even escapes your own comprehension, but still I say that you
should rejoice because of your alienation from the world and
those many material things which, as you see so plainly, hold
the minds of others to the exclusion of everything which is
of the Spirit . . .

In the days of old there was one greatly " inspired ", so
you would say, who taught much concerning spiritual gifts and
the things which are of God. I speak of one called Paul and
he tonight is in this little room trying to help you, trying by
love and prayer to still those many sadnesses which assail the
mind of the body.

In his day, dear children—as all will see in perusing that
which he wrote—he more than all the rest tried to explain to
man those powers which were hidden and imprisoned within;
those mighty gifts of the Spirit which indeed indicate in a way
which no one can deny that close and intimate link between
the child and his Father. I would like all those who read
these records to ponder still more on the many digressions
regarding the things of the Spirit which were peculiar to this
faithful servant of the Master; I want them to read and to
re-read again—laying aside as much as possible the physical
mind—to read with the mind of the Spirit when they will see,
slowly at first but in growing degree, that he who was called
Paul put into words much which escaped the discernment of
others—escaped that spiritual discernment which he declared
was essential in order to explore those things which are of
God.

My children, much was written in those early days of
what you call the Christian era—much was written which only
now is being uncovered to man; yet had not those words
been written aforetime there would be many today who would
bar the Truth because of that exclusion. And so, as always,
building for the far future he—dominated by the Holy Spirit
—put on record not only statements but explanations regarding the gifts of the Spirit which have been given to man . . .

R

Yes ! tonight there are many here who away back in the long ago trod a difficult path, and I want you in your regard to the pioneers of the great Truth to remember always that for the most part they climbed the steep hill to God by faith and by faith alone. Many were shut off from what you call the intellectualities of physical life; they lived in a very humble way, and those who were born to ease saw, by God's grace, that only by laying aside that which came too close to the earth could they attain to the heights.

You see, dear children, that the physical setting of the so-called Saints was very ordinary, was much like the common lot of the majority today—not very much of anything and yet, as seems so strange to the unthinking mind—required to lay even that little aside because the quest which lay before them was holy indeed.

And while I am speaking on this I would like to say one word about the contrast which has been presented to you in the lives of two, both sorely stricken yet one apparently sur-rounded with all those mitigations which should be forth-coming in times of physical tribulation, and the other poor, yes ! and rather forsaken by those you think should out of common humanity do the most.

Well, dear children, referring to my remarks last week regarding Divine justice, I can assure you with a light heart that Divine justice will be worked out down to the tiniest de-gree. Your respect for one whose life of toil has left little behind in a material way—that respect, dear children, is en-tirely on the side of the Spirit. Cannot you see this because here are indications of a fine nature, because the past has held much work—aye ! and some sorrow too—cannot you see that by the very fact that such a one calls out not only your com-passion for his plight but that deep admiration for the qualities held and treasured by the soul, that the Spirit is at work un-consciously though it may be to the physical mind which holds him.

There was one who told you that ere she passed out those of the Bright Throng had gathered to her (Mrs. Grant) and I tell you tonight that could you but see things as they are you would know that the lack of the physical and the material brings a correspondingly greater power from those sent by God to tend and care for His beloved. Put all thoughts aside as to the seeming injustice, and hold on to your greater knowledge—that in the Hands of God he is safe, safe and cared for in a way no words can express.

Yet think not that the other is not under God's care as well but as you must know, when the world still holds those who are free are, as it were, pushed a little far off, and because the desire for their presence is not there so they wait until the Spirit realises its great need.

And then, dear children, I would say just one word about the qualities which are possessed and which have been shown in the daily life of the one (Davis) to whom your sympathy goes out so freely, and indeed is God-blessed in its passage.

Now, dear children, there are those in your little world who do not understand the inner meaning of good workmanship and here it is that I want to show you that the good workmanship which is individual and the good workmanship which is admired and insisted upon in others, are quite different things.

Children, this man is a " good servant " and I want you to take those words in their highest and finest sense—a good servant not only to his master, but in a gigantic way a good servant to himself. Children, I have told you that the lowest kind of work, in the world sense, is hallowed by the way in which it is done; I have said to you that because work of a certain character goes against the grain causing even physical repulsion, if that work is done well then indeed it is beautiful, it is holy in a manner no words can express.

" Ah, yes ", you will say to me, " but this man knows nothing of religion in its religious sense ", and I answer that ignorant though the mind of the body may be the Spirit within was strong enough to insist on good workmanship, and because he toiled with a consciousness that the best was required of him so he shall see, in God's good time, that his humble occupation has produced order and harmony which cannot be explained.

Oh ! my dear children, I know your hearts go out to these forgotten ones, and I thank God for it; I know if you could you would lift them out of their need, but that lack shall bring them recompense a million times over in the days to come; and remember my words—that God knows His own and God has him under His care.

Children, I cannot let this point be ignored. There are many in the world who have a love of order which perhaps appears to others as carried to an extravagant extent, yet listen to me. Thousands and thousands have that faculty—the determination that order shall be the rule of others, yet placed in similar circumstances they would not find within themselves an equal love of orderliness which would induce them to labour in like degree . . .

Children, in the realms of the Spirit order and harmony is everywhere—on every side, but it is contributed individually. Those who have the power to command others, those who have many at their beck and call these, though careless and heedless in their own actions, insist with a severity which is almost cruel on perfect exactness in others. They have much to learn, yet mark you this: that because those underlings suffer under the discipline imposed, by the very formation of such habits done under compulsion, these, when they are free, will step into harmony and order—into that perfection of harmony and order which is everywhere in the realms of the Spirit.

Cannot you see my point ? The one who is in your thoughts possessed the gift—I call it a gift—and by labour and close attention he was in every sense " a good servant " not only to those for whom he worked but a far, far better servant to that Spirit within of which at this stage his physical mind is unconscious. I want you to take this in its widest sense; I want those who have this sense of order to try and extend their sympathy to those in whom as yet it is not so fully developed; yet I must say that if it is their own possession, worked for and striven for in the past, then indeed when they are free they will find themselves one in the perfect harmony which is the keynote of the Spirit realms . . .

And now, dear children, I have a more interesting subject—so you will think—to discuss, yet as we go on you will see that these remarks of mine indirectly had their bearing upon the greater topic.

Children, tonight I am going to endeavour to tell you a little about that much misunderstood word, or subject, Telepathy; and I want you to give me your undivided attention because as usual I must take you entirely out of the physical into the spiritual if I am to give you even in the least degree a true idea of what lies within that word Telepathy.

Children, there are many in the world today who have not studied the method by which this holy communion is set into being—there are very many who quite idly (yes ! it is a form of idleness) dismiss the whole subject under the word Telepathy; and yet if you pursued the subject with them, quite easily you could drive them back against their last post when they would be forced to admit that very little was known, or had been proved, about that misleading gift of Telepathy.

First of all, dear children, I want to touch upon Hypnotism because in the many experiments which have been carried out, the power of one mind over another has been used in some cases to a damaging extent. Dear Children, those who possess the power to dominate and control the will of others —these hold a very grave responsibility. It is not wise that anyone either in the world of the flesh or in those vast ranges outside, should ever have the power to dominate and control the mind of another. I have told you before that we—although imbued with an immense power by God—that we in the Spirit are unable to influence the thought even of a tiny babe except by love, and that love is real love in which self never must find a place.

Yet there have been those, and there are some today, who possess this tool of controlling the minds and the actions of others; and, dear children, it is necessary for me to make this quite clear—that power is not of the good but rather of those who are out to destroy. If the power is used for the mitigation of suffering, if it is put into action in order to protect the weaker from itself, then the gift is hallowed indeed, but how seldom is it used in this way . . .

Confuse not this force with the power of the Spirit, with those who are used directly by the Great Healer to bring healing to others, for with these—when they get out of touch with God—their power goes. You have had this illustrated again and again: that the gifts of the Spirit cannot bide when the heart and mind are really estranged from God . . .

Children, you see to what I am leading your thoughts. It is a fact, and a very sad one as well, that it is impossible for anyone to be able to dominate the mind of another without damage coming to the one so used—so far as the physical organ is concerned—and far more damage to the other because that damage is done to the greater self.

Then, dear children, we pass on to what I regard as the next stage—that transference of thought between two who are linked together by sympathy if not by love; and this, dear children, goes on in a way totally unimagined by the greatest enthusiast of the practice. It has been in action from the very beginning of creation and to it there is no end, because in the realms of the Spirit thought takes the place of speech in the sense that speech seems cumbersome in comparison.

Now, dear children, I said that this transference of thought goes on in a very comprehensive way, but I want you to realise that quite independently of arrangement, or even of those love-thoughts which are directly focussed on another —independently of all this, thought transference or telepathy is everywhere, in every road of life because it is a spiritual law.

Children, I have tried to tell you something about Thought and I have warned you that thoughts are definite things, that they have individual formation and substance of their own. Is it so hard for you to grasp that even a child is sending out a multitude of thought-forms which intermingle with the countless millions which are on every side ?

Now listen to me ! Every temperament is keyed to certain vibrations of thought and feeling, and because temperament is individual and " attractive " so do people gather unto themselves those thoughts which are nearest their own. But, dear children, forget not this: that many thoughts are weak in power, they have no depth in them. There are those in your little world who are classed as the " shallow ", and the word expresses exactly the thoughts to which I am referring. You would be surprised if with the eyes of the Spirit you could see some of the thoughts which such as these send out. They are, to use a crude illustration, like the unfinished drawing of a tiny child—chaos, for the most part.

You see how I am trying to prepare your minds for the understanding of what lies beneath that wonderful law of the Spirit which acts so perfectly and yet, to you, quite automatically in your daily life. As the individuality of a person develops so also do their thoughts gain in formation and finish, and this applies both to the bad thoughts as well as to the good . . .

And then I take you one step further and I ask you to try and visualise those thoughts which are of love—the unselfish thoughts, the thoughts of sympathy, of help and of healing. And so gladly I tell you that these thoughts, because they are charged by power direct from God—these thoughts are a million times stronger and have a million times more vitality in them than the greatest intellectual thought which ever man has sent out.

I want you to consider this: that everyone unconsciously is practising telepathy; I want you to realise just a little of the gigantic character of thought transference one to the other; and here again we bring in that greatest force for evil or for good there is: I speak of influence—the influence that each one has upon the other. Now, dear children, it would seem to you quite reasonable that the more sensitive the individual, the more likely are they to be suitable instruments through which the practice of telepathy could be illustrated, and this is so. Here, dear children, I would like to bring in a purely physical fact: It is common knowledge that those who are what you call highly strung—the sensitive, that these are affected directly and sometimes disastrously by changes in climatic conditions. It is a fact, and as I go on I will show you how impossible it would be that this should be otherwise . . .

Children, imagine if you can even a square inch of what you call " vibrations "—what this appears like, remembering the conglomeration, the multitude of thoughts which it contains. Then take a room or a building or, again, think of this great big world, as it seems to you !

Children, that which man calls Telepathy is in evidence everywhere only in a way so gigantic that it is overlooked; yes ! because it is everywhere its significance is overlooked, and here, dear children, we bring in somewhat as a side issue those experiments with sound-waves and what can be received apparently without any in between agency at all.

Children, each one of you are receivers and transmitters, only no instrument is required and it is totally unnecessary to wait for certain hours or certain occasions in order to get the

connection you desire. I want you to think of it like this:
Right down through nature, even with the smallest insect,
telepathy is practised in a way not yet unfolded to the mind
of man. " Instinct " it is called—that instinct with which the
Creator has endowed everyone from the least to the greatest,
from the lowest (using earth language) to the strongest and
the purest.

Children, that word instinct is simply a rough translation
of one or other of the many spiritual laws which dominate
your world and ours; and forget not that spiritual laws concern not only mankind but because God is the Creator of all,
" Spirit " runs through everything that can be thought of—
through everything that has been and will be . . .

I must leave it to you to think out for yourselves how
this spiritual law is, as it were, automatically always in use
between the cruder forms of creation, right up through each
" kingdom " forgetting not the flowers and the trees . . .

Now, dear children, we come back to yourselves, and I
tell you that as man develops so will this gift of telepathy
come into its own. Even now where love is strong, again and
again thoughts sent from the far away reach the one to whom
they belong—perhaps unconsciously—but there are many who
are sufficiently evolved who can, as you put it, " pick up "
fragments of the thoughts so sent in their direction.

And the next step is this—so natural, leading on in a
perfectly practical, commonsense way—the thoughts, dear
children, which your loved and loving ones in the Spirit send
towards you. Have I not said that even as the rain so are these
thoughts showered down upon you—that symbolical rain of
love; and sometimes—ah ! very often—they fall all around
you to the ground, as you would say, shedding their beauty
on those same vibrations but not finding a lodgment in your
minds, because the things of the world, its many distractions
and disturbances held you too tight and you did not know
what you were missing . . .

You see, dear children, that when man talks of thought
transference for the most part he is totally ignorant of what
this implies. Those trivial—yes ! from our point of view
they are intensely trivial—those experiments which have been
undertaken with so much gravity, these because they concern

the things of the earth alone not only demonstrate but little but, as it were, have the power to throw dust over the spiritual vision of those who think they would like to know more.

Now, dear children, I have shown you in very rough outline something of what underlies that word Telepathy, yet the point I have not yet touched upon is its relation to this sacred communion which is going on now so widely between those who are held by the body and those who are free in the Spirit.

Well, dear children, think over my words and you will see at once that it is rather beside the question of Telepathy; in fact, its concerns are so definitely—not in an opposite direction—but in an entirely individual direction that you realise that the two gifts operate in a different way.

Children, in regard to those who seek out these instruments of God (mediums) and ply them with questions—many of a very misleading character and, sad to relate, put with the express purpose of proving the one so used as unfaithful to her trust—such as these questioners very often cover both their own lack of spirituality as well as the lack of complete satisfaction they have experienced by saying that " telepathy " is the explanation of the facts so gained. Well, dear children, telepathy in those cases is going on in rather a terrible way. The doubter and the scoffer by the very fact of his unworthy thoughts, by his concealed distrust of the one he wishes to use, he—all unconsciously to himself—is contacting with and attracting those out of the body who are like-minded to himself. If the " conditions " could be seen with the physical eye such a one would be aghast at the companionship he had brought around him, and because these instruments of God— so delicately poised so at the mercy of those who are brought into their vibrations, yes ! so at the mercy of such as these if God is not definitely in their hearts and minds—these suffer in proportion, and the gift which they possess is not able to demonstrate itself with the freedom which the Giver intended . . .

I want you to mark this well. There have been many of your own acquaintance who have gone to these instruments with faith and with trust in their hearts, and they have received a hundredfold in return. Distrust—that hypocrisy of the mind which while the lips say: " I seek the truth " yet says

itself: " I seek to prove it false "—these get what they bring
themselves, for here are those who are attuned to finer vibrations than the physical world presents and because they are as
you say, direct " mediums " between the coarser and the finer,
so they must suffer by the ignoble actions of others . . .

Children, when you come here it will seem to you thus:
That the communion between those in the body and those who
have laid it aside is such an extraordinarily natural, simple
thing; and when you look at what you call telepathy—at that
mighty thought transference which is going on in a way no
words can express, you will with reason think that it is a very
difficult subject indeed to understand. Not so to us because
remember, we are well grounded in those laws which govern
Spirit life, whether that Spirit life is free or whether it is in-
tangled in the depths of the earth. Yet recollect my words
that every moment of your life you are receiving direct
thoughts from those who love you in the Spirit. The telepathy
which goes on between the Great Father and His children is
continuous. One thought of God makes the contact complete; even one thought of love or compassion for a brother or
a sister in your daily life makes the contact between you and
the Great Heart of Love complete. You cannot take it in
but these thoughts of Love are, as I have said, rained down
upon you wherever you may be, whatever your thoughts, whatever your actions . . .

It seems to me, dear children, that tonight I have only
touched on such a little of this great subject, yet the time has
sped and I cannot say much more now, yet to those who have
held the thought in their mind as to telepathy relating to this
work I bid them think again and get things into their right
position. Those who have passed on are able to use the physical organs of the trained and the prepared, and for the most
part they refer to their thoughts and to their attitude towards
life when on earth. I want the doubters to consider this aspect and to give telepathy its rightful place, and once they
have done that they will find that the two gifts are quite
separate in their working; both God given, both harmonising
but in effect, in action they are separate and complete in themselves.

And then, dear children, I bring you back to the thought
of order and harmony in daily life. You will realise ere this

that only by precision—which is a physical expression of harmony—could your little world or the many realms of the Spirit continue producing and progressing. You see, my little ones, that God's Mind is perfect and because that Mind is perfect only that which harmonises with perfection could emanate from it. The conditions on earth may be distressing and destructive because of the disharmony which humanity, by forsaking its quest, has brought upon itself; yet in spite of that obvious disharmony the spiritual laws set into being by God work on in perfect order, unchanged, unchangeable, protecting man from himself as far as he will allow it, renewing and recharging every second of time. And only by this perfect precision, this exquisite harmony would it be possible that those who stray should be gathered back into the Home they have forsaken . . .

You see, dear children, man wars against the greater self within and so long as this feud goes on so suffering comes, but because God is the God of harmony so by the power of that same telepathy—that thought transference, man will be brought back to that same Harmony from which he started out to learn his lessons and gain his own experiences.

Perfect is the Mind of God, perfect is that which is of God within you, and because of that Perfection within so the evolving stages go on, and as the spiritualisation of the soul-body takes place so the Spirit is able to link itself—just a few threads at first—but to link and knit itself to that Perfection and Harmony to which it rightly belongs . . .

Children, think it out for yourselves; try and grasp something of the great gift which is your own and which is in the possession of all, and then go back to the one I named first—to that same Paul and read between the lines. Ponder o'er his life, on his many visions, on his fight against the attitude of the world and the Light which came to him, on those many truths which he struggled so hard to put into human language that might convey to the mind of man something of the wonder of the Mind of God . . .

And as you think, so your appreciation of the Divine Mind will grow; and as you think again so you will realise how limited is the physical mind and how generous is the Mind of the Father—all-thoughtful, all-love, and His children (so many of them) misunderstanding the purpose and the plan;

so often thinking of their Father as one who but represents what they would be if His powers were their own . . . I have told you, dear children, that the Father-Mind is not like ours yet as humanity goes on, by suffering, by work, by emancipation so, by God's grace, shall man represent in a fragmentary way something of the beauty and the humility of the Great Giver of all . . .

And now I go. Keep a firm hold over the conditions here; they are as you would say of the " finest "; treat them gently and with respect for God has blessed us all in this happy communion tonight . . .

Spirit Consciousness

MY little children, we meet together in this sweet way some-what sooner than you anticipated, but I want you to realise that things do not " happen " in the earth sense—that they are God-directed and by acquiescing to His will you are contributing your little which, in time to come, shall be seen as great and beautiful as well. So then, my little ones, re-member this always and for ever—that the next step and the next is God's will and if you allow physical inclination to intervene then indeed you are breaking that perfect harmony which has been set into action in order to bring you out of the wilderness into the promised Land of Revelation.

Oh, my children, take this to heart—and there are some who know that I address them direct (medium and note-taker). Do not hinder those who are piloting the ship out of the har-bour of the earth across the sea of experience into that harbour which is Home indeed ! Hamper them not by thoughts of doubt—by those ever ready objections which fly to the mind. Remember that in times of danger or when direction seems a little vague to you, that those in the Spirit charged with power from the Great Pilot of all—they know best because they have seen the future.

So, my children, let your minds at this moment sink into that deep river of God's Love and say to yourselves: " All is well because Christ is leading me on !" My child (Dorrie) I speak to you with special emphasis tonight. I am endeav-ouring, and those who love you are endeavouring to steer the little craft of your life into safe waters. Cast not the rudder of faith aside ! Never question " Can I do this, can I do that ?" Say instead: " God needs me for His work ", and you shall see —oh ! with so much joy I say it—you shall see that the Father knows how to look after His little ones.

Tonight, dear children, I ask you all to lay desire aside. I did so before but then it was God's will that those who loved you should speak to you in person. Tonight we are a little farther on and I beg you to concentrate on the Work and the Work alone, when you shall see that by the very absence of the visible and definite presence of those linked to you by the closest ties of the Spirit—by their absence you have knit yourselves to them far more closely than if they had spoken. That is another spiritual law—the laying aside of the lesser in order to gather to yourselves the greater; yes ! you shall see what it means to work for God in God's way, putting aside the desires of the heart.

My children, tonight I have another little inch of that long furrow of knowledge to lay open before you and I ask for your kind attention so that the links may remain unbroken, so that God's will may be accomplished.

Last week, dear children, we discussed together that subject which has raised much speculation: I speak of thought-transference, what you in your world call Telepathy; and following on that which I was able to convey—so limited, so fragmentary, it is true—I want you tonight to think with me awhile on Spirit-consciousness—that consciousness of " something of God " within.

Now, dear children, as you were told, even in the lowest forms of creation " Spirit " must be, in the sense that nothing which is, which has been, or which will be can have existence without the power of God in it and around it. Tonight, however, I am taking you a long way from nature pure and simple, and I want you to focus your attention on man—maybe the " children " of humanity—but those who indeed come under the heading of mankind.

Once again you get the trinity of thought. Here is that instinct, that intuition, that Spirit-consciousness which, as we see it, are the three big steps which lead to God . . . Yet confuse not my meaning. Although to some it is possible only to experience that which you term instinct, yet by the gracious will of the Father many there are who on stepping free from the physical tabernacle find that Spirit-consciousness was their own. Yes ! though they knew it not, though the physical mind bound and fettered them, though the knowledge of the world was as an unopened book; yet such is the Mind of God that He taking the simple impulses, the sacrifices, even that rebelling against the sense of imprisonment—taking these, by the magic of His Love, they are shown in their true guise as " consciousness " not only of God the Creator but of the gift of Divinity within . . .

Oh ! my children, more and more do I implore you to cast aside those conceptions of the world—those hundred and one barriers between man and man, those restrictions of race, of creed and still more so of learning—I entreat you to try and get God's view of the ones who toil and, it seems to them, toil in vain, shut in by the darkness of the physical mind, uncouth both mentally and spiritually it would appear, yet because of their hardships, because of the very lack of ameliorations in physical life, so they demonstrate the strength and the courage of the Spirit within . . .

Ah ! let those who make sweeping assertions as to " instinct " take care, because instinct, in a crude form perhaps, is indeed that Spirit-consciousness, without which no one can climb the hill to God. And when those same instincts drag man away from the Light into the twilight, again I say: Judge not but pray, for there are those allied to the destructive forces who indeed play upon that very sensitiveness with which the child of nature is endowed. And here, dear children, I want you to give full value to the sensitiveness of those same primitive races; how again and again they are forced to rely on that which is within, for which they can find no reason and of which they can give no explanation; but as you have been told those in the Spirit, directed by God, by that " instinct ", by that very sensitiveness are able in a measure to protect and guide them. Physical though instinct may be, it is spiritual as well and that is what the majority forget.

Now, dear children, it is quite possible with the untutored types of humanity—for these to possess in an enormous degree that which is regarded as " intuition ", and here it is that I want to make it quite clear that the gifts endowed by God work separately, operate on an entirely individual basis from the physical mind and the knowledge it may contain.

Have I not shown you that instinct, that " sensitiveness " to conditions—for which no explanation in physical language is available—that this is protection for those who are not in a position to protect themselves ? Again I say that intuition —the capacity for pushing aside material facts and, as it were seeing in the distance the light of direction—that too is solely and only part of the spiritual equipment. How often have you found that by obeying unquestioningly the Voice—that influence coming from you know not where—that you have achieved greater and better results than by long hours of mental concentration ? And, mark you, this faculty is within all; the gifts of the Spirit are not scattered here and there as favour directs. God in giving of Himself to you, to me and to the countless millions that have lived on your little plane—God gave with both Hands equally to all. Yet there have been those who listening to the shadows have allowed themselves to be diverted out of the straight and shining path, and the darkness of the forest has closed them in; and darkness and light are as you must see enemies in every sense there could be. Yes ! Light is the enemy of darkness because it must destroy it, and darkness knowing that Light in the end shall prevail—that darkness, by subtle means, with the wile of the serpent, seeks to shade the Light so that the true Vision is gone, so that God's gifts may lie within unused, untried . . .

Keep these points clear in your mind: that valuable as knowledge may be, attractive as all those accomplishments of the physical mind may appear to you, the greatest gift of all is within—the greatest gift that could ever be thought of is consciousness of the love of the Father and of the kinship there is between you . . .

So, my children, I ask you to guard those intuitions— not to dismiss them as imagination or as accounted for by physical conditions but to guard and to tend them, realising that delicate plants need understanding, need care, need suitable food in order to bring them into the beauty which God intended that the flowers of the Spirit should possess.

And then, dear children, I want to speak to you about that Spirit-consciousness which I am so anxious to forward and to strengthen, and the importance of this cannot be over estimated because what is not accomplished now must be done in time to come when those gifts will be wanted for use by the Master. And it is just like this: there you will be with the One you love best, and in your hands you will find the tools of service but they won't be bright or ready for use. Yes ! and this is what causes the greatest grief of all ! Opportunities on every side, all those wonderful things that you longed to do when in the body, made possible; nay, they are waiting to be done; and the children of the earth because they still remain children are hampered and hindered, they have then to set to work to do that which might so easily have been done before . . .

Does this sound hard ? Then, my children, I have infinite comfort for you all. I tell you that there is not one of you who, when you are free, shall not thank God that you are free indeed; yet in order to make this possible I beg you to prepare still more because of the wonderful future which awaits you.

In regard to the unfoldment of the Spirit, most of you instinctively—aye ! mark that word " instinctively "—have found the key and is it not that of service to your brothers and sisters who, as yet, are further down the hill than yourself ? —that service which is entirely of the Spirit, that giving out of love—so hard to do it seems to some. yet when they are in the atmosphere of love they find that so naturally the love flows out from them to contact and to join with the love which is all around . . .

So, dear children, I would tell you for your instruction that by quiet concentration on the things of the Spirit, by spreading the truth regarding the things of the Spirit among others, by doing the next thing, by holding on to the promise of God that He will guide you, you can—without any of those mental attainments which now seem so attractive to you— you can indeed be " conscious " not only of God in your life but of His mighty power and His creative thought within you—within that which is restricted indeed. And mark you this: that God expects His children as well as entreats His children to come closer to that which His Holiness represents. Many there are who would warn you that the cultivation, or the wish to cultivate those higher, stronger powers which are Divine—they would warn you that this is presumptious indeed; but Christ says to you as He said to us in the days of old: " Follow Me " and He was God !

My children, as the days go on you will find almost in a miraculous way that the physical mind will hold you still less and less: you will find that you will look at nature with new eyes, you will look at humanity with new love, and because of

S

this you will understand—yes ! understand a little more of what is in the Heart and Mind of the great Father . . .

And now, my children, I am going to leave you for a little while, yet in speaking at so brief a length I am definitely calling upon that Spirit-consciousness within: I am saying to each and every one " Teach yourself, for within you is something of the greatest Teacher of all !"   And if you endeavour to put God first, so the light of revelation shall stream down upon you and you will indeed realise in all its sweetness, in all its wonder, what it is to be a child of God . . . And now I go.

Forgiveness

MY little children, once more the days have flown and we gather together in love; and I want to try and impress upon you tonight something of the far-reaching love there is between us.

You little realise it, but all the time—every hour of your life you are seeking or you are feeling the loss of Christ. My children, lest there should be misunderstanding I want to make it quite clear that those times when you feel the Father is a little removed from you—this is but trying the love which is within your hearts; yet it should not be necessary for me to tell you that Christ is always and for ever within your personal vibrations . . .

Yes! there are days which are sweet indeed—when you feel close to the things of the Spirit, when the world and its many fractious details pass over and beyond you and leave no mark behind. These days are "good days"; but, my little ones, if your faith could survive the days of chill those days would be far better still.

It is difficult, I know. It seems strange to the searching mind of man that with the desire for this close contact with Christ, the shadows should be allowed to intervene; but, my children, these tests must be put, and the one who still seeks after the Master in spite of feeling at times that he has lost the direct way into Love—he that still seeks shall not only find, but in the by-and-bye he shall see with so much joy that those periods of chill tightened and strengthened the link between him and his God . . .

Tonight, dear children, I want to direct your attention to a question which has caused misgivings in the minds of many —yes! and there have been those who have laid the subject aside because, as it were, they came to a wall in which they found no door.

Children, I am going to tell you a little, just a very little,

about the underlying meaning of that wonderful word—of
that most beautiful quality which you call " Forgiveness ".
Yes ! the word comes up so often. In daily life where so
many warring interests are in evidence there is much to forgive and there is much to forget; yet my children, the world
and even those who wish to love The Master have scarce
touched on the outer covering of that comprehensive quality
of Forgiveness.

Children, I speak tonight with so much understanding of
the past and I want you in listening to my words to say to
yourself—" Zodiac is thinking of me and Zodiac is trying to
help me because his love is mine " . . .

Children, as the years go on, mercifully the remembrance
of wrongs committed by others against you—mercifully this
remembrance grows less; and this is another law of the Spirit
because the Father is unwilling that the ones who have taken
on this burden, out of love for Him, should bear it for all
time.   You find it so among yourselves.   There was a time
when memory was all too keen; when a chance word, when
the sight of a forgotten thing brought back in all its force, in
all its agony as well, that which had been done against you
in the days of long ago.

Children, our Saviour Christ, realising how much each
one has to forgive the other put in His own prayer that most
protective sentence: " Forgive us . . . as we forgive them ".
And oh ! my children, though there may be many who have
thought that was hard indeed, yet tonight I am going to show
you for your heart's comfort how wonderfully like Love it
was and is.

First of all, dear children, I have to remind you that God
as your Father separates Himself from that gift of Forgiveness
in the sense that it is applied on earth. If I tell you that God
does not forgive then you will gain an entirely false impression; but if I say that God does forgive then, again, the impression is not according to truth.   Between the Father and
His child the position is this—and I speak tonight under the
direct authority and instruction of the One who created us
all—that where Love is, forgiveness does not exist; and if
there are some who would challenge this statement then I
turn them to their own heart and mind.   I say to them: Do
you not know that love when forgiveness as forgiveness is

mockery, because even as the blow is struck—though you suffer through your love—the love surges up and dominates, and by its very strength overwhelms every other thought ?

Children, though you may " sin ", as you call it, the Father neither forgives nor withholds His forgiveness, but the Father throws around you again and again those mighty rays of His Love, and if your ears could hear the Voice which for ever is speaking to the heart of man, you would know that the Father was claiming you as His own !

Yet, dear children, I must not keep back anything from you. You have been told already that before the stronger self, which is within each one, you indeed tremble with fear and apprehension. This is no exaggeration; there are no words in your language which could portray the feelings which come to all when spiritual sight is their own and they are faced with the past. I make no reservations at all because you must know that the nearer we are, that the higher we have climbed the hill of achievement so because of our greater Spirit-consciousness the appalling multitude of our failures face us. You have noted again and again with those who come back and speak to you—speak to you with a joy you will never know until you are free yourself—that those who, as you say, have done " the best ", express—with a sincerity which cannot be denied—their great regret, their overwhelming sense of failure towards their greater selves. And that must be so; therefore, dear children, remember always that the position is this: That God your Father neither " judges " you nor does " forgiveness " in the earth sense, ever come into the relationship between you. These many expressions regarding forgiveness which appear in the sacred record were used solely and only to try and dissipate that deeply rooted belief that God Almighty was the Ruler and Condemnor . . .

It is difficult for you in this generation to realise anything of the relationship between the children of the earth and the One God Jehovah of old. Very little love came into it from man's side, and although God's Love was shown in such a bountiful way right through the ages, yet the teaching and the training was entirely on lines of fear and of punishment. Forgiveness of sin was almost a foreign idea to the majority—it was a term so vague that it conveyed very little to the mind even of the student; it was, for the most part, " attrition "

which controlled; but when the Master came that greatest
change of all was brought into active being, for once the
Love of Christ had pierced the physical mind attrition was
displaced by a contrition too deep, too far-reaching to be explained . . .

My children, I have had to go into this rather at length
but it is necessary for you to gain some idea of the attitude of
mind in those early days, with its many forms of bondage and,
most of all, with the minds and the lives of the people controlled and guided by those who had very little notion of
God as the Creator and none at all as the Father of Love.

Children, you have learnt a little about the effect of forgiveness, particularly in regard to the influence it has on the
progress of those who have finished their experience in a
body of flesh. I want tonight to put into words what is not
understood in its simplest form by those who are investigating
this great Truth.

You have been told that if a man or a woman has injured another and has not sought to right the wrong, when
they pass out of physical life that deed done in such spiritual
ignorance, has to be worked out with pain and with effort.
You are conscious too that it is a dangerous thing to withhold
forgiveness because it blocks the progress of the one who is
beyond your ken, in the sense that no visible act of theirs can
right the wrong.

Well, dear children, as I am so anxious that you should
learn a little more regarding Divine justice, there is one point
which I should like to make clear. True it is that those who
have passed out of the body are hindered and hampered in a
most terrible way by the lack of forgiveness from those on
earth; yet, dear children, is it not more in harmony with God's
Love when I explain that although this unforgiveness hampers,
it is in one direction alone !

Think you like this: When you are free from the body
there are a multitude of things which have to be done; there
are those so-called " sins " of commission and of omission and
these, each one, have to be made good in order that the pattern
of the life may be true to the design of the God-Spirit within.

You see the point ? It will appeal to you at once that it
would be grossly unfair if the absence of the necessary forgiveness should hinder the progress of the soul, now gifted

with spiritual sight, in any direction but the one concerned. It is like this: You know that during daily life now and again you come upon an intricate piece of work and try how you may you cannot conquer certain difficulties which, at the time, seem insurmountable. And so if you are wise, after putting a certain amount of effort into the accomplishment, you leave it for a while and do some of those many other tasks which await your attention. And then when the mind has had a little rest and distraction back again you come to the obstinate piece of work; you put a little more effort into it, and as time goes on, perhaps a fresh idea comes to you and at last, in conjunction with all the help that is around you, you finish that which you began with so much doubt and misgiving—you finish what has cost you dear, but you finish it in the end . . .

Children, that is exactly the position in regard to those who have injured another and who have not righted the wrong during the time they were on earth. And this explains much; it explains why as the years go by the sense of injury grows dimmer in the mind of the one so injured, and at last—thank God !—the time comes when they can say: " Not only have I forgiven but I've almost forgotten as well " . . .

Perfect is the Mind of Love ! There is no mistake so grievous which cannot be rectified when consciousness—that Spirit-consciousness comes to the one who has struck.

Another point, dear children, is this: There are many in the world who with quite a worthy motive, scruple not to destroy both love and happiness in the life of another. There are those, I know, who out of lack of thought and—alas and alas !—from evil intent deal these blows, little reckoning the consequences which must follow. But at the moment I am speaking of the conscientious ones; and, children, do not confuse that word " conscientious " with Spirit-consciousness, because often when such as these come here they find that the Spirit was fettered indeed.

Blows received in this way are perhaps harder to endure than those which are done out of malicious intent because it is hard to be hurt by those who, as you think, should have been the first to defend and to aid.

And while I am referring to this I want to touch on those who have struck you perhaps more deeply than any others. I speak to you, Annie my child, (Mrs. Moyes)—I am referring to those poisoned darts which as it seems to you have been aimed directly at this most precious work for God . . . You see, dear children, it says something for human nature when I can state that the sharpest blows of all are not those aimed at your heart and mind but those directed against the quest of the Spirit within . . .

Well, dear children, have I not told you that because man has been gifted with free-will God cannot interfere with the mischievous thoughts of others, but He can do this—and it is going on in a way so gigantic that no words can express it—He can take the very evil intent and use it to bring you gain ! You have had this evidenced amongst your friends in the little yesterday and it gave you joy to see, even as the blow was struck and the victim trembled under its fierceness, how God's Love shone forth and that which was infinitely greater in value than what had been taken away came as a direct result . . . So God moves amongst those who try and do His will . . .

My children, will you try and look at it like this: In regard to those who from any motive have injured you to believe that if you could see things as they really are the only feeling you would have for them would be infinite compassion, and " forgiveness " would cease to have any meaning between you. I am speaking of the big things and I am speaking of the small ones: You cannot either intentionally or through carelessness injure another without immediately creating regret for the days which are to come; and that is why what you call remorse is such a wonderful gift. Yes-! when you come here you will thank God for those minutes, those hours of remorse, for the times when you felt all drab and ugly within, for the times when you wished with all your heart that you could be washed clean of those thoughts which, even now, you realise are totally unworthy of your real self.

The gift of remorse !—and when it comes but seldom during physical life it means simply that for these unfortunate victims of the shadows, a terrible accumulation awaits them when the body is laid aside . . .

So, my children, I want you to turn over in your mind the little I have told you about forgiveness and about the responsibility of withholding it. In everyday life, could you see things as they are, you would know that each has much to forgive and, what is harder still, much to forget ! . . . I am speaking, dear children, of those who have entered into the arena of experience—the vast majority of toilers, those who every day come up against seemingly most terrible injustices; and very often because they do not know the truth—because there is no one to tell them, bitterness enters in and the heart and mind becomes estranged from God, although God is never estranged from them . . .

Children, over the past, over those most unnecessary blows, so it seems to you, I want you to take the bigger view. I want you to take the bigger view. I want you not to say merely: " I have forgiven " but to try and build up in your mind real compassion for the ones who have sought to hinder you in your upward climb . . .

When you come here you will see what forgiveness has produced, and it is in this connection that I bring in that phrase in the sacred prayer: " Forgive us . . . as we forgive ". Herein, as I said before, is a most wonderful protection. Christ, knowing the attitude of mind of those to whom He spoke, realising in full the power of traditional thought, sought to harmonise—to link together attrition and contrition, so that each one unconsciously to themselves should be building better than they knew . . .

You see, dear children, that nothing which happens is just between two; there is always the third and the third is Christ. Cannot you visualise this: Two enemies endeavouring to strike one another and Christ seeking to defend them both and, at the same time, receiving the blows of each . . . That is the position, literally—not drawing upon the imagination one iota. Nothing you do is individual, nothing you do is confined to two, nothing you think or feel, or fail to be, or wish to be can exclude Christ, your Companion, for within you is that Divinity which makes it impossible, even if God wished it, to dissociate Himself from your life . . .

Children, there is so much I could tell you in regard to this wonderful quality of forgiveness yet even while I use the word I have to say that to the awakened soul it has no meaning at all. And when you lay the body aside and you look back over the past—over your own life and over all those lives which were linked to you—you will find that forgiveness has no place in regard to them; but as the soul stands stripped of pretence, stripped of all those misconceptions built up during physical life, then, dear children, you will find, as we all find, that it is very hard to forgive your lesser self.

Keep the point clear in your mind. Once spiritual sight is your own, forgiveness in regard to others will have no meaning, but in regard to yourself it will have a deeper, wider meaning than you ever guessed . . .

But oh ! I would not leave one tiny cloud of sadness on your minds. You see, dear children, that in the Spirit nothing is hidden; all who are there bear in intelligible form the history of their past life as shown in the pattern of the soul-body. And strange it is to those so critical in physical life—strange it is to such as these that never one word of surprise at another's failure is heard. No ! things go too deep for that. If mistakes have been made then, because the one concerned is desperately in need of help, so you focus your love upon them seeking, with them, to make straight that which has gone awry; and while you are doing that someone is doing the same to you, and that is universal ! Yet need I tell you—you who have learnt so much—that only by Christ and through Christ could we have either the love or the power to help ourselves and others . . .

Oh ! my children, be glad that you have chosen the hilly way ! Cannot you see how this preparation now is going to save you untold journeyings in the days to come ? Cannot you see that by linking yourself to God and to His messengers, you are uncovering that buried Spirit in a way which it would have taken you aeons of time to accomplish when the body was laid aside.

And here I bring in that point which so often is overlooked. Progress out of the physical body is infinitely slower than when the body binds. And the reason for this must be apparent to all. The imprisonment of the flesh, the closed eyes of the Spirit—for the most part, the unconsciousness of the why and the wherefore, the crudeness and the coarseness of the physical vibrations—all, as it were, being burdens which the soul is carrying, by the very fact that they exact so much in suffering and in misunderstanding these burdens take you on in a way it is impossible to describe.

In the Summerland, dear children, beauty is on every side and knowledge, as you have been told, simply waits to be made your own; but because conditions are so much easier, cannot you see that the compilation of effort and of endurance is infinitesimal in comparison with life on earth . . .

Children, these conditions are not what you would call " spiritually advanced "; they are more or less those into which the ordinary uninspired, unawakened soul enters. The ones who have jogged along—neither doing great things nor stooping to those which are base—into the Summerland they pass and sometimes much time elapses before the desire comes to them and to go over the past and to seek to retrieve the time so wasted.

I know, dear children, that you long for the physical experience to be over, but I entreat you to try and get this in its right perspective—to do your best to grasp the enormous value of the tool (physical body) which is placed in your hands, and to thank God that the Spirit was strong enough not to choose the easier path, but that the Spirit had the Divine wisdom to try and make the best use of the years which, as you will see presently, have really passed so quickly.

My children, I implore you all to keep your thoughts away from that sad subject—that longing to be free of the cumbersome tiresome painful body; that deep, deep longing —which really is remembrance—the longing to be in your rightful Home and to forget. yes ! and to forgive the anguish of physical life . . .

Oh ! my children, God understands this in a way no words can tell, but if your wish were granted then indeed would the Spirit mourn—mourn that so much had been thrown away, so much had been sacrificed when the whole of Eternity lies in front of you . . . Yes ! dear children, every month, every week, every day of your bondage counts for great things in the Spirit, and while I assure you that if you laid the body aside ere this night had flown joy and brightness would be your own, yet I must say that because the Spirit is ambitious indeed instead of that wonderful peace for which you crave, regret would be your portion.

Does that sound a contradiction of terms ? I tell you that happiness and brightness would be your own, but oh ! dear children, so many are in this position, it is because the happiness and the brightness reminds them so much of God that they suffer regret in an extreme measure, because they did not do a little more when the opportunity was in their possession . . .

My children, even with the longest life on earth as the years pass it seems that time has sped in a flight so fast that they are surprised to find that physical age has crept over them. When you come here the experience of the earth life will represent to you such a tiny portion of time that you will marvel that so much could be accomplished, and, much more, how you could have grieved over anything so passing, so transitory in its course.

Therefore tonight, dear children, I want you to draw out of the vibrations the joy of the Spirit and to try and make it your own—to allow the consciousness to penetrate your physical mind that although it seems that you are banished from the dear Home-land, yet those of the dear Home-land are sharing your exile with you, that they will never leave you and that they come not empty-handed . . . Roses may be fair, sweet their fragrance but, oh ! the flowers of the Spirit cannot fade; they are charged with eternal life and these, symbolical of so much you could not understand, these for ever are being brought to you even by many you know not—those who passed out of the body right back in the deep pocket of time . . .

So, my children, gather unto yourselves something of the " blessings " which lies all around and be certain and sure that you are never left, that we are bound to you by every tie there could be, and that Love walks with you—that the Saviour is never too busy, never too occupied with the tragedies and disasters to look after His little ones during the daily round, and this of course applies to all. You cannot understand it neither can we, because it is one of those secrets of Divinity, but Christ is literally and actually the Companion of all, linked to the Spirit within which is of Him; and though the way may be long or short, though the hill may be steep or gradual, Christ is never absent from any experience which humanity goes through . . .

So my last words in this connection are these: Remember the place God holds in your life; remember that He is the " third " in every partnership of gladness or of sorrow there may be; that in forgiving others and in covering up the wounds you are indeed contributing to His joy, and—what will appeal to you still more—you are saving the Heart of Love one pang less ! . . .

Now, my children, I will go. Help by your thoughts and keep Christ's image centred in your midst . . .

Printed in the United States
134077LV00002B/127/A